REVISED & UPDATED

WASHINGTON

THE 34 BEST WHITEWATER RIVERS

WHITEWATER

by
Douglass A. North

Photography by Lorrie H. North

The Mountaineers

9 8 7 6 5
6 5 4 3 2

Published by The Mountaineers
1001 SW Klickitat Way, Suite 201, Seattle, Washington 98134

Published simultaneously in Canada by Douglas & McIntyre, Ltd., 1615 Venables Street, Vancouver, B.C. V5L 2H1

Published simultaneously in Great Britain by Cordee, 3a DeMontfort Street, Leicester, England, LE1 7HD

Manufactured in the United States of America

Edited by Dana Fos
Cover photographs: *Popeye* on the Middle Sauk; (smaller inset) Surfing the Chiwawa.
All photographs by Lorrie H. North unless otherwise credited
Cover design by Elizabeth Watson
Book layout by Bridget Culligan Design
Title photo: Digging into *Another Roadside Attraction* on the Methow

Library of Congress Cataloging in Publication Data:
North, Douglass A.
Washington whitewater: the 34 best whitewater rivers/by Douglass A. North.—Rev. and updated.
p. cm.
Rev. of Washington whitewater 1 published 1988 and Washington whitewater 2 published 1987.
Includes index.
ISBN 0-89886-327-9
1. Rafting (Sports)—Washington (State)—Guide-books. 2. Whitewater canoeing—Washington (State)—Guide-books. 3. Washington (State)—Description and travel—1981—Guide-books. I. North, Lorrie H. II. Title.
GV776.W2N67   1992
797.1'22—dc20

91-39562
CIP

Contents

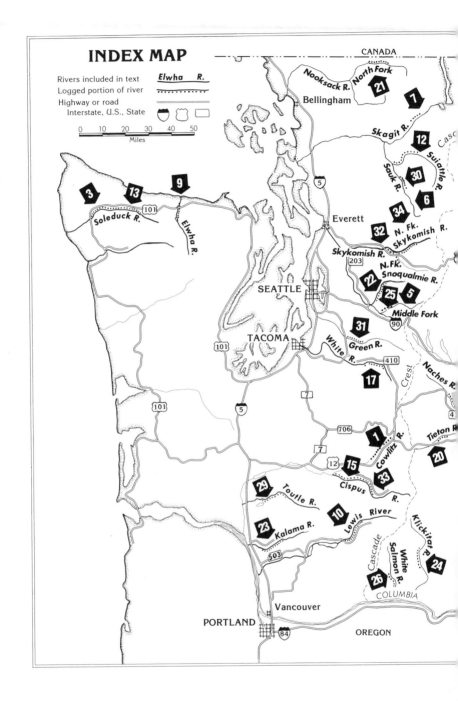

INDEX MAP

Rivers included in text   *Elwha R.*
Logged portion of river   ⋯⋯⋯⋯
Highway or road
     Interstate, U.S., State

0   10   20   30   40   50
Miles

CANADA

Nooksack R.   North Fork   **21**
Bellingham   **7**
Skagit R.   **12**   Casc
Suiattle R.
Sauk R.   **30**
6
34   N. Fk.
Everett   **32**   Skykomish R.
Skykomish R.   N. Fk.
203   Snoqualmie R.
22
25   **5**
SEATTLE   Middle Fork
90
31   Green R.
TACOMA   White R.   410
Naches R.
17   Crest   4
7
5   706   **1**   Cowlitz R.   Tieton R.
12   **15**   **20**
7   Cispus   **33**
29   Toutle R.   R.
23   **10**   Lewis River   Klickitat R.
Kalama R.   White Salmon R.   **24**
503   Cascade   **26**
COLUMBIA
Vancouver
PORTLAND   84   OREGON

3   **13**   **9**
101   Soleduck R.   Elwha R.
101
101
5

4

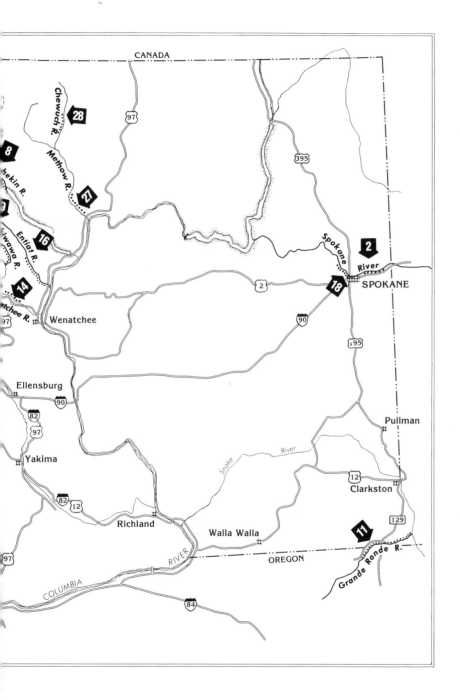

CANADA

Chewuch R.

28

97

8

Methow R.

Chelan R.

27

Entiat R.

16

395

Spokane

River

2

Wenatchee R.

14

97

Wenatchee

2

18

SPOKANE

90

Ellensburg

90

I 95

82

97

Pullman

Yakima

Snake

River

12

Clarkston

82

12

129

Richland

Walla Walla

11

COLUMBIA RIVER

OREGON

Grande Ronde R.

97

COLUMBIA

84

Preface

River guidebooks take two basic approaches. One paints a general picture of the river, provides the essential information on put-ins, take-outs and river difficulty, and leaves the reader to explore the river himself. The other approach provides the reader with all of the verifiable information possible on the river, including descriptions and locations of rapids, landmarks and possible campsites. Each approach has advantages and disadvantages; some people may prefer one to the other.

The principal advantage of the less-detailed guidebook is that it forces the boater to rely on his own resources. Its advocates point out that river channels constantly change, so recording the location of all rapids and landmarks as if they were static could be misleading.

The detailed river logs in this book obviously place it in the second category. These logs have several advantages:

1. They allow the boater who has never run the river to figure out where he is.

2. They allow boaters to choose put-ins and take-outs for the part of the river they wish to run.

3. They provide a graphical representation of the difficulty and intensity of each part of the trip.

4. They allow government agencies to precisely locate the important rapids and the most scenic sections for river conservation purposes.

5. They keep the author honest. Providing a detailed river log is impossible without having actually run the river, usually several times. Some authors are willing to include in their guidebooks rivers they have heard about but have never run. Their "information" is often woefully inaccurate.

The first *Washington Whitewater*, published eight years ago, and *Washington Whitewater* 2, published five years ago, have been well received. This revision combines the two volumes and updates the information on put-ins and take-outs (and man-made changes such as the Tieton dam), and notes several changes that occurred on the rivers as a result of the floods of November 1990.

An important reason for writing a guidebook is to promote river conservation. *Washington Whitewater* and *Washington Whitewater* 2 have introduced many boaters to the beauty and excitement of the rivers of this state. They have helped build a constituency of boaters to protect these rivers. A politically vigorous group of Washington boaters is vital to saving our free-flowing rivers. Over 100 dam license applications are pending for hydroelectric projects on Washington rivers. In a few years, the bottom 1.7 miles of the Cispus River will disappear beneath the slack wa-

Whitewater and Green Mountain on the Upper Middle Fork Snoqualmie

ters behind the Cowlitz Falls project. A battle now rages to save the lower 5 miles of the Cispus from de-watering by a hydroelectric project. There have been dams proposed on many of the rivers in this book, including the Cowlitz, Chiwawa, Skagit, Middle and North Forks Snoqualmie and Skykomish. To save these rivers, boaters must actively oppose these projects.

Washington Whitewater is designed to promote continued river conservation work. It will introduce you to many new rivers and, hopefully, get you involved in their protection. Concerned whitewater boaters in Washington have formed the Rivers Council of Washington to advocate the value of free-flowing rivers and the fish, wildlife, and recreation dependent upon them. The Rivers Council has taken an active role in the Northwest Rivers Study conducted by the Power Planning Council to determine future dam sites in the Northwest. We have intervened as a party in Federal Energy Regulatory Commission dam licensing proceedings, participated in the planning process with the National forests and, along with several other conservation groups, campaigned for a Wild & Scenic Rivers bill for Washington.

If you enjoy Washington's rivers, get involved! Contact:

Rivers Council of Washington
1731 Westlake Ave. N., #202
Seattle, WA 98109
(206) 283-4988

Acknowledgments

This book is dedicated to the hard-working volunteers and staff of the Rivers Council of Washington who keep these rivers flowing free for all of us to enjoy.

I would like to express my love and appreciation to my wife Lorrie. Without her tolerance of my mania for rivers, this book would not be possible.

I would like to give special acknowledgment to Terra Hegy for her assistance in this revision.

I also gratefully acknowledge the assistance and kind permission of John Garren to use the river log system that he developed in *Oregon River Tours* and *Idaho River Tours*. He developed much of the river data in the introduction to explain the background and use of the river log system.

Finally, thanks go to Professor Joel M. Andress and geography students Shane Straga, George Stuart, Julie Lacefield, Robert Adams, Cheryl Beedle, Hank Riddle and Julie Houston at Central Washington University, who drew the maps for this book.

Introduction

This guidebook is for intermediate, advanced and expert rafters or kayakers who already know the basics of controlling their boats in rapids. It is *not* for beginners to use by themselves. If you do not already know how to handle a raft or kayak in class 2 water, you are not yet ready to undertake the trips in this book without expert help. The beginning boater should look first to books on technique and equipment, such as the *Whitewater River Book* by Ron Watters.

Because it is essential to know the water level of a river in order to run it safely, I selected rivers for which representative gauge readings are available. To increase the likelihood of a pleasant experience for everyone, I chose rivers that normally have sufficient water to allow you to run them in a raft for at least three weeks from April through September.

Although some smaller rivers have enough water to be boated nearly every year, their frequent logjams make boating difficult. I have excluded rivers with insufficient flow to move the logs to one side of the river. This does not mean that you will never encounter a log all the way across these rivers, but it is unusual. However, you should always remain alert.

Washington Whitewater describes nearly all the rivers in this state that (1) have significant whitewater, (2) allow rafting, as well as kayaking during the warm months of the year, (3) have fairly reliable water level information available on them and (4) do not suffer from chronic logjams.

River Classification

There are formal, recognized methods of classifying rivers according to difficulty. This allows the beginning boater to select rivers, or sections of rivers, within his capability. The following is a summary of the International River Classification System.

Class 1. Easy and Novice

Sand banks, bends without difficulty, occasional small rapids with waves regular and low. Correct course easy to find. River velocity less than hard backpaddling speed from 0–4 miles per hour. Spray cover or decking for canoes unnecessary. River drop approximately 0–5 feet per mile.

Class 2. Medium or Intermediate

Fairly frequent but unobstructed rapids, regular waves, easy eddies and river bends. Course easy to recognize. River velocity occasionally exceeding hard backpaddling, velocity from 2–6 miles per hour. Spray covers for canoe useful. River drop 5–15 feet per mile.

Class 3. Difficult or Advanced

Maneuvering in rapids necessary. Powerful eddies, standing waves, course difficult to read, scouting may be required, lining should be considered. Canoes require spray covers. River drop 10–25 feet per mile. River velocity 4–8 miles per hour.

Class 4. Very Difficult or Expert

Difficult broken water, long extended rapids, standing waves and eddies, powerful hydraulics, course difficulty requires scouting, lining may be necessary. River drop exceeds 30 feet per mile. River velocities over 6 miles per hour.

Class 5. Exceedingly Difficult

Extremely complicated rapids with powerful hydraulics. River conditions are only attempted by the very experienced.

Class 6. Dangerous

River running involves substantial hazard to life.

It is almost impossible to rate a whole river under this system, but the classification is useful in describing a particular rapid. Generally, any major rapid is class 3 or more and should be approached with some caution. Ratings in this book are conservative. Thus, if there is a question between two rating classes, the higher rating is used.

You should keep in mind that each rapid differs slightly at every water level. However, the same rapids present the most serious challenges on a given stretch regardless of the water level. Ultimately, it is your responsibility to match your ability to the river you intend to run.

In order to provide some help to you in evaluating the difficulty of the rivers in this book, the trips are described from the *least* to *most* difficult—from the Cowlitz to the North Fork of the Skykomish. The runs are grouped into three sections: intermediate, advanced and expert. An intermediate boater knows the rules of whitewater safety, understands hypothermia and basic river hydraulics, and can control his boat in moderate rapids—class 2 with some easy class 3. The intermediate runs either have rapids no more difficult than class 2 or the major rapids can be easily inspected from the road before putting in, allowing you to decide whether you are capable of running them before you start.

An advanced boater thoroughly understands river hydraulics, runs class 3 rapids with confidence and has good river-reading skills. All of the advanced runs have either demanding class 3 rapids that cannot be easily seen from the road or have nearly continuous class 2 and 3 rapids that require substantial experience to run safely.

An expert boater has excellent river-reading skills, runs class 3 rapids without scouting and remains confident in class 4 water. The expert runs involve class 4 rapids and, often, nearly continuous class 3.

Boaters in open canoes should approach these rivers with great caution.

Know your whitewater abilities! (Kevin O'Brien photo)

The intermediate rivers can be canoed by very good canoeists, after careful scouting. All the advanced rivers have class 3 rapids that will swamp an open canoe. Only expert whitewater canoeists running the river at low water are likely to make it down these rivers with both themselves and their canoes intact. The expert rivers verge on being impossible to canoe even for expert whitewater canoeists.

Decked canoes are capable of running any water that a kayak can, and all references to kayaks in this book include decked canoes as well.

Washington Rivers

Boaters from other states who are not familiar with continuous rapids should approach Washington rivers with caution. In many other parts of the country, the rivers are pool and drop with substantial stretches of calm water between the rapids. Very few Washington rivers are pool and drop. Most have continuous fast water that offers little opportunity to recover from an upset before the next rapid. Some of the rivers have such continuous rapids that eddies are rare enough to be landmarks.

Getting your money's worth out of a hole

Washington rivers have continuous fast water because their river valleys are fairly broad and smoothly sloped. The valleys were formed by glaciers in the last ice age and have the U-shape characteristic of glacial valleys. Washington had particularly heavy glaciers in the last ice age due to its northern location and its heavy precipitation.

Because the glaciers carved broad valleys with even gradients, Washington's highway engineers have built roads along nearly all of the major river valleys in the state. (Due to dense vegetation, however, the roads are not usually visible from the rivers.) This is in contrast with other states (such as California, Oregon and Idaho) that have large river valleys with no roads in them. Often the river valleys in these states are narrow defiles cut solely by the river's erosion. Thus, highway engineers have frequently avoided the river valleys in favor of the plateaus between.

Selecting a River

Know your abilities and select a river suitable for your skill level. Generally at least one intermediate, advanced or expert run is at a runnable water level at all times from April through July. The Runnable Seasons table (following) will help you pick a river that is likely to be at a good water level.

RUNNABLE SEASONS

Trip		Recommended Water Level (in cubic feet per second) and Gauge Location	Month											
			J	F	M	A	M	J	J	A	S	O	N	D
1	Cowlitz	1,400–3,200 Packwood							█					
2	Upper Spokane	2,000–19,000 Spokane				█	█	█						█
3	Lower Soleduck	1,200–3,000 McDonald Bridge	█	█	█	█	█	█				█	█	
4	Naches	1,200–2,600 Cliffdell					█	█						
5	Upper Middle Fork Snoqualmie	1,200–3,500 Middle Fork	█	█		█	█						█	
6	Upper Sauk	4,000–10,000 Sauk				█	█	█	█					
7	Skagit	1,500–5,500 Newhalem	█	█	█					█	█	█	█	
8	Stehekin	1,500–5,000 Stehekin				█	█	█						
9	Elwha	1,200–2,600 McDonald Bridge	█	█	█	█	█	█	█			█	█	
10	Lewis	1,200–2,800 Randle	█	█	█	█						█	█	█
11	Grande Ronde	1,500–9,000 Troy	█	█	█	█								█
12	Suiattle	2,500–9,000 Sauk	█	█	█	█	█	█	█			█	█	
13	Upper Soleduck	1,200–3,000 McDonald Bridge	█	█	█	█						█	█	█
14	Wenatchee	4,000–13,000 Peshastin				█	█	█						
15	Lower Cispus	1,400–4,000 Randle	█			█	█					█	█	█
16	Entiat	5,500–11,000 Peshastin					█	█						
17	White	1,000–3,400 Buckley	█	█	█								█	█

RUNNABLE SEASONS

	Trip	Recommended Water Level (in cubic feet per second) and Gauge Location	Month											
			J	F	M	A	M	J	J	A	S	O	N	D
18	Lower Spokane	4,000–19,000 Spokane	■	■	■	■	■	■	■					■
19	Chiwawa	4,000–10,000 Peshastin					■	■	■					
20	Tieton	1,000–2,500 Rimrock									■			
21	North Fork Nooksack	600–1,300 North Fork					■	■		■	■			
22	Snoqualmie, North Fork	600–1,600 North Fork	■										■	■
23	Kalama	1,100–3,200 Kalama	■	■	■									■
24	Klickitat	1,700–3,500 Pitt				■	■							
25	Middle Middle Fork Snoqualmie	1,500–3,000 Middle Fork	■										■	■
26	White Salmon	600–1,300 Underwood						■	■	■			■	■
27	Methow	3,000–11,000 Pateros					■	■	■					
28	Chewuch	5,000–10,000 Pateros						■	■					
29	Toutle	1,500–3,500 Tower Road				■	■	■	■			■	■	
30	Middle Sauk	4,000–9,000 Sauk						■	■	■				
31	Green	1,100–2,300 Howard Hansen	■	■	■									■
32	Skykomish	2,000–5,000 Gold Bar	■	■	■	■					■		■	■
33	Upper Cispus	1,500–2,600 Randle					■	■	■					■
34	Skykomish, North Fork	6,000–12,000 Gold Bar						■	■					

Water Level

Water level is one of the most important factors a boater should consider. There is a relatively narrow range of water levels for any river that makes for a good trip. Below some minimum level, the stream velocity decreases, the rocks (stream roughness) become more troublesome and the trip more difficult. Conversely, above a certain level, the stream velocity becomes so high and the river hydraulics so powerful as to make safe boating impossible. This is particularly true on rivers with very high average slopes, like many of those in this book.

Fortunately, government agencies maintain a large system of stream gauges on almost all major rivers. The gauge heights are translated into cubic feet per second, abbreviated as cfs, a measure of the volume of water passing by the gauge in one second. Each whitewater trip in this book is referenced to a specific water level on the particular trip, along with recommended water levels. I have tried to use representative gauges wherever possible. Sometimes it has been necessary, however, to use a gauge on another part of the river, because it is the only one from which up-to-date readings can be obtained.

Kayakers can usually run a river at a lower water level than rafters; thus, many of the descriptions mention a lower minimum water level suitable for kayakers. The recommended level is the one for rafts because kayakers will also generally find the higher water level more enjoyable, with better holes to play in.

You can check on the current water level by calling the tape-recorded message prepared by the National Oceanic and Atmospheric Administration (NOAA) at (206) 526-8530. The tape is updated every morning from April through November. From December through March, the tape provides Steelheader's Hotline information on river levels. For some rivers I have listed another agency that can provide gauge information as well. The tape should be your main source of information because the other agencies are primarily concerned with flood control and warnings and do not welcome calls from river runners. Call them only if you cannot get the information you need from the tape.

The Runnable Seasons table shows you the time of year when the average flow of the river is within the recommended water level. Of course, the river frequently varies from the average flow, so check the water level. Since most people like to boat in the warm months of the year, the times listed as best at the beginning of each chapter are only the warmer months.

Slope

River slope is usually measured by boaters in feet of river drop per mile. It can be scaled from conventional U.S. Geological Survey contour maps. Steep slopes have high river velocity and will usually, but not nec-

A steep slope and high water can make for big rapids on the lower Methow.

essarily, have difficult rapids. The slope listed at the beginning of each chapter is the average for the trip.

Most of the trips in this book have high average slopes,. Many famous whitewater trips in other states have more gentle slopes. The Colorado in the Grand Canyon has a slope of 8 feet per mile, the Salmon River in Idaho 12 feet per mile. In this book, the Lower Spokane, Lower Soleduck and Skagit have a slope in this range, but the rest of the trips have much higher slopes. ranging up to the North Fork of the Skykomish at 56 feet per mile. High slopes make for faster trips and more constant whitewater.

Roughness

River roughness greatly influences river difficulty. The rocky, "rough" stream channel provides the basis for a wide variety of stream hydraulics that form rapids.

A relatively uniform stream slope and smooth channel (such as the Cowlitz) usually provide easy river boating. Rough channels with steeper river slopes often end up with names like Boulder Drop, White Lightning, Mercury and Jaws.

RELATIVE USE

River	Commercial Use	General Use
1 Cowlitz	None	Light
2 Upper Spokane	Light	Heavy
3 Lower Soleduck	Light	Moderate*
4 Naches	Light	Light
5 Upper Middle Fork Snoqualmie	None	Light
6 Upper Sauk	Light	Moderate
7 Skagit	Moderate	Moderate
8 Stehekin	Light	Light
9 Elwha	Light	Moderate
10 Lewis	None	Light
11 Grande Ronde	Moderate	Moderate
12 Suiattle	Heavy	Heavy
13 Upper Soleduck	Light	Light*
14 Wenatchee	Extreme	Extreme
15 Lower Cispus	Moderate	Moderate
16 Entiat	None	Light
17 White	Light	Moderate

*Soleduck use is light before and after fishing season and moderate during fishing season when many fishermen are on the river in drift boats.

RELATIVE USE

River	Commercial Use	General Use
18 Lower Spokane	Light	Moderate
19 Chiwawa	Light	Moderate
20 Tieton	Extreme+	Extreme+
21 North Fork Nooksack	Light	Moderate
22 Snoqualmie, North Fork	None	Moderate
23 Kalama	None	Light
24 Klickitat	Light	Moderate
25 Middle Middle Fork Snoqualmie	Light	Moderate
26 White Salmon	Moderate	Heavy
27 Methow	Heavy	Heavy
28 Chewuch	None	Light
29 Toutle	Light	Light
30 Middle Sauk	Moderate	Moderate
31 Green	Light	Moderate
32 Skykomish	Heavy	Heavy
33 Upper Cispus	Light	Light
34 Skykomish, North Fork	Light	Light

+Tieton use is extreme only in September. It is light in June, when the river often reaches runnable levels.

Difficulty

The factors of water level, slope and roughness are the major criteria to consider in evaluating river difficulty. All of these factors play a role in the formation of rapids, and rapids are the principal determinant for river difficulty. Several other factors are more subjective, such as ease of rescue, water temperature or remoteness of the river. Indirectly, all of these factors are considered when evaluating the rapids' classifications.

Once you have found a river of suitable difficulty and water level, look at that chapter and see whether the scenery, camping and rapids descriptions suit your needs. If you seek solitude, consult the Relative Use table.

Length of Runs

Some of the runs are much longer than others and lend themselves to overnight trips if you would like to do some river camping. The Grande Ronde and Klickitat would make good overnight trips, as would the Upper and Middle Sauk, the Upper and Lower Cispus or the Upper and Middle Snoqualmie, run as one trip. The following table lists the length of each trip.

White Lightning *adds excitement to a potential overnight trip on the Upper and Lower Cispus.*

WHITEWATER RUNS*

INTERMEDIATE RIVERS		ADVANCED RIVERS	
River	Length of Run in miles	River	Length of Run in miles
1 Cowlitz	8	**18** Lower Spokane	6
2 Upper Spokane	6	**19** Chiwawa	15
3 Lower Soleduck	7	**20** Tieton	12
4 Naches	26	**21** Nooksack North Fork	8
5 Upper Middle Fork Snoqualmie	7	**22** Snoqualmie, North Fork	6
6 Upper Sauk	8	**23** Kalama	10
7 Skagit	9	**24** Klickitat	18
8 Stehekin	10	**25** Middle Middle Fork Snoqualmie	8
9 Elwha	6	**26** White Salmon	7
ADVANCED RIVERS		**27** Methow	26
10 Lewis	6	EXPERT RIVERS	
11 Grande Ronde	45	**28** Chewuch	13
12 Suiattle	13	**29** Toutle	10
13 Upper Soleduck	24	**30** Middle Sauk	10
14 Wenatchee	19	**31** Green	14
15 Lower Cispus	15	**32** Skykomish	7
16 Entiat	14	**33** Upper Cispus	9
17 White	14	**34** Skykomish, North Fork	11

*This ranking is based on the difficulty of controlling your boat. Estimating the danger to swimmers in the event of upset would be different. As an example, the White's log jams present a great danger of death to swimmers who may be swept into them. Thus, it requires less skill to boat the White than the Lower Spokane, but there is greater danger boating the White.

The river logs show the landmarks you can see from the river.

Using the River Map and Log

The river map and log contain most of the information you need on the river. Both the log and map use the standard river convention of placing upstream at the bottom of the page and downstream at the top so that the log and map show the river flowing away from you. The maps and logs correlate so that you can see where you are on both simultaneously by referring to river miles. River miles are counted from the mouth so that they go down in number as you go down the river.

The river log depicts features that can actually be seen by a boater on the river. Thus, some of the maps show features that are useful reference points but do not appear on the logs, and some of the text refers to features that are not on the logs because these features can't be seen from the river. The maps often show a larger area than indicated on the logs so that the user can get oriented more easily for making shuttles.

The log and map can be taped on the cowling of a kayak or the frame of a raft. Only a few symbols are necessary to describe most of the things a boater can identify on the river. Of course, it isn't possible to follow the log while running a river with continuous difficult rapids such as the Gorge section of the Green River or the North Fork Skykomish. On these rivers, you consult the log whenever you stop, and check on the landmarks that you need to remember for the next portion of the trip.

Remember that the river logs are not engraved in stone. River channels can change overnight with flood, landslide, earthquake or even a big tree falling across the river. If you see anything peculiar, such as freshly toppled trees that still have green leaves on them piling up around a bend, get out and scout from shore!

The river logs are measured in units of time rather than distance. This is because the speed with which a boater progresses downriver changes frequently as the slope of the riverbed changes. Time remains constant, however, and you can easily gain a sense of how long it will take to get to the next rapid in comparison with how long it took you to get to the last one. I don't expect that you will actually use a watch to time your progress downriver, but only that the log will give you a feel for how long it will take you to get to the next point of interest.

In planning your trip, you should expect that the total time on the river, including stops, will be about one and one-half to two times the amount of time shown on the log.

Symbols for the Logs

Unimproved boat ramp		Pilings	☼
Put-in or take-out		Rock or hole	✳
Light boat put-in or take-out		Highway next to river	
Building		Tree leaning from bank	
Dam		Powerline or cable crossing	
Bridge over river			
Bridge over tributary stream		Rapid — Class 1	●
		Class 2	●
		Class 3	●
Stream entering river		Class 4	●
Island		Class 5	●
Potential campsite		Railroad Bridge	
Campground		Footbridge	

Relative Drift Time

The relative drift time for various boats differs significantly. Log times in this book are for a 10-man raft at a particular river stage. (If you wonder why a raft was always used, try keeping track of time while taking detailed notes and paddling a kayak.) For the same type of boat and approximate river stage there is little difference in time. Kayaks, however, move downriver about one and one-half times faster than a raft (unless they are playing in a hole, of course); consequently, kayakers should find that it takes them only about two-thirds of the time shown in the log to cover any portion of the run.

Safety

Anyone using this book on a river should already be very familiar with whitewater safety. Just as a reminder, however, the following points should be borne in mind.

1. Wear a lifejacket at all times. The biggest cause of death on a river, bar none, is the failure to wear a lifejacket. Everyone should wear a Coast Guard-approved type I, III, or V lifejacket.

2. Never boat a river beyond your ability. You should always be capable of running the hardest rapid on the stretch of river that you intend to run. Know the River Classification System and your ability.

Make sure you have the proper safety equipment.

Can you handle Class 4 drops? Know your abilities!

3. Never boat a river at too high a water level. This is probably the next biggest killer after failure to wear a lifejacket. Consequently, this book recommends a range of water levels for each river and tells you where to call to find out the gauge readings.

4. Always be aware of the threat of hypothermia. It is nearly always necessary to wear a wetsuit or drysuit when running the rivers of western Washington. Most of the water in these rivers is recently melted ice and snow. Hypothermia strikes in three to five minutes. Wetsuits are often necessary in eastern Washington, too, and wool or polyester pile clothing should always be kept handy.

5. Always boat with an organized group. There should be at least two boats in your party if both are large rafts (larger than six-man) and at least three boats if any are not large rafts. Everyone in the group should be trained in how to rescue boaters in the event of upset.

6. Be aware of the danger presented by sweepers and strainers. Sweepers and strainers are downed logs and brush in the river. They present a much greater danger of death to swimmers than do rocks because the water flowing through them can easily pin a swimmer under water. Boaters must be careful to stay away from brush and logjams.

7. Be aware of the danger presented by dams and weirs. These man-made river obstructions create perfect hydraulics that can prove deadly with only a 2-foot drop. They are the second most dangerous obstacles on a river after sweepers and strainers.

8. Wear a helmet at all times when you kayak and in class 4 or 5 water when you raft. The rocky channels generally present in class 4 or 5 rapids pose a considerable danger to the head of anyone thrown out of a boat. Kayakers should wear helmets at all times because of the ease with which they may suddenly find themselves upside-down.

Because of the difficulty of these runs, kayakers should be familiar with the Eskimo Roll, and all boaters should be prepared to remove a boat pinned on rocks.

Whitewater rafting and kayaking entails unavoidable risks that every river runner assumes, realizes and respects. This guide assumes that you understand those risks. The fact that a section of river is described in this book and is rated for difficulty does not mean that it necessarily will be safe for you. Rivers vary greatly in difficulty and in the amount and kind of preparation needed to enjoy them safely. And because rivers are dynamic systems, conditions frequently change with the weather, seasons and other factors.

You minimize the risks by being knowledgeable, prepared and alert. There is not space in this book for a general treatise on whitewater rafting or kayaking, but a number of good books and courses teach these skills. It is essential that you be aware both of your own limitations and of existing conditions at the time and place of your outing. If river conditions require greater skill or experience than you possess, or if factors such as weather or the condition of your craft, yourself or your companions are such as to dangerously increase the risk of running a river, change your plans. It is better to have wasted a day or two than to invite serious injury or fatality.

These warnings are not intended to warn qualified whitewater boaters off the rivers described in this guide. Many people enjoy safe kayaking or rafting trips down these rivers every year. However, one element of the beauty, freedom and excitement of river running is the presence of risks that do not confront us at home. When you kayak or raft down a whitewater river, you take on those risks. You can meet them safely, but only if you exercise your own independent judgment and common sense.

River Ethics

Part of river conservation is making sure that your enjoyment does not degrade the river's natural qualities or harm its fish and wildlife. If our children and grandchildren are to enjoy our rivers and the wild creatures that visit them, we must take care to leave the river environment no worse than we find it. To ensure the enjoyment of our rivers for everyone, keep the following rules in mind.

1. Respect private property. Don't put in, take out or stop on private property without the owner's permission. Certainly, don't take anything, such as fruit or wood. Nothing will restrict our use of rivers faster than alienating local landowners.

2. Don't leave anything behind. This applies to litter, equipment and even evidence of fire. Pack it all out.

3. Use a stove or firepan. Use of fire is not common on Washington rivers

Always boat in an organized group.

because nearly all rivers can be run in one day, but if you have a fire, put it in a firepan. A firepan prevents charring the ground and killing the micro-organisms in the soil. It also makes packing the ashes out with you easy, and no one can tell that you had a fire. Always have a shovel along (in addition to your bailing bucket) anytime you have a fire.

4. Dispose of human waste and waste water above the high water mark. It will decompose faster if buried in the top 6–8 inches of soil. Pack out all toilet paper in a plastic sack. Use biodegradable soap.

5. Respect the privacy of others. Don't stop to eat or camp where others have stopped; find your own site downriver. Keep quiet while passing other groups on the river; they may be appreciating nature's tranquility.

6. Don't disturb wildlife. Many animals and birds nest and feed along rivers and can be seriously disturbed by boaters coming unnecessarily close, perhaps to take a picture.

River shorelines are a particularly fragile and much used environment. Treat them with respect so that we can continue to enjoy them in the future.

River Protection Programs

There are two major programs available to protect Washington's rivers from dams and development and to preserve them for fish, wildlife, recreation and scenery.

National Wild & Scenic Rivers Act

Under the Wild & Scenic Rivers Act, a segment of a river is eligible to become part of the Wild & Scenic Rivers system if it is free-flowing and has one or more outstandingly remarkable values (such as scenery, fish and wildlife, recreation, geology, history, culture or ecology). To become "Wild & Scenic" the river most often has to be designated by an act of Congress. Congress usually requires that a study of the river be done before it is added to the system. The study can be done either at the direction of Congress or by a federal land-managing agency (such as the Forest Service) as part of its planning process.

National Wild & Scenic River segments are classified according to how much development they have along them. *Wild* river segments can be accessible only by water or by trail and have very few human-made structures along them. Although there are some Washington river segments that qualify as wild, none have yet been designated. Roads can parallel *Scenic* river segments as long as they are generally not visible and there are very few bridges or buildings along them. In Washington, the Sauk, Suiattle, Cascade and White Salmon have the only Scenic River segments designated under the Act. *Recreational* river segments can have a great deal of development along them if, at the same time, they have outstanding natural river values. The Skagit and lower Klickitat (near the Columbia Gorge) are designated as Recreational river segments.

National Wild & Scenic designation protects a river from all dams and water projects and limits further development along its banks. State and local governments control development. The general idea is that homes, farms and cabins already there can stay, but new building should be back from the bank, where it can't be seen from the river. The act prohibits the use of condemnation to acquire land if over half the land along the river is already owned by the government; this is true for all the rivers that have homes on them proposed for Wild & Scenic designation in Washington. After designation, a management plan is drawn up for the river in order to protect its scenery, fish, wildlife and recreation.

Washington State Scenic Rivers Program

The state Scenic Rivers Program protects scenic rivers of special value to the citizens of Washington State. Rivers must be added to the program by an act of the state legislature. The Committee of Participating Agencies oversees the program and is charged with making recommendations to the legislature on new rivers to be added. The program is administered through the state Parks and Recreation Commission. The commission has recommended 18 rivers to the legislature, including several in this book: Soleduck, Nooksack, Green, Cispus, Methow, Wenatchee and Klickitat.

The state Scenic Rivers Program directly affects only state, city and county land. It does not affect private land, but it does direct local governments (which administer the zoning and shorelines management programs) to act in a manner consistent with the Scenic Rivers Program. Federal agencies that license or build dams are required to consider whether or not a river is in this program, but they can decide to build a dam even though the river is in the state program.

After a river is added to the state Scenic Rivers Program, a management plan for the river is drawn up. State Parks and Recreation has involved recreational users and local citizens in drawing up a management plan for the original river in the system: the Skykomish (along with the North Fork, Beckler, and Tye). The Little Spokane was added in 1991.

The state program is definitely weaker than the national Wild & Scenic Rivers Act, but it is a good choice for those rivers (such as the Green, lower Methow and lower Wenatchee) where there is no federal land and where federal protection is therefore unlikely. State designation makes money available to acquire river access, camping and picnicking sites, which can lessen conflicts with local landowners.

The state Scenic Rivers Program deserves our support. If you would like to help protect rivers under it, contact the Northwest Rivers Council (listed in the Preface) or:

The Green River would make an excellent addition to our State Scenic Rivers Program.

Steve Starlund
Washington State Scenic Rivers Program
Washington State Parks and Recreation Commission
7150 Cleanwater Lane
Olympia, WA 98504

Department of Wildlife Conservation Licenses

The Washington State Department of Wildlife requires everyone over 16 using its river access sites to have a license. You can have a fishing, hunting or conservation license. A conservation license is issued for a calendar year and in 1991 cost $10. You can use it an unlimited number of times within the year. It entitles you, your spouse and any children under 18 accompanying you to park at and use the department's river access points (mentioned in this book on the Wenatchee, Methow, Klickitat, Soleduck, Grande Ronde, Toutle and Skykomish). Anyone using a department access site without a license will be ticketed by a department officer.

INTERMEDIATE RIVERS

1

Cowlitz

Logged at -	1,500 cfs Packwood gauge
Recommended water level -	1,400 to 3,200 cfs
Best time -	Late June to late July
Rating -	Intermediate
Water level information -	NOAA Tape (206) 526-8530
River mile -	134.8 to 126.5; 8.3 miles
Time -	2 hours, 9 minutes; 3.9 mph
Elevation -	1,255' to 1,050'; 25' per mile

La Wis Wis to Packwood

The first mile and a half of this trip are very beautiful. You will pass between towering rock walls and under the branches of virgin evergreens that overhang the channel. The crystalline water collects in deep green pools, then flows into straightforward, fun rapids. Enjoy this portion of the trip—once the Muddy Fork of the Cowlitz joins the channel, the scenery is much less spectacular.

The name Cowlitz comes from an Indian name that had many different spellings but was applied both to the river and to the Salish tribe that lived along its banks. Its exact meaning has been lost, but it is roughly translated as "capturing the medicine spirit" since the tribe used a prairie along the river for young braves to commune with the Great Spirit.

Getting There

The Cowlitz runs along US 12, 67 miles east of I-5. To reach it from western Washington north of Tacoma, take State Routes 410 and 123, which cross Cayuse pass east of Mt. Rainier. If you are planning a trip between November and April, call 1-976-ROAD (35-cent charge) before you set out to be sure the pass is not closed by snow.

Put-ins and Take-outs

To reach two of the three popular put-ins, you will have to enter La Wis Wis Campground, clearly marked on US 12. Note that the campground is only open from Memorial Day weekend through mid-November. If you

There are beautiful cliffs along the upper Cowlitz.

would like to get into the area at any other time, call the Packwood Ranger Station, (206) 494-5515.

Small groups with lightweight boats may want to use the uppermost put-in. To reach it, take the first right after entering the campground. The put-in is a narrow and fairly steep 15-foot path to the river, near the bridge over the Clear Fork of the Cowlitz. You can't park here, and you will have to unload the boats quickly, then drive to parking elsewhere.

Large parties and groups needing to inflate rafts will want to drive straight ahead on the road into the campground. Beyond some campsites is the put-in, just below the confluence of the Clear Fork of the Cowlitz and the Ohanapecosh rivers.

You can also put in or take out at Jody's Bridge, about a mile from US 12 on Forest Service 1270 road. The road turns off US 12 about 2 miles south of La Wis Wis Campground and 4.5 miles north of Packwood. Coming from the north, the road leaves US 12 just beyond a yellow highway sign indicating a road leaving the opposite side of the highway from 1270 and going to Lava Creek.

To reach the take-out, turn off US 12 in the middle of Packwood onto the Skate Creek Road. The take-out is on the left bank, just downstream from the bridge over the river.

Water Level

The Cowlitz is a good run at 1,400 to 3,200 cfs on the Packwood gauge. Canoeists and kayakers may be able to run it down to about 1,200 cfs if they don't mind hitting a few rocks.

Cowlitz
Packwood Gauge
Recommend 1,400 to 3,200 cfs

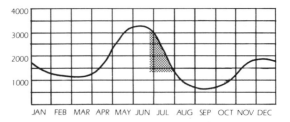

Special Hazards

None.

Scenery

The first 1.5–2 miles of the trip are breath-taking. Many kayakers and canoeists may want to run the upper section to Jody's Bridge, then take out and go back up to run the section again. The scenery deteriorates as soon as the Muddy Fork of the Cowlitz River joins the channel. It's interesting to watch the water of the Clear Fork mix with the silt-laden Muddy Fork, but within 200 yards, the whole river is gray. The channel becomes braided and winds constantly around many islands and gravel bars. However, from the wider river channel, you will have good views of Mt. Rainier and the surrounding mountains.

Camping

Because La Wis Wis Campground is large, you will probably be able to find sites there except on holiday weekends. It is a beautiful campground—a fee is charged.

If you are with a large group or want a more private site, ask at the Packwood Ranger Station, (206) 494-5515. Sites are available near Jody's Bridge and up State Route 123, along the Ohanapecosh near Mt. Rainier National Park. But don't camp on the land along the river below log time 45 minutes; it is generally privately owned.

Rapids

The rapids on this trip are straightforward, and you won't need to scout them except at water levels higher than those recommended. You will encounter the most difficult maneuvering at the two head-walls at log time 15 minutes. You will have to be positioned in advance to pull off first the right bank and then the left bank. The rapid at log time 1 hour, 50 minutes, provides the largest waves of the trip in a drop that funnels all the river's water through a gap about 35 feet wide.

The banks of the upper part are heavily forested.

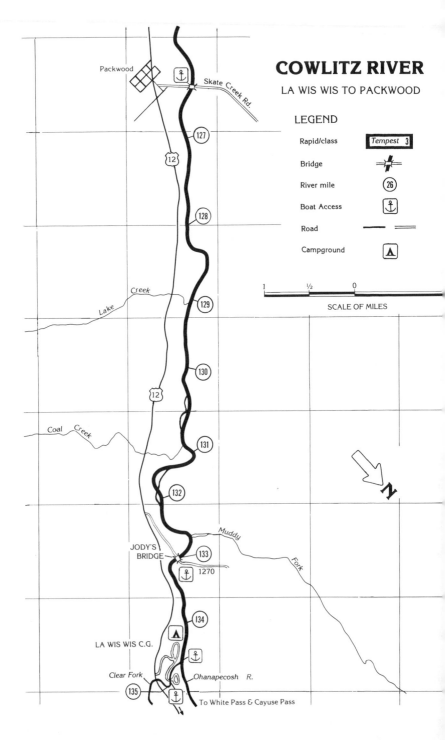

COWLITZ RIVER
LA WIS WIS TO PACKWOOD

LEGEND

Rapid/class	*Tempest* 3
Bridge	
River mile	26
Boat Access	
Road	
Campground	A

SCALE OF MILES

Packwood
Skate Creek Rd.
127
12
128
Lake Creek
129
130
12
Coal Creek
131
132
Muddy Fork
JODY'S BRIDGE
133
1270
134
LA WIS WIS C.G.
Clear Fork
Ohanapecosh R.
135
To White Pass & Cayuse Pass

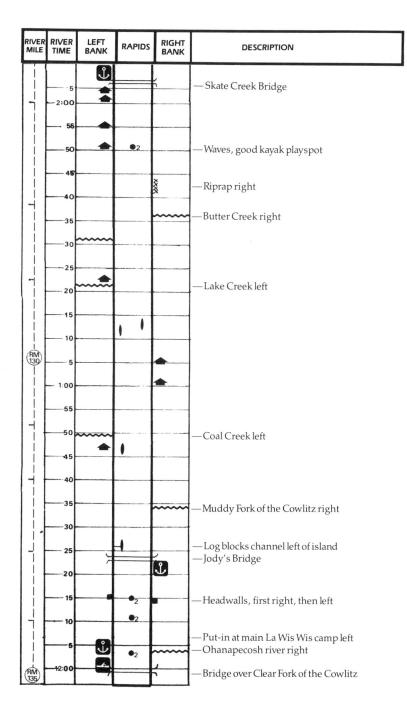

RIVER MILE	RIVER TIME	LEFT BANK	RAPIDS	RIGHT BANK	DESCRIPTION
	5				—Skate Creek Bridge
	2:00				
	55				
	50		●2		—Waves, good kayak playspot
	45				
	40				—Riprap right
	35				—Butter Creek right
	30				
	25				
	20				—Lake Creek left
	15				
	10				
RM 130	5				
	1:00				
	55				
	50				—Coal Creek left
	45				
	40				
	35				—Muddy Fork of the Cowlitz right
	30				
	25				—Log blocks channel left of island
	20				—Jody's Bridge
	15		●2		—Headwalls, first right, then left
	10		●2		
	5				—Put-in at main La Wis Wis camp left
	12:00		●2		—Ohanapecosh river right
RM 135					—Bridge over Clear Fork of the Cowlitz

2

Upper Spokane

Logged at	-	13,000 cfs Spokane gauge
Recommended water level	-	2,000 to 19,000 cfs
Best time	-	April through July
Rating	-	Intermediate
Water level information	-	Washington Water Power (509) 489-0500 (Ext. 2141)
River mile	-	92.7 to 86.3; 6.4 miles
Time	-	1 hour, 10 minutes; 5.5 mph
Elevation	-	2,000' to 1,905'; 15' per mile

Harvard Park to "Walk-in-the-Wild" Park

The Upper Spokane provides good playspots and is also the classic training run for Spokane boaters. The name Spokane comes from a chief of the local Indian tribe who identified himself to early fur traders as Illim-Spokane or "chief of the sun people." You'll usually find sun when running the Spokane in May or June, when the water levels are good. The trip is just class 2, but at lower water levels, a lateral wave in Sullivan Rapids can cause trouble for open canoes.

Getting There
The Upper Spokane is paralleled by I-90 east of Spokane.

Put-ins and Take-outs
The put-in is reached by taking exit 296, labeled Liberty Lake, Otis Orchards, from I-90. Go north toward Otis Orchards 0.2 mile to the bridge over the river. Harvard Park is just downstream from the bridge on the right bank.

The take-out at Walk-in-the-Wild Park is reached by taking exit 289, labeled Pines Road, Opportunity, from I-90. Go north on Pines Road 0.8 mile, and turn right on the tree-lined road to Walk-in-the-Wild Park. Bear right when you come to the Y 0.7 mile down the road and right again onto a gravel road at a Y 0.1 mile farther. Turn left after another 0.1 mile, going through a narrow concrete overpass to the river.

An alternative put-in or take-out can be made on the right bank downstream from Sullivan Bridge by taking exit 291 from I-90 onto Sullivan Road.

You can lengthen the trip by 1.5 miles of class 1 water down to Plante Ferry State Park. The take-out there is on the right bank of the river, reached from Spokane by taking Upriver Drive.

Water Level

The Upper Spokane provides a good run at levels between 2,000 and 19,000 cfs. Above 19,000, the drops begin to wash out and there are very few playspots. In late June, the gates on the dam at Post Falls, Idaho, are gradually closed and the river drops rapidly. The sun is strong enough to warm the water significantly by mid-June, making it quite pleasant.

Sullivan Rapids *has some good playspots.*

Spokane Gauge
Recommend 2,000 to 19,000 cfs

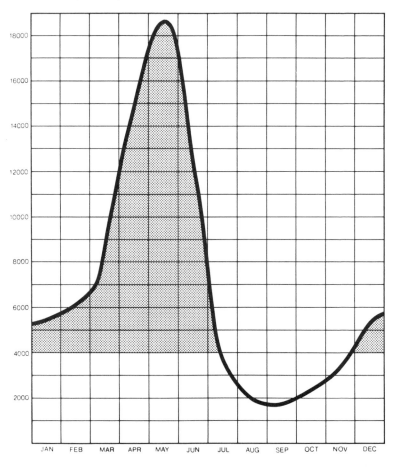

Special Hazards

There are no significant rapids on this section of the river, yet people are killed on it nearly every year when they go tubing without lifejackets. It's a big river; treat it with respect.

Scenery

Although the run is very near Spokane, much of it is fairly pretty with scattered pine forests and a boulder-strewn riverbed, particularly in the section from river log time 40 minutes to 1 hour.

The Upper Spokane is very popular with novice rafters.

Camping

Camping facilities are available at Riverside State Park, along the Spokane, downstream from the city. See the chapter on the Lower Spokane for directions to the park.

Rapids

The rapids on this stretch are no more than class 2, though Sullivan Rapids can cause problems for inexperienced boaters. You can scout on the right bank.

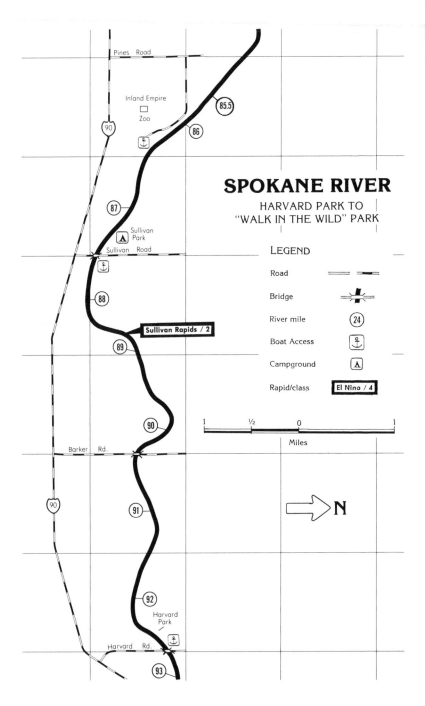

SPOKANE RIVER

HARVARD PARK TO "WALK IN THE WILD" PARK

LEGEND

Road	
Bridge	
River mile	(24)
Boat Access	
Campground	(A)
Rapid/class	El Nino / 4

Pines Road

Inland Empire Zoo

85.5

86

90

87

Sullivan Park

Sullivan Road

88

Sullivan Rapids / 2

89

90

Barker Rd.

90

91

92

Harvard Park

Harvard Rd.

93

Miles

N

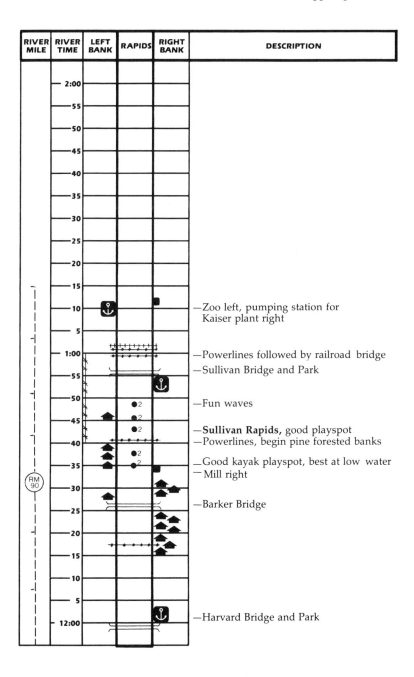

RIVER MILE	RIVER TIME	LEFT BANK	RAPIDS	RIGHT BANK	DESCRIPTION
	2:00				
	55				
	50				
	45				
	40				
	35				
	30				
	25				
	20				
	15				
	10				—Zoo left, pumping station for Kaiser plant right
	5				
	1:00				—Powerlines followed by railroad bridge
	55				—Sullivan Bridge and Park
	50				—Fun waves
	45		●2		
			●2		—**Sullivan Rapids,** good playspot
	40		●2		—Powerlines, begin pine forested banks
	35		●2		—Good kayak playspot, best at low water
RM 90	30				— Mill right
	25				—Barker Bridge
	20				
	15				
	10				
	5				
	12:00				—Harvard Bridge and Park

3

Lower Soleduck

Logged at -	2,000 cfs McDonald Bridge gauge (early May)
Recommended water level -	1,200 to 3,000 cfs (varies)
Best time -	April to mid-June
Rating -	Intermediate
Water level information -	NOAA Tape (206) 526-8530
River mile -	29.9 to 23.1; 6.8 miles
Time -	2 hours, 2 minutes; 3.4 mph
Elevation -	330' to 260'; 10' per mile

Salmon Hatchery to Salmon Drive

The Soleduck is named after the Sol Duc Hotsprings near its headwaters in Olympic National Park. The Indian Spelling, Sol Duc, means "sparkling water." Indians believed that the water had magical, medicinal powers. Whatever the healing powers of the hotsprings may be, a trip on the river can be healing to the soul. The clear water, overhung by lush trees festooned with moss, teems with salmon and steelhead and flows through largely untouched banks. The Soleduck has magic.

Getting There
US 101 parallels the Soleduck from a few miles north of Forks nearly to Lake Crescent, some 34 miles west of Port Angeles.

Put-ins and Take-outs
The put-in is the boat ramp at Soleduck River Salmon Hatchery near Sappho, some 12 miles north of Forks. From either direction the turn-off is about 0.2 mile after crossing a bridge over the Soleduck. Turn south on the dirt road, and take an immediate right in the direction pointed by the small, white "Hatchery" sign. Take the gravel road parallel to the river downstream about 1.5 miles to the hatchery. The boat ramp is to your right.

The take-out is at another boat ramp just off Salmon Drive. Take the turn-off marked Salmon Drive from US 101. The turn-off is about 6 miles north of Forks or about 6.5 miles from the turn-off to the salmon hatchery. Salmon Drive cuts along the side of the hill down to a bench of land by the river and there turns directly away from 101. Follow it toward the

The Lower Soleduck can be canoed if your canoe has flotation and you are an experienced whitewater paddler.

river for a couple hundred yards, and take a right at the stop sign. Drive parallel to the river for another 0.3 mile and you will reach the Department of Wildlife boat ramp. A Department of Wildlife conservation license is required.

Water Level

No gauge has up-to-date reports on the Soleduck, so the water level must be judged by the McDonald Bridge gauge on the Elwha, the next basin over. The Elwha gauge provides a fairly good indication of conditions on the Soleduck, but certainly not an exact measurement. The Elwha gets more snow run-off than the Soleduck, so a higher reading is needed on the McDonald Bridge gauge later in the season than early on. What you are looking for is a somewhat greater-than-average flow in the spring. It

The Soleduck is lined by lush vegetation.

is usually present after a good rain or after a couple days of hot weather that melts the snow. Recommended minimum and maximum levels for the Soleduck in spring are as follows:

	April	May 1–15	May 16–31	June 1–15	June 16–on
Min	1,200	1,500	1,800	2,100	2,400
Max	2,400	3,000	3,600	3,700	3,900

You have to use some good sense in making use of this table. It is based on average weather conditions. For example, in early May, it if has been colder and wetter than normal, look at the April figures. If it has been hotter and drier than normal, however, look at the late May figures. Also note that these are the recommended boating levels; you can scrape down the river with a lot less. Fishermen regularly take their drift boats down the Soleduck at least through mid-June every year, but they're looking for good fishing, not good boating.

McDonald Bridge Gauge
Lower Soleduck
Recommend 1,200 to 3,000 cfs

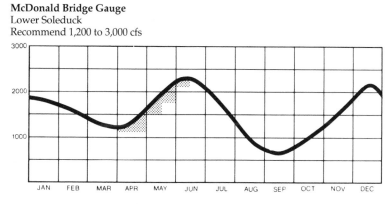

Most of the Soleduck rapids are boulder gardens.

Special Hazards

Fishermen are not really a special hazard, but remember that they were here first. Stay out of the way of their lines, particularly if they have a fish

The channel with the most water is often close to the bank.

on. Fishing season usually lasts from winter through March and begins again in late May, continuing through July. April and early May are good times to boat the Soleduck without getting in the way of the fishermen.

Scenery

The Soleduck is a very beautiful river with lots of wildlife living in its stream and along its banks. Except for scattered cabins, the thick foliage screens away the sights and sounds of civilization. I've seen deer, ducks, salmon and bald eagles while threading through bouldery drops and drifting on crystal clear pools.

Camping

Campsites provided by ITT Rayonier are available in the Tumbling Rapids Recreation Area right across US 101 from the turn-off to the salmon hatchery. Tumbling Rapids is usually open only from Memorial Day weekend through Labor Day, however. The State Department of Natural Resources (DNR) Wahlgren Memorial Campground, about 3 miles east of the turn-off to the salmon hatchery, toward Port Angeles on US 101, is open throughout the year.

Rapids

The mild rapids on this trip could be negotiated by good whitewater canoeists. They mostly consist of rock gardens, requiring considerable threading through boulders, but they do not have powerful hydraulics. **Tyee Rapids** provides some waves that can swamp a canoe, however.

Below the logged run, the river is almost entirely class 1, except for three class 2 rapids in the lower 23 miles of the river: Shuwah Rapids, at the mouth of Shuwah Creek, about a mile below Salmon Drive; Double Rapids, a few miles farther down, just below the US 101 bridge near Forks; and a rapid just above the mouth of the river. This lower section also has pleasant scenery, but homes and cabins along the banks are much more common and nearly all the land is privately owned.

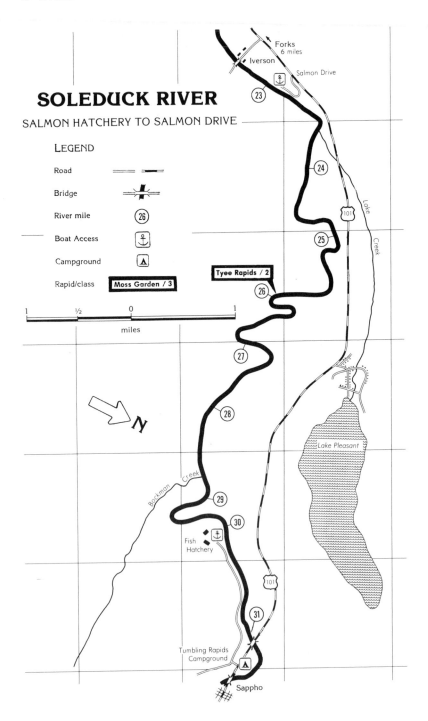

SOLEDUCK RIVER

SALMON HATCHERY TO SALMON DRIVE

LEGEND

Road

Bridge

River mile   (26)

Boat Access

Campground

Rapid/class   Moss Garden / 3

1   ½   0   1

miles

Forks
6 miles
Iverson
Salmon Drive

23

24

101

25

Tyee Rapids / 2

26

27

28

Lake
Creek

Lake Pleasant

Brockman   Creek

29

30

Fish
Hatchery

101

31

Tumbling Rapids
Campground

Sappho

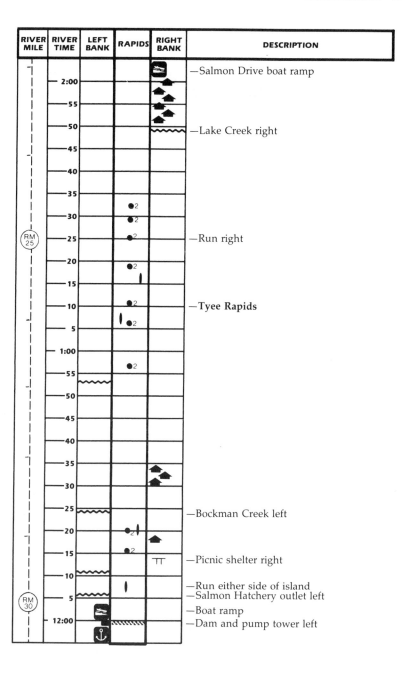

RIVER MILE	RIVER TIME	LEFT BANK	RAPIDS	RIGHT BANK	DESCRIPTION
					—Salmon Drive boat ramp
	2:00				
	55				
	50				—Lake Creek right
	45				
	40				
	35				
	30		●2		
RM 25	25		●2		—Run right
	20		●2		
	15				
	10		●2		—Tyee Rapids
	5		●2		
	1:00				
	55		●2		
	50				
	45				
	40				
	35				
	30				
	25				—Bockman Creek left
	20		●2		
	15		●2		—Picnic shelter right
	10				
RM 30	5				—Run either side of island
					—Salmon Hatchery outlet left
	12:00				—Boat ramp
					—Dam and pump tower left

4

Naches

Logged at - 2,400 cfs Cliffdell gauge
Recommended water level - 1,200 to 2,600 cfs
Best time - Late April to late June
Rating - Intermediate
Water level information - NOAA Tape (206) 526-8530
Bureau of Reclamation
(509) 575-5854
River mile - 43.4 to 17.6; 25.8 miles
Time - 3 hours, 56 minutes; 6.6 mph
Elevation - 2,485' to 1575'; 35' per mile

Sawmill Flat to Tieton River

The Naches derives its name from an Indian word meaning "plenty of water." While this is dry country, there is usually plenty of water in the Naches during the May and June boating season. The upper part of the river is in the Wenatchee National Forest in a canyon lined with basalt cliffs and pine-forested hillsides. The lower end of the run is in stark desert country, but the rapids become more exciting. The Naches often has sun and warm temperatures in May and June, when the water levels are good.

Getting There

The Naches is about 19 miles northwest of Yakima, flowing parallel to State Route 410. From the Puget Sound area, take Route 410 over Cayuse and Chinook passes, checking pass conditions before you leave in the fall or spring. (Often the roads aren't cleared of snow until late April or May.) The State Department of Transportation, (206) 464-7165, can tell you what to expect.

Put-ins and Take-outs

If you'd like to put in at the beginning of the logged run, you can do it easily at the picnic area of the Sawmill Flat Campground. When you look up and see the nice class 2 rapid just above the picnic area, though, you may want to look for a vacant campsite farther upriver and put in there.

Another convenient put-in or take-out point is the Cottonwood Campground. Or, you may want to use the fairly easy put-in/take-out just

There are lots of fun, class 2 rapids on the Naches.

downstream of the upper Nile bridge on the left bank. The turn-off to the bridge is about 5.5 miles below Cottonwood Campground and about 14 miles above the turn-off for US 12.

If you'd just like to run the Horseshoe Bend stretch, you can put in at a wide gravel turn-out along the road just below the log bridge at river time 3 hours, 5 minutes. It is rough, but it's the only place available.

The bottom take-out is almost directly below the US 12 bridge over the river. To reach it, take a left off US 12 about 0.2 mile past the bridge as you head toward White Pass. You'll find yourself on a poor dirt road, and if you bear left as it branches, it'll take you back to the bridge.

Water Level

You'll get a good run on the Naches when the water is from 1,200 to 2,600 cfs on the Cliffdell gauge. Kayakers and canoeists may enjoy the run down to 1,000 cfs. You can run the river above 2,600 cfs, but there are likely to be few eddies.

Naches
Cliffdell Gauge
Recommend 1,200 to 2,600 cfs

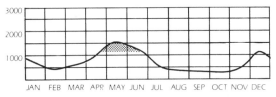

Special Hazards

Downed trees and **brush** sometimes block the smaller channels between islands, particularly in the section of the river from the lower Nile bridge to the class 3 rapid below it—about log time 2:40 to log time 2:54.

Scout the **dam** at log time 3:40 carefully. You'll be able to see it, and the building next to it, from the highway. You can scout, line or run the dam on the right, but remember that it's very dangerous to run any dam because the hydraulics can easily trap and hold anyone swimming in the river. Unless you're thoroughly familiar with river hydraulics and rescue techniques, do not run the dam, no matter how easy it looks to you.

There is a very dangerous **dam** about 0.25 mile below the take-out. Do not run it under any circumstances.

Scenery

In May and June, the area above the upper Nile bridge is often thick with wildflowers, and throughout the boating season, you'll enjoy the beautiful basalt cliffs that line much of the upper portion of the river. Don't be disappointed to find signs of civilization, however; although the area is nearly all National Forest land, there are many private cabins and bridges across the river.

Spelunkers might want to take a side trip when they reach Boulder Cave picnic area on the right bank of the river, about log time 10 minutes. A 0.75-mile hike will take you up to Boulder Cave, fascinating to explore because Devil Creek runs through it.

Below upper Nile bridge, the pine forests disappear as the land becomes drier. You'll leave behind the cliffs and notice the valley's widening. But the trip ends with a bang. A spectacular canyon, narrow and dry, forms the Horseshoe Bend area near the end of the run, and it has the best rapids of the trip. Beyond, the land is so dry that you should watch for cactus at the take-out.

Camping

There's ample space at the Sawmill Flat and Cottonwood campgrounds, where it'll cost you about $6 per campsite to pitch a tent. Nearly

Bridges are the major landmarks on the river. (Leroy Gunstone photo)

all the land below Cottonwood Campground is privately owned, so don't camp there without permission from the landowner.

Rapids

You can see the most difficult rapids on the Naches from the highway, and it'll be easy for intermediate boaters to determine if this run suits their abilities. Intermediate boaters and canoeists should carefully study **Cottonwood** rapid, just below Cottonwood Campground, and the **Horseshoe Bend** area before running them. **Sticks and Stones** rapid at log time 2:53 is only listed as a class 3 because it's difficult to run some of the channels on the right side between the islands. You can identify it by the large boulders on the right, and intermediate boaters and canoeists should stop and scout it.

Canoeists should be able to handle the river above Horseshoe Bend easily but should be careful around Cottonwood rapid. Only expert canoeists are likely to make it through Horseshoe Bend without swamping and capsizing.

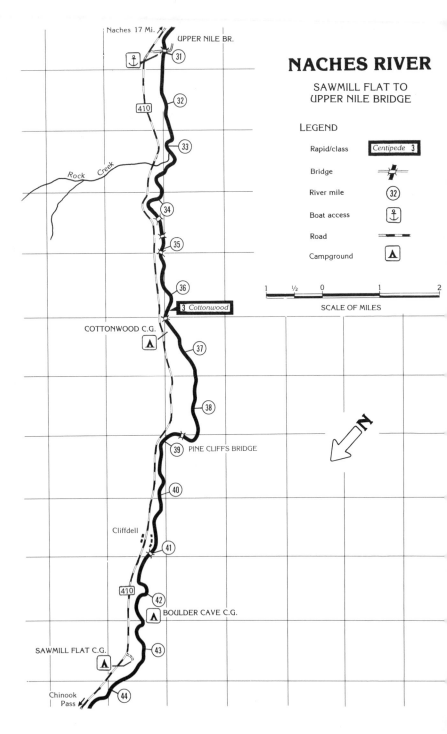

NACHES RIVER

SAWMILL FLAT TO UPPER NILE BRIDGE

LEGEND

Rapid/class	Centipede 3
Bridge	
River mile	32
Boat access	
Road	
Campground	

SCALE OF MILES

Naches 17 Mi.

UPPER NILE BR.

410

Rock Creek

3 Cottonwood

COTTONWOOD C.G.

PINE CLIFFS BRIDGE

Cliffdell

410

BOULDER CAVE C.G.

SAWMILL FLAT C.G.

Chinook Pass

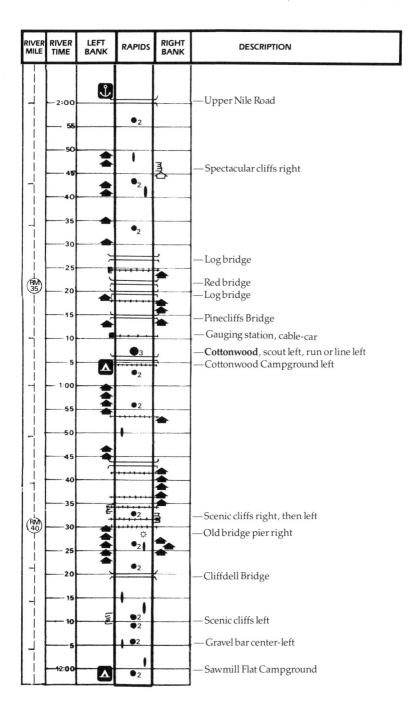

RIVER MILE	RIVER TIME	LEFT BANK	RAPIDS	RIGHT BANK	DESCRIPTION
	2:00				—Upper Nile Road
	55		●2		
	50				
	45				—Spectacular cliffs right
	40		●2		
	35				
	30		●2		
	25				—Log bridge
RM 35	20				—Red bridge —Log bridge
	15				—Pinecliffs Bridge
	10				—Gauging station, cable-car
	5		●3		—**Cottonwood**, scout left, run or line left —Cottonwood Campground left
			●2		
	1:00				
	55		●2		
	50				
	45				
	40				
	35				
RM 40	30		●2		—Scenic cliffs right, then left —Old bridge pier right
	25		●2		
	20		●2		—Cliffdell Bridge
	15				
	10		●2 ●2		—Scenic cliffs left
	5		●2		—Gravel bar center-left
	12:00		●2		—Sawmill Flat Campground

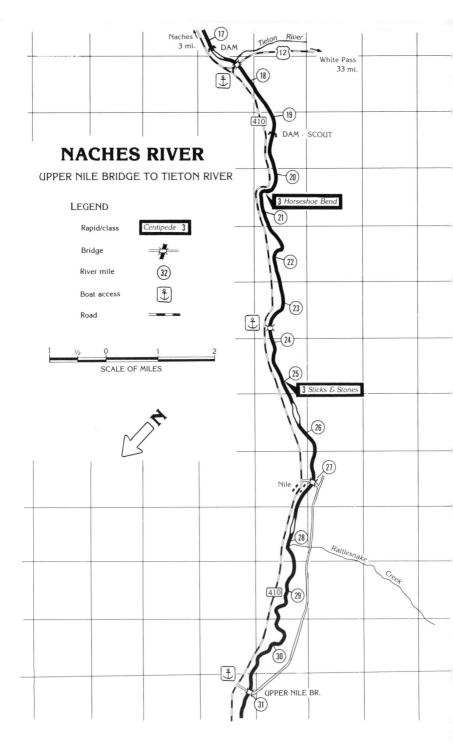

Naches
3 mi.

DAM

Tieton River

White Pass
33 mi.

410

DAM - SCOUT

NACHES RIVER

UPPER NILE BRIDGE TO TIETON RIVER

3 *Horseshoe Bend*

LEGEND

Rapid/class   *Centipede* 3

Bridge

River mile

Boat access

Road

3 *Sticks & Stones*

1   ½   0   1   2

SCALE OF MILES

N

Nile

Rattlesnake

Creek

410

UPPER NILE BR.

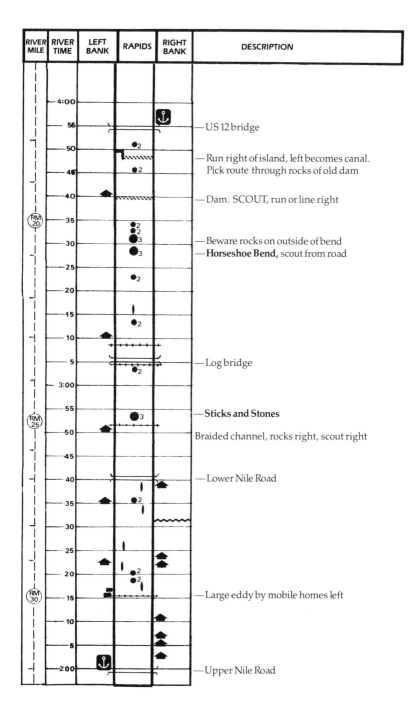

RIVER MILE	RIVER TIME	LEFT BANK	RAPIDS	RIGHT BANK	DESCRIPTION
	4:00				
	55			⚓	
					—US 12 bridge
	50		●2		
					—Run right of island, left becomes canal.
	45		●2		Pick route through rocks of old dam
	40				—Dam. SCOUT, run or line right
RM 20	35		●2 ●2		
	30		●3 ●3		—Beware rocks on outside of bend
	25				—**Horseshoe Bend,** scout from road
	20		●2		
	15				
	10		●2		
	5				—Log bridge
	3:00		●2		
RM 25	55		●3		—**Sticks and Stones**
	50				Braided channel, rocks right, scout right
	45				
	40				—Lower Nile Road
	35		●2		
	30				
	25				
	20		●2 ●2		
RM 30	15				—Large eddy by mobile homes left
	10				
	5				
	2:00	⚓			—Upper Nile Road

Mount Garfield is stunning from the put-in.

5

Upper Middle Fork Snoqualmie

Logged at	-	1,300 cfs Middle Fork gauge
Recommended water level	-	1,200 to 3,500 cfs
Best time	-	April through early July
Rating	-	Intermediate
Water level information	-	NOAA Tape (206) 526-8530 King County Public Works (206) 296-8100
River mile	-	64.3 to 57.1; 7.2 miles
Time	-	2 hours, 10 minutes; 3.3 mph
Elevation	-	1,020' to 850'; 24' per mile

Taylor River to Concrete Bridge

The Upper Middle Fork provides a near wilderness trip within an hour's drive of the Seattle metropolitan area. With stunning mountain views and only one difficult rapid (which can be portaged with some difficulty), the Upper Middle allows intermediate boaters to get a feeling for the sort of experience that draws more advanced boaters to the few difficult overnight whitewater trips in the western United States.

There have been numerous development and logging proposals for the Middle Fork Valley and the Pratt Valley. To help stop this development of a prime scenic area, contact the Rivers Council of Washington (listed in the Preface) and help make the Middle Fork a Wild & Scenic river.

Getting There

Take exit 34 (Edgwick Road) from I-90 and turn north under the freeway. On your left is Ken's Truck Stop. Continue about 0.2 mile north past Ken's and take a right at the T intersection. In about 0.9 mile, the road divides and then rejoins again in 1.2 miles. Just beyond, the pavement ends. Continue a little over 3 miles more to the concrete bridge over the river.

Put-ins and Take-outs

The old take-out a quarter mile above the bridge has been closed, so the only take-out available is beside the bridge. The river-left side of the bridge provides potential take-outs both above and below the bridge, but the one below the bridge may be blocked and the one above is very steep.

Rainy Creek Drop *provides the major whitewater of the trip.*

An alternative take-out, which is at log time 1 hour, 28 minutes, can be reached by turning off toward the river on the unmarked dirt road that is 1.65 miles above the turn-off to the lower take-out. This is 0.55 mile above mile marker 6. This road requires a high-clearance vehicle and reaches a beach in about 0.2 mile. This take-out is also on private land, but the public is allowed to use it. Be wary of parking your vehicle on the "beach." Rapidly rising water can flood these sand and gravel bars.

To reach the put-in, continue on up Forest Service 56 road along the north side of the Middle Fork. About 5 miles above the lower take-out (or 3.5 above the upper take-out) Forest Service 210 road turns off to the left. Check your odometer at the 210 road sign, because the put-in is at the end of a 50-foot unmarked dirt road turning off toward the river just under 1 mile from this sign.

Water Level

You can scrape down the Upper Middle with as little as 800 cfs, but it's much more enjoyable with at least 1,200. Above 3,500 cfs the river approaches flood stage and most of the eddies are gone.

Upper Middle Fork Snoqualmie
Middle Fork Gauge
Recommend 1,200 to 3,500 cfs

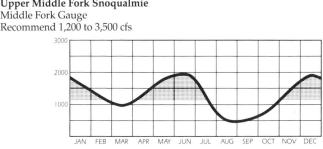

Special Hazards

Keep a sharp eye out for **logs** blocking the channel.

Scenery

On a clear day the scenery is outstanding. There are breath-taking views of Mt. Garfield above the put-in (between the Upper Middle and the Taylor rivers), Preacher Mountain and Russian Butte to the south and Green Mountain to the north. The Pratt River valley is revealed as a dramatic cleft between Preacher Mountain and Russian Butte in the middle of the run. Both the Upper Middle and the Middle Middle should be given Scenic river status in our national Wild & Scenic Rivers system.

Camping

The only designated campground along the Middle Fork is operated by the state's Department of Natural Resources at Mine Creek, a couple of miles below the take-out (see Chapter 25). However, people are welcome to camp anywhere on national forest land—at the put-in, for example. This trip could be combined with the Middle Middle (see Chapter 25) for an overnight trip, so several potential riverside campsites are marked on the log.

Rapids

Most of the rapids on the Upper Middle are straightforward class 2 drops. **Rainy Creek Drop**, however, has some good-sized waves and ends in a head-wall. It can be portaged (with some difficulty) on the right bank. The bank is steep and rocky, but there is a very nice eddy to put in below the drop. Watch for the river plunging down out of sight toward the left bank as the sign for this rapid.

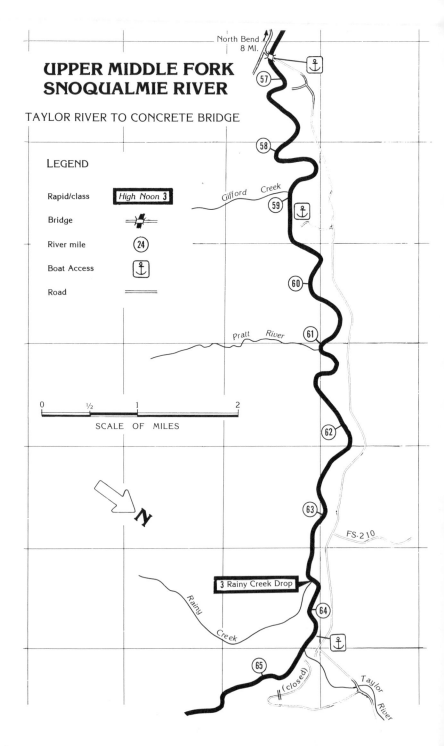

UPPER MIDDLE FORK SNOQUALMIE RIVER

TAYLOR RIVER TO CONCRETE BRIDGE

North Bend
8 MI.

LEGEND

Rapid/class   High Noon 3

Bridge

River mile   (24)

Boat Access

Road

Gifford   Creek

Pratt   River

0   ½   1   2
SCALE   OF   MILES

N

FS-210

3 Rainy Creek Drop

Rainy   Creek

(closed)

Taylor   River

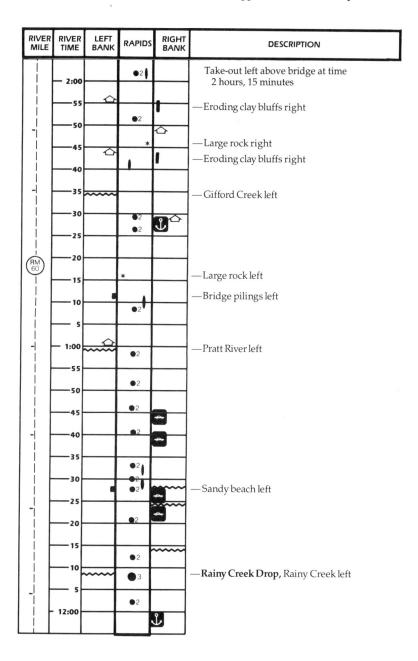

RIVER MILE	RIVER TIME	LEFT BANK	RAPIDS	RIGHT BANK	DESCRIPTION
	2:00		●2		Take-out left above bridge at time 2 hours, 15 minutes
	55				—Eroding clay bluffs right
	50		●2		
	45		*		—Large rock right
	40				—Eroding clay bluffs right
	35				—Gifford Creek left
	30		●2		
	25		●2		
	20				
RM 60	15		*		—Large rock left
	10				—Bridge pilings left
			●2		
	5				
	1:00				—Pratt River left
			●2		
	55				
	50		●2		
	45		●2		
	40		●2		
	35				
	30		●2		
			●2		
	25		●2		—Sandy beach left
	20		●2		
	15				
	10		●3		—**Rainy Creek Drop,** Rainy Creek left
	5		●2		
	12:00				

6

Upper Sauk

Logged at - 7,500 cfs Sauk gauge
Recommended water level - 4,000 to 10,000 cfs
Best time - May to July
Rating - Intermediate
Water level information - NOAA Tape (206) 526-8530
River mile - 40 to 31.7; 8.3 miles
Time - 2 hours, 4 minutes; 4.0 mph
Elevation - 1,125' to 900'; 27' per mile

Bedal Campground to White Chuck

Running through the thick forest of western Washington, the Sauk River offers both exciting paddling and marvelous scenery. The nearby crags of the Cascades are snow-covered most of the year, and wildlife is often present. You are likely to see deer and waterfowl and perhaps an occasional otter or bear. The Sauk is protected as a scenic river under the national Wild & Scenic Rivers Act.

Getting There

The best route to the upper Sauk is through Darrington, about 65 miles northeast of Seattle on State Route 530. To reach the Mountain Loop Highway heading south out of town to the Upper Sauk, go one block east of the 90-degree bend in the main road in Darrington, turn right and then, after several blocks, left at a T intersection. Follow the signs to "Mountain Loop Highway, Granite Falls." About 8.5 miles south of Darrington, the road crosses the Sauk just above the mouth of the White Chuck.

Put-ins and Take-outs

To reach the take-out, turn left, off the Mountain Loop Highway, about 200 yards after crossing the Sauk. You will cross the White Chuck and reach the river access site just below the mouth of the White Chuck.

To avoid running Rock Road, the most difficult rapid at the end of the trip, park at the trailhead for the Beaver Lake Trail. This trailhead is up a short road that runs up the Sauk opposite the turn-off to the access site below the White Chuck. The trail runs along an abandoned road right-of-way next to the river for several hundred yards. The riverbank is steep but provides a take-out for those who don't mind carrying their boats some distance.

To reach the put-in, continue up the Mountain Loop Highway, which soon becomes a one-lane gravel road. About 8 miles up the road, turn right into Bedal Campground and reach the river through one of the campsites.

Water Level

Although kayakers or canoeists might be able to run the river at 3,000 cfs on the Sauk gauge, 4,000 cfs is about the minimum flow necessary for rafts. The maximum recommended flow is 10,000 cfs on the Sauk gauge. Above this level, the river approaches flood stage and there are very few eddies. The best water levels for the trip are found from May through July. Later in the summer the river is likely to be low. Pay close attention to the effects of the weather on the water level. A hot day or a good rain can cause the Sauk to rise exceptionally fast and make a day-old gauge reading completely inaccurate.

The river discharge levels on the Sauk gauge are much larger than

There are breathtaking mountain views from the Upper Sauk. (Keith Gunnar photo)

what is actually present in the Upper Sauk. The gauge is located below the entrance of both the White Chuck and the Suiattle rivers on the Sauk. The percentage of water shown on the Sauk gauge that is actually flowing in the Upper Sauk varies by month as follows:

May	June	July	August
29%	27%	24%	20%

Upper Sauk
Sauk Gauge
Recommend 4,000 to 10,000 cfs

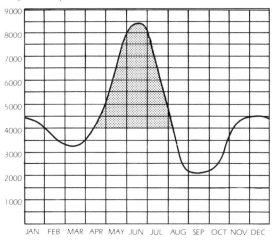

Special Hazards

Logjams are a great hazard on the Upper Sauk. Recently there have been logs completely crossing the river in at least one place every year. These logs are often left by high water at a height that allows the boater to pass underneath them, but they present a very serious hazard.

Scenery

The forest lining the riverbanks is untouched, and the views of the mountain peaks are some of the most stunning ones you'll see on any river. The water is a clear green, and the rocks of the riverbed can be clearly seen as you drift above them. You can see salmon and steelhead spawning here in July and August.

Camping
There are Forest Service campgrounds at the put-in and at Clear Creek, downstream along the Middle Sauk.

Rapids
The most difficult rapid on the trip is right at the end. **Rocky Road** can be viewed from the bridge across the Sauk just above the White Chuck. If you are an intermediate boater, you should inspect the rapid before your trip to determine if it is suitable for you. Generally the most exciting rapids are at the beginning and the end of the trip with a scenic float in-between. This river should be canoed only by experts who can avoid being swamped in the rapids at the beginning and the end of the trip.

Rocky Road *provides an exciting end to the trip.*

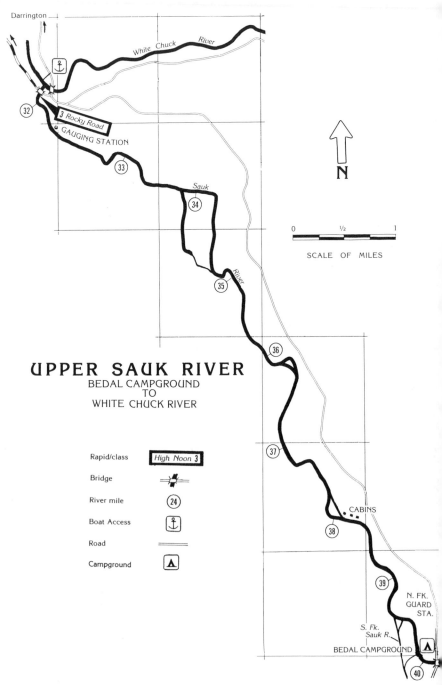

UPPER SAUK RIVER
BEDAL CAMPGROUND
TO
WHITE CHUCK RIVER

N

SCALE OF MILES

0	½	1

Darrington

White Chuck River

3 Rocky Road

GAUGING STATION

Sauk River

CABINS

N. FK. GUARD STA.

S. Fk. Sauk R.

BEDAL CAMPGROUND

Rapid/class   High Noon 3

Bridge

River mile   24

Boat Access

Road

Campground

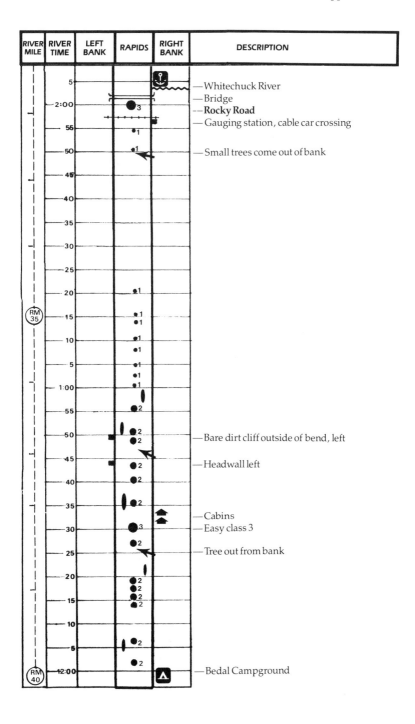

RIVER MILE	RIVER TIME	LEFT BANK	RAPIDS	RIGHT BANK	DESCRIPTION
	5			⚓	—Whitechuck River
	2:00		●3		—Bridge
					--**Rocky Road**
	55				—Gauging station, cable car crossing
	50		●1		
			●1		—Small trees come out of bank
	45				
	40				
	35				
	30				
	25				
	20		●1		
RM 35	15		●1		
			●1		
	10		●1		
			●1		
	5		●1		
			●1		
	1:00		●1		
	55		●2		
	50		●2		
			●2		—Bare dirt cliff outside of bend, left
	45		●2		—Headwall left
	40		●2		
	35		●2		
				🏠	—Cabins
	30		●3		—Easy class 3
	25		●2		—Tree out from bank
	20				
			●2		
	15		●2		
			●2		
	10				
	5		●2		
			●2		
RM 40	12:00			▲	—Bedal Campground

7

Skagit

Logged at - 2,500 cfs Newhalem gauge
Recommended water level - 1,500 to 5,500 cfs
Best time - August to October
Rating - Intermediate
Water level information - NOAA Tape (206) 526-8530
River mile - 92.8 to 83.9; 8.9 miles
Time - 2 hours, 8 minutes; 4.2 mph
Elevation - 473' to 355'; 13' per mile

Goodell Creek to Copper Creek

The Skagit River area is full of wonders. Paddle the river in early fall and you'll see salmon spawning. Paddle it during the winter months and you'll often be treated to the sight of bald eagles. Although the Skagit is dam-controlled (by Seattle City Light's Ross, Diablo and Gorge dams), the river and surrounding area have remained so pristine that they are part of a national recreation area (NRA) attached to North Cascades National Park. The NRA does not prohibit dam construction, however, and Seattle City Light's proposed Copper Creek dam would turn this whole run into a reservoir. This section of the Skagit should be added to the national Wild & Scenic Rivers system (joining the rest of the river below Bacon Creek) so that it remains free-flowing.

Permits for the river are self-issued at the Goodell Creek Campground (the put-in). The National Park Service ranger at Marblemount can answer questions about the permits.

Getting There

State Route 20 (the North Cascades Highway) parallels the Skagit.

Put-ins and Take-outs

The put-in is at Goodell Campground, near the Seattle City Light town of Newhalem (a corruption of the Indian word meaning "goat snare"). There's a steep take-out beside a wide turn-out along the highway, about 2 miles above Bacon Creek. If you have lightweight boats, you may want to take out here, because it's located at the end of the whitewater. The best take-out is at the end of Copper Creek Road, which leaves the main highway 0.9 mile east of Bacon Creek Bridge, just before a yellow state highway sign. Turn right on the dirt road and go 0.2 mile to the riverbank.

You will encounter much quiet beauty while drifting on the Skagit. (Leroy Gunstone photo)

Water Level

This section of the Skagit is nearly always runnable because it's regulated by dams. However, you might scrape your raft on the rocks if you run at levels below 1,500 cfs on the Newhalem gauge. A maximum level of 5,500 cfs is recommended because above that point there are few eddies, and the hydraulics on the S curves become very powerful.

Keep in mind that Ross Dam is there to produce electricity. Thus, discharge from the dam will be higher during weekdays and peak electricity demand periods. Water levels will drop when the demand for power drops.

There are fine views from the Skagit.

Skagit
Newhalem Gauge
Recommend 1,500 to 5,500 cfs

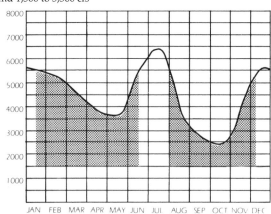

Special Hazards

None.

Scenery

Views of the nearby Cascades and abundant wildlife are the primary attractions of this trip from Goodell Creek Campground until log time 1:25. You'll see high, jagged peaks and deer, coyotes, foxes and raccoons that live in the surrounding forest. You may also see an occasional bear, beaver or otter, and geese, ducks and trout are present almost all year.

Camping

If all the campsites at Goodell Creek Campground (the put-in) are taken, try Newhalem Campground, on the south side of the river, across the bridge at Newhalem. It has 129 sites and is rarely full. Camping along the river is prohibited.

Rapids

Much of the river is considered class 1 to 2. But at **Shovel Spur** (the Portage or S-bends) the whitewater becomes more exciting; that rapid is considered class 3 at low to moderate levels, class 4 at higher levels.

You'll approach Shovel Spur at log time 1:25. You can scout the entire rapid from State Route 20, and intermediate boaters should scout the rapid before putting in to see if they have the skills to run it. (The highway is above the riverbank, so you'll have a bird's-eye view of the rapid.)

The only eddies in this stretch of the river are near the left bank. Because the drops are on left bends in the river, you'll want to scout them from the left bank. Generally, you can run them by starting right, then moving to the center so you won't be driven into the right bank.

Shovel Spur *is the whitewater highlight of the trip. (Kevin O'Brien photo)*

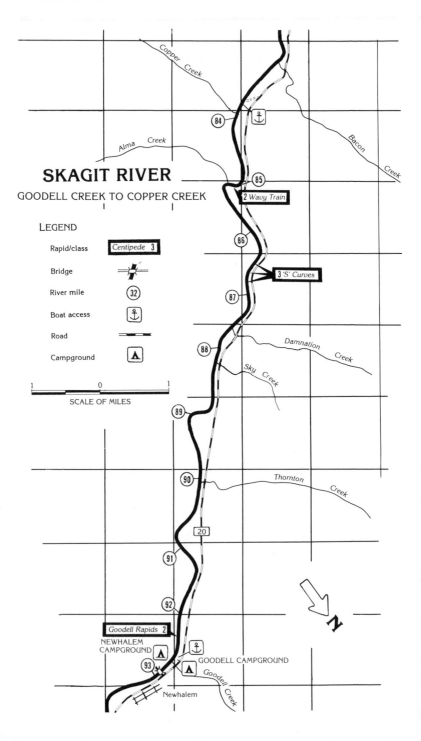

SKAGIT RIVER

GOODELL CREEK TO COPPER CREEK

LEGEND

Rapid/class · Centipede 3

Bridge

River mile · 32

Boat access

Road

Campground

SCALE OF MILES

2 Wavy Train

3 'S' Curves

Damnation Creek

Sky Creek

Thornton Creek

20

Goodell Rapids 2

NEWHALEM CAMPGROUND

GOODELL CAMPGROUND

Goodell Creek

Newhalem

Copper Creek

Alma Creek

Bacon Creek

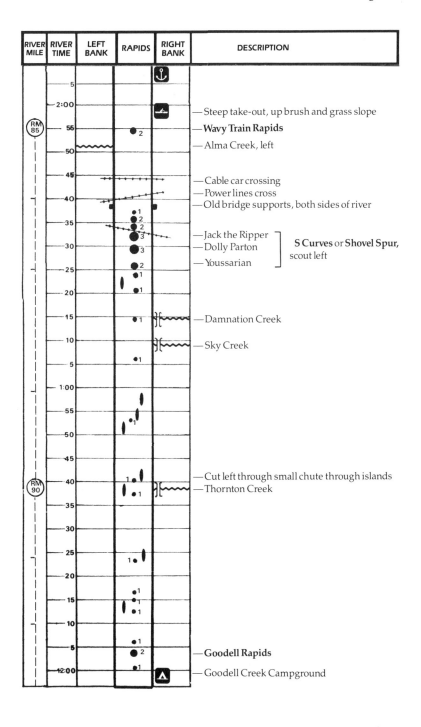

RIVER MILE	RIVER TIME	LEFT BANK	RAPIDS	RIGHT BANK	DESCRIPTION
	5			⚓	
	2:00				—Steep take-out, up brush and grass slope
RM 85	55		● 2		**Wavy Train Rapids**
	50				—Alma Creek, left
	45				—Cable car crossing
	40				—Power lines cross
					—Old bridge supports, both sides of river
	35		●1 ●2 ●2		—Jack the Ripper
	30		●3 ●3		—Dolly Parton
	25		●2 ●1		—Youssarian
	20		●1		
	15		●1		—Damnation Creek
	10				—Sky Creek
	5		●1		
	1:00				
	55		●1		
	50				
	45				
RM 90	40		1●, ●1		—Cut left through small chute through islands
	35				—Thornton Creek
	30				
	25		1●		
	20				
	15		●1 ●1 ●1		
	10				
	5		●1 ●2		—**Goodell Rapids**
	12:00		●1	⛺	—Goodell Creek Campground

S Curves or Shovel Spur, scout left

Lake Chelan can be breathtakingly still in early morning.

8

Stehekin

Logged at -	2,500 cfs Stehekin gauge
Recommended water level -	1,500 to 5,000 cfs
Best time -	May to August
Rating -	Intermediate
Water level information -	Chelan County Public Utility District (PUD) (509) 663-8121
River mile -	10.1 to 0; 10.1 miles
Time -	1 hour, 50 minutes; 5.5 mph
Elevation -	1,525' to 1,100'; 42' per mile

Agnes Creek to Lake Chelan

The Stehekin is one of the most remote boatable rivers in Washington. Because of transportation difficulties, it is a particularly good run for small inflatables. Only the first 0.5 mile of the logged run involves serious whitewater (and that part can be easily avoided by putting in downstream a bit) but the scenery and campsites are gorgeous. Stehekin means "the way through" and the valley was a travel route through the mountains for the Indians.

Miners came to the Stehekin in the 1880s to work claims that went by such names as Black Warrior, King Solomon and Emerald Park. The valley was homesteaded in the 1890s and soon became a mecca for tourists and hikers. The valley is now part of the Lake Chelan National Recreation Area, attached to North Cascades National Park and administered by the National Park Service.

Getting There

Getting there, as they say, is half the fun. In the case of the Stehekin, it's an adventure: you can't drive. There's no road to the Stehekin. Access is via the *Lady of the Lake* or the *Lady Express*, large passenger boats operated by the Lake Chelan Boat Company, Box 186, Chelan, WA 98816, (509) 682-2224. From March 15 to October 31 the boats run up and down the lake once a day, but call before you go, to check. (Off-season the *Lady Express* runs only Monday, Wednesday, Friday, Saturday and Sunday.

Unfortunately, the boats will not take kayaks. A barge that can trans-

There are many great hikes into the mountains out of Stehekin.

The Lady of the Lake *tied up at Stehekin Landing.*

port your kayak travels up and down the lake every other week, but you'll have to make advance arrangements. If you have use of a powerboat, you could easily launch it on the lake and make the 55-mile trip to the Stehekin landing yourself. This is also a good means if you want to take a dog; the commercial boats don't take pets.

The commercial boats do take rolled and packaged rafts, bundled paddles and lifejackets, but the maximum size for a single piece of baggage is 70 pounds (self-bailing rafts can probably meet this limit by unlacing the floor and thwarts and transporting them separately)

The *Lady of the Lake* leaves Fields Point Landing, about 1/4 way up the south side of Lake Chelan, at 9:45 A.M., arrives at Stehekin at 12:30 P.M., leaves Stehekin at 2:00 P.M. and gets back to Fields Point at about 4:45 P.M. Round trip fare in 1995 was $21. The *Lady Express* leaves Fields Point at 9:20 A.M., arrives at Stehekin at 10:45 A.M., leaves Stehekin at 11:45 A.M. and returns to Fields Point at 1:20 P.M. Round-trip fare on the *Lady Express* in 1995 was $39. You can also book a combined trip, going up on one boat and back on another for $38.50 round trip. For those who prefer not to attempt to transport all their equipment, contact the Lake Chelan Boat Company for a guided float trip.

Once you reach Stehekin landing, you have to get up the river. The Park Service operates shuttle vans ($5.00 each way to High Bridge; you'll need only a one-way ticket) that will carry you and your gear. (The vans won't take kayaks or pets, however.) The Park Service shuttle leaves at 8:00 A.M. and 2:00 P.M. Depending on the season, additional buses leave at 11:15 A.M. and 2:15 P.M.

The Park Service asks that you make reservations to ride the shuttle van, more than two days in advance, by writing to: Shuttle Bus Reservations, National Park Service, Box 7, Stehekin, WA 98852 or by calling (360) 856-5703, ext. 14, from 8:00 A.M. to 4:30 P.M. weekdays. No reservations are needed for the buses. For more information, call the Park Service office in Chelan at (509) 682-2549.

Put-ins and Take-outs

Your shuttle van driver will usually be willing to make short detours along the way to see the sights, such as the 312-foot Rainbow Falls and a log cabin still in use as a one-room schoolhouse.

If you're camping, I recommend a stop at Harlequin Campground on your way upriver to drop off your camping gear. Harlequin is below all of the rapids on the river, so on your way downriver you can stop and load all your gear in the boat without fear of waves getting it wet. Having your gear in the boat allows you to paddle down the lake to a beautiful, boat-access-only campground at Weaver Point. Before leaving home for a Stehekin trip, it's a good idea to pack so that you can quickly separate your camping gear to be dropped off at Harlequin.

After the stop at Harlequin, head upriver to your choice of two put-ins. The lower, more frequently used one (all of the commercial rafting trips use it) avoids the difficult rapids noted at the start of the log. It's located on an unmarked dirt turn-off toward the river about 0.3 mile below Bullion Camp; your driver should know where it is. The bank is fairly steep and the eddy small, but it's the best put-in on the upper river.

The upper put-in is even steeper and tougher. To reach it, continue upriver about 0.5 mile (well past Bullion Camp) to where the road begins to climb up and away from the river (High Bridge is so named because the bridge is high above the river which is in a tight gorge). You'll have to assemble your gear on the road and slide it down the rocks into the river. Park Service shuttle vans cannot drop you off at the upper put-in because there is no place to park.

Water Level

The Stehekin provides a fun trip between 1,500 and 5,000 cfs, on the Stehekin gauge. At flows above 3,500 cfs approach the part of the river above the lower put-in with great caution. It's very fast, has big holes and little opportunity to rescue anyone in the water.

No current readings can be obtained from the Stehekin gauge, but

Chelan County PUD (509-663-8121, ext. 4360) can tell you the inflow into Lake Chelan for the previous day in cfs. The Stehekin provides the following percentages of the Lake Chelan inflow: April–June 67 percent, July 77 percent, and August–October 87 percent.

Stehekin
Stehekin Gauge
Recommend 1,500 to 5,000 cfs

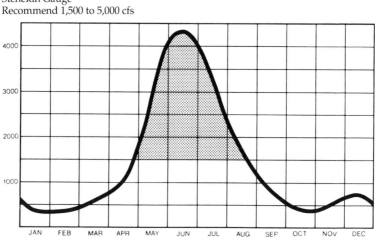

Special Hazards

Downed trees and logs are frequent hazards on the Stehekin, so stay alert. The river can also switch channels from year to year. Ask the Park Service or the commercial rafters at Stehekin landing about recent channel changes. In recent years, it has been necessary to take a small, new channel that you enter at about log time 1 hour, 25 minutes.

Scenery

The scenery is some of the finest to be found on any eastern Washington river. Lake Chelan, an Indian name meaning "deep water," is 1,500 feet deep (placing the bottom 400 feet below sea level) and the deepest blue imaginable. It snakes between the towering, snow-capped crags of the North Cascades. The Stehekin valley, carpeted with beautiful, semi-open pine and fir forests, is flanked by mountain cliffs. From the green-tinged river you have beautiful views of the mountains and valley, including another chance to see the spectacular 312-foot Rainbow Falls.

Camping

Camping on the lake is available at Weaver Campground. The Park Service shuttle provides access to campgrounds along the river at Harlequin and High Bridge.

Rapids

I've rated the Stehekin run intermediate because most boaters will want to start their trips at the lower put-in. Cascade Rapids can make a trip from the upper put-in an advanced or even expert run depending on the water level. Don't attempt to run **Cascade Rapids** until you have thoroughly scouted them from the bank.

From the lower put-in, all of the rapids are straightforward class 2 or less and should not present you with any problems.

If you'd like to look at some really crazy water, go to High Bridge and look at the stretch from High Bridge on up.

Rainbow Creek Falls *can be seen from the Stehekin River.*

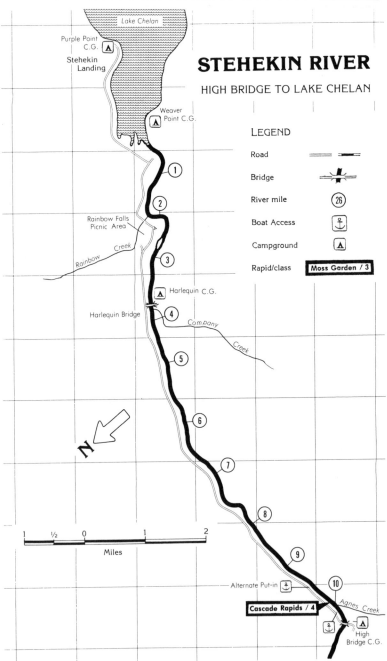

STEHEKIN RIVER

HIGH BRIDGE TO LAKE CHELAN

LEGEND

Road	
Bridge	
River mile	26
Boat Access	
Campground	
Rapid/class	Moss Garden / 3

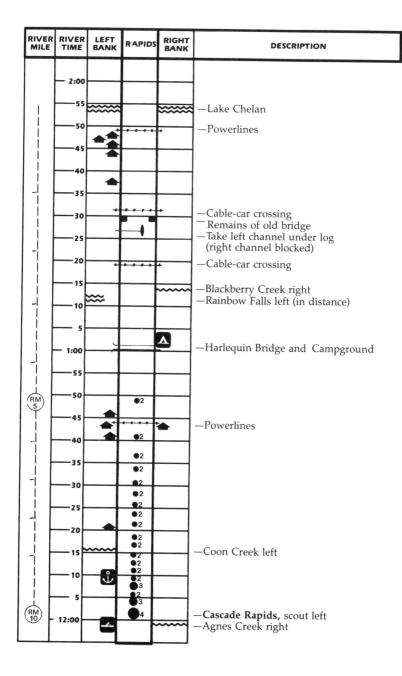

RIVER MILE	RIVER TIME	LEFT BANK	RAPIDS	RIGHT BANK	DESCRIPTION
	2:00				
	55				—Lake Chelan
	50				—Powerlines
	45				
	40				
	35				
	30				—Cable-car crossing
					—Remains of old bridge
	25				—Take left channel under log (right channel blocked)
	20				—Cable-car crossing
	15				—Blackberry Creek right
	10				—Rainbow Falls left (in distance)
	5				
	1:00				—Harlequin Bridge and Campground
	55				
RM 5	50		●2		
	45				—Powerlines
	40		●2		
	35		●2		
	30		●2		
	25		●2		
	20		●2		
	15		●2		—Coon Creek left
	10		●2		
	5		●3		
RM 10	12:00		●4		—**Cascade Rapids,** scout left
					—Agnes Creek right

9

Elwha

Logged at - 1,500 cfs McDonald Bridge gauge
Recommended water level - 1,200 to 2,600 cfs
Best time - April through July
Rating - Intermediate
Water level information - NOAA Tape (206) 526-8530
River mile - 13.4 to 7.5; 5.9 miles
Time - 1 hour, 22 minutes; 4.4 mph
Elevation - 400' to 205'; 32' per mile

Upper Elwha Dam to US 101

The Elwha provides summer boating in a very natural Olympic river valley with fine views of the surrounding mountains. Elwha means "elk" in the local Indian tongue and the valley is an important wintering place for the large Roosevelt elk. If you put in at Altaire Campground, you'll encounter rapids that are exciting but not very difficult. Above Altaire, **Gorge Rapids** is a challenge to the best of boaters.

Getting There

US 101 crosses the Elwha about 7 miles west of Port Angeles.

Put-ins and Take-outs

The take-out is on the right bank just downstream of US 101, on land belonging to the Elwha Resort. The store owned by the resort is right along the highway. Ask at the store for permission to use the take-out.

To reach the put-in, take the road running up the east bank of the river into Olympic National Park. About 1 mile into the park, the road is right along a bend in the river. Here is **Fisherman's Bend**, the most difficult rapid on the lower part of the river; you may want to scout it on the shuttle.

About 1.5 miles beyond Fisherman's Bend, the road crosses the river. Altaire Campground is to your right just beyond the bridge. The boat access area is at the downstream end of the campground.

If you wish to run the gorge, continue up the road beyond Altaire Campground. About 0.2 mile beyond the bridge over the river, an overgrown dirt road turns off to the left underneath the powerlines. Park on the main road, walk about 50 yards down the powerline access road and cut left to the river to get a look at **Gorge Rapids**. It's a nasty drop that has killed several people, mostly local people attempting to run the river with inadequate equipment.

To get to the upper put-in, continue up the main road. About 0.75 mile from the bridge over the river, you will come to a gravel road leading left, downhill to the powerhouse. A sign says "Private Road, Authorized Vehicles Only. No Camping." Park along the main road and carry your equipment about 200 yards down the gravel road to the river.

Water Level

The Elwha is a good trip between 1,200 and 2,600 cfs. Canoes and kayaks can probably scrape down on 800 cfs, but rafts would run aground. Over 2,600 cfs, there are very few eddies and rescue becomes difficult.

Elwha
McDonald Bridge Gauge
Recommend 1,200 to 2,600 cfs

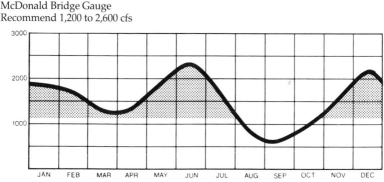

Special Hazards

Logs in the Elwha frequently block some of the smaller channels between the numerous islands. Stick to the channels with the most water. **Gorge Rapids** is a very difficult rapid, approaching class 5 at some water levels. It should not be taken lightly, and no one should run the upper portion of the river without scouting it first.

Scenery

The banks of the Elwha are heavily forested and you get many fine mountain views. The gorge just above the bridge near Altaire Campground is particularly pretty.

The deer and elk heavily affect the vegetation in the forest. This is graphically demonstrated on the left bank at log time 29 minutes. Land in the eddy there and walk back through the woods for 100 yards. There you'll find a small part of the forest fenced off by a 12-foot-high wire

The Elwha flows through a steep, forested valley.

fence as an experiment. In contrast to the knee-high underbrush you have been walking through, the fenced-off area is choked with dense brush 15 feet high. In most of the forest each year, the deer and elk efficiently "mow" the underbrush.

Camping

Camping is plentiful in the Elwha valley. Just above Fisherman's Bend is Elwha Campground and just above the bridge is Altaire Campground. A fee is charged for camping at each.

Rapids

I rate this trip intermediate because most people will want to put in at Altaire Campground. This trip is *not* intermediate if you run **Gorge Rapids**, then it is an expert trip.

The lower part of the river is all class 2 except for **Fisherman's Bend**, a straightforward class 3 easily scouted from the road.

Gorge Rapids is a real hair curler. Before you get to it, you have to run a substantial class 3 rapid, pock-marked with numerous big holes. Then you negotiate a sharp left bend, staying to the inside (left side) of a large rock in the middle of the channel. This brings you to Gorge Rapids proper.

Mid-way through the rapid is a large keeper hole extending out from the right bank two-thirds of the way across the river. Just below the hole is a large boulder, about one-third of the way out from the left bank.

A quarter of the water jams through a 2-foot-wide slot to the left of the big boulder; there's no room there. How do you avoid the keeper hole on the right and get back to the right of the boulder? It's real tight. But you've got some help from a pillow wave that forms in front of the boulder. Rafts have to ride up on the wave, pull hard right and pivot to the right, running the bottom of the drop backward to make it. Kayakers will need a strong backferry to get through. Check it out, make your own plans, and if it looks too tough, put in at Altaire.

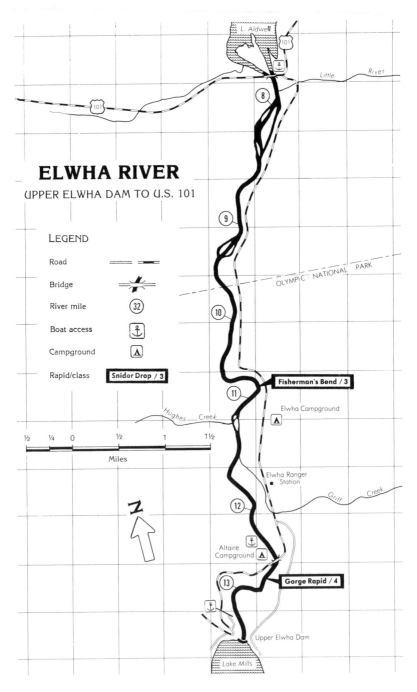

ELWHA RIVER

UPPER ELWHA DAM TO U.S. 101

LEGEND

Road	
Bridge	
River mile	(32)
Boat access	
Campground	(A)
Rapid/class	Snidor Drop / 3

L. Aldwell

Little River

Snidor Drop / 3

Fisherman's Bend / 3

Elwha Campground

Hughes Creek

Elwha Ranger Station

Grift Creek

Altaire Campground

Gorge Rapid / 4

Upper Elwha Dam

Lake Mills

OLYMPIC NATIONAL PARK

½   ¼   0   ½   1   1½

Miles

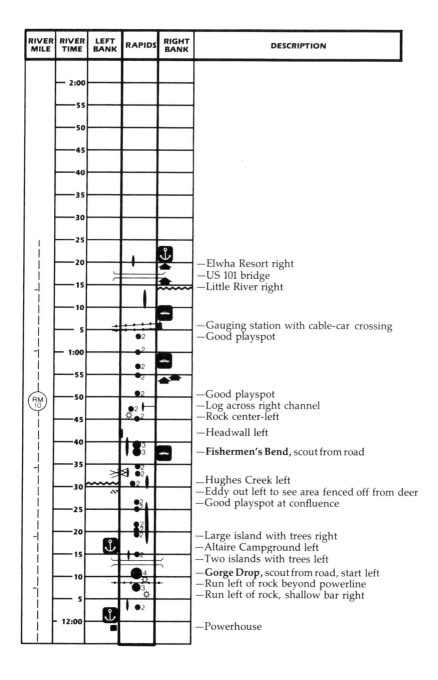

RIVER MILE	RIVER TIME	LEFT BANK	RAPIDS	RIGHT BANK	DESCRIPTION
	2:00				
	55				
	50				
	45				
	40				
	35				
	30				
	25				
	20				—Elwha Resort right
	15				—US 101 bridge
					—Little River right
	10				
	5				—Gauging station with cable-car crossing
					—Good playspot
	1:00				
	55				
	50				—Good playspot
					—Log across right channel
	45				—Rock center-left
	40				—Headwall left
	35				—Fishermen's Bend, scout from road
	30				—Hughes Creek left
					—Eddy out left to see area fenced off from deer
	25				—Good playspot at confluence
	20				—Large island with trees right
	15				—Altaire Campground left
					—Two islands with trees left
	10				—Gorge Drop, scout from road, start left
					—Run left of rock beyond powerline
	5				—Run left of rock, shallow bar right
	12:00				—Powerhouse

RM 10

ADVANCED RIVERS

10

Lewis

Logged at - 1,300 cfs Randle gauge
Recommended water level - 1,200 to 2,800 cfs (varies)
Best time - April through early July
Rating - Advanced
Water level information - NOAA Tape (206) 526-8530
River mile - 64.7 to 59.2; 5.5 miles
Time - 1 hour, 30 minutes; 3.7 mph
Elevation - 1,155' to 1,015'; 25' per mile

Rush Creek to Eagle Cliff Bridge

A trip on the Lewis provides you with gorgeous scenery, including one of the most beautiful sights on any Washington river: Curly Creek Falls. Curly Creek drops 60 feet in a thundering cascade into the Lewis through two natural stone arches. You can paddle or row your boat right under the falls in a setting that seems to be right out of a Tarzan movie. The mist from the falls keeps the area lush in spectacular greenery. The trip is short, with moderate whitewater, but well worth making for the scenery. The Lewis is named for A. Lee Lewis, who homesteaded near its mouth.

Getting There

Take exit 21 from I-5 at Woodland and follow State Route 503 some 32 miles east to Cougar. This town's name was selected from a list of animals submitted by townspeople to the Postal Service. Cougar is famous as the place where D. B. Cooper bailed out of an airliner following the first skyjacking of modern times.

From Cougar continue east on the Forest Service 90 road some 20 miles to the Pine Creek Information Station. Shortly beyond the information station the 90 road turns to the right to Eagle Cliff Bridge.

Put-ins and Take-outs

The take-out is just above the bridge on the right-hand side.

To reach the put-in, continue across the bridge and up the 90 road approximately 4.5 miles to where the 51 road turns off to the right toward Carson. About 0.95 mile beyond the intersection, you will cross a bridge

Curly Creek Falls (note the two natural stone arches)

Rigging a boat near the mouth of Rush Creek

over Rush Creek (signed). Another 0.15 mile beyond the bridge, turn downhill toward the river on an unsigned dirt road. The road switchbacks 0.8 mile to a point near Rush Creek, where you bear right onto the branch that turns upriver 0.15 mile and ends at the put-in. It may be necessary to carry your equipment for the last 0.1 mile. From the put-in, you'll want to ferry across the river passing to the right of a gravel bar in the center of the river.

For an alternate put-in, turn off the 90 road onto Forest Service 9039 road. This road turns off the 90 road about 4.3 miles from Eagle Cliff Bridge or about 0.2 mile short of the intersection with the 51 road. Approximately 0.8 mile down this road, you will cross the river on the bridge that appears at log time 29 minutes. The put-in trail on the upper side of the bridge on the right bank is steep, but not too difficult.

Kayakers may wish to consider a put-in much farther upriver where the 90 road crosses the river near Cussed Hollow. This is near river mile 71, making the trip about 12 miles. This portion of the river is very beautiful with no signs of civilization. The water is mostly class 2–3 with two difficult stretches. The first is at a sharp left bend in the river, just beyond a small creek entering on the left, a little over 2 miles into the trip. Here is class 4 at most water levels but it can be read easily. The other difficult stretch comes about 2 miles farther, just above the mouth of Big Creek. Here the river rushes through a tight gorge filled with huge boulders. Since the gaps between the boulders are often no more than 4–5 feet wide, this gorge is impassable to rafts (with the possible exception of small paddle rafts). Kayakers, however, may be able to run the gaps or else carry their boats around the 200-yard gorge on the trail on the right bank.

Water Level

No gauge on the Lewis gives current water level reports. There is a gauge, however, at Randle on the Cispus, which is the next drainage to the north. This gauge provides a reasonably accurate measure of conditions on the Lewis. The Cispus drains more high snowfields than the Lewis and therefore has more summer flow than the Lewis. Flows in the Lewis amount to the following percentages of flow in the Cispus: January and February 123 percent, March and April 94 percent, May 83 percent, June 75 percent; July 64 percent, August 82 percent, September 74 percent, and October through December 102 percent.

These percentages translate into the following recommended minimum and maximum water levels for the Lewis:

	Jan–Feb	Mar–Apr	May	June	July	Aug	Sept	Oct–Dec
Min	750	1,000	1,100	1,200	1,400	1,100	1,200	900
Max	1,600	2,100	2,600	2,800	3,000	2,500	2,800	2,000

Lewis
Randle Gauge
Recommend 1,200 to 2,800 cfs

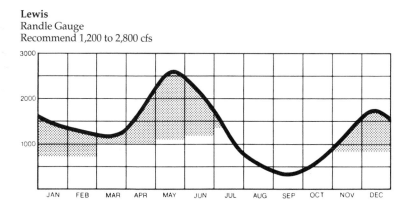

There's a good playspot near the bridge at the take-out.

Special Hazards

Many logs clutter the Lewis at high water. The positions of the logjams change from year to year and you should keep a sharp lookout for logs blocking the channel.

Scenery

The scenery on this trip is magnificent. Besides Curly Creek Falls, which is worth the trip by itself, there is the smaller Miller Creek Falls just downstream and a beautiful, tight gorge extending approximately from river mile 63 to 62. The whole trip above river mile 61 is quite natural, with the bridge as the only sign of civilization. Unfortunately, clearcuts come into view below mile 61. This land was clearcut and not replanted in the late 1960s when Pacific Power and Light planned a huge dam at Eagle Cliff, the take-out. This project, which would inundate the logged run, is not dead—only placed on hold until economics permit completion. Support Wild & Scenic protection of the Lewis to prevent destruction of this beautiful river.

The shuttle provides views of Mt. St. Helens, and paddlers may wish to take a side trip to view Lower Falls on the Lewis upriver from the trip described here. The Lewis plummets 35 feet in a spectacular curtain of whitewater just downstream from Lower Falls Campground, located about 1.5 miles beyond the bridge over the river at Cussed Hollow on the 90 road.

Camping

Camping is plentiful. There are campgrounds at Lower Falls, Swift Camp (about 1.5 miles west of the ranger station) and at Beavertail Recreation Area (about 1 mile east of Cougar).

Rapids

The most difficult rapid of the logged trip is **Eagle Cliff Drop**, which can be easily inspected from the take-out. The river below Rush Creek is a fairly easy whitewater trip but has some good playspots and beautiful scenery.

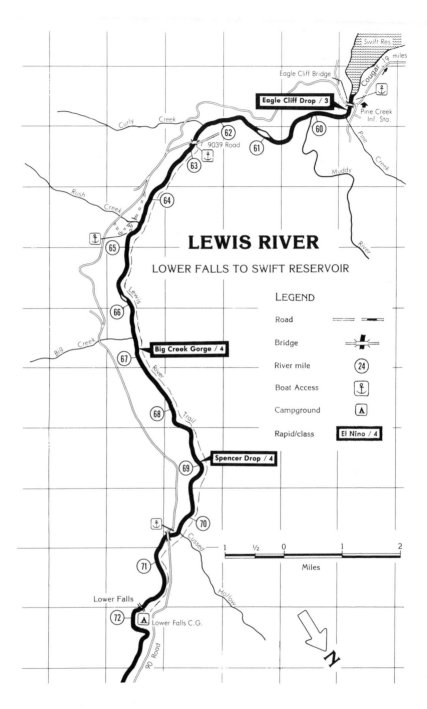

LEWIS RIVER

LOWER FALLS TO SWIFT RESERVOIR

LEGEND

Road	
Bridge	
River mile	24
Boat Access	
Campground	
Rapid/class	El Nino / 4

Eagle Cliff Drop / 3

Big Creek Gorge / 4

Spencer Drop / 4

Miles

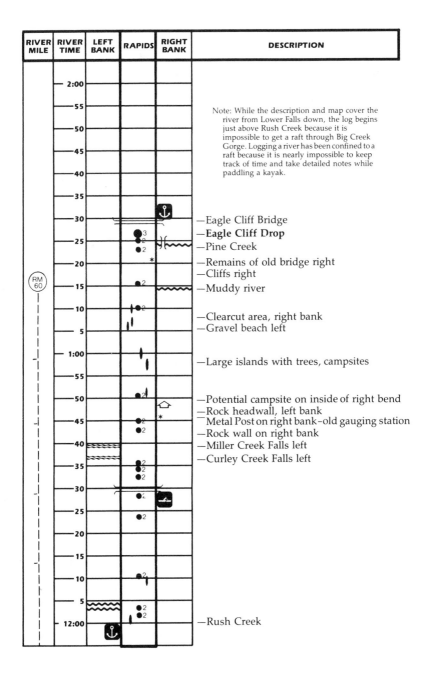

RIVER MILE	RIVER TIME	LEFT BANK	RAPIDS	RIGHT BANK	DESCRIPTION
	2:00				
	55				Note: While the description and map cover the river from Lower Falls down, the log begins just above Rush Creek because it is impossible to get a raft through Big Creek Gorge. Logging a river has been confined to a raft because it is nearly impossible to keep track of time and take detailed notes while paddling a kayak.
	50				
	45				
	40				
	35				
	30				—Eagle Cliff Bridge
	25				**Eagle Cliff Drop**
					—Pine Creek
	20				—Remains of old bridge right
					—Cliffs right
RM 60	15				—Muddy river
	10				
	5				—Clearcut area, right bank
					—Gravel beach left
	1:00				
	55				—Large islands with trees, campsites
	50				—Potential campsite on inside of right bend
					—Rock headwall, left bank
	45				—Metal Post on right bank–old gauging station
					—Rock wall on right bank
	40				—Miller Creek Falls left
	35				—Curley Creek Falls left
	30				
	25				
	20				
	15				
	10				
	5				
	12:00				—Rush Creek

Dry hillsides rise up and up from the Grande Ronde.

11

Grande Ronde

Logged at -	7,000 cfs Troy gauge
Recommended water level -	1,500 to 9,000 cfs
Best time -	April to mid-July
Rating -	Advanced
Water level information -	Portland River Forecast Center (503) 249-0666
River mile -	45.3 to 0; 45.3 miles
Time -	8 hours, 3 minutes; 5.8 mph
Elevation -	1,585' to 815'; 17' per mile

Troy, Oregon to Snake River

The Grande Ronde provides Washington boaters with a southwestern United States-style touring river. Here you'll find strange desert rock formations in a canyon over 3,000 feet deep. There is no road access to a portion of the run through a rugged canyon, making for pleasant picnicking and camping. The rapids are all class 1 or 2 difficulty, except for the Narrows, a series of three class 3 rapids near the end of the trip at river mile 4.5. The good beaches and generally sunny spring and summer weather make this a fine camping river. Bring sunscreen because the sun is intense.

The 44-mile trip upriver from this run (from Minam on the Wallowa river to Troy) is covered by John Garren in his guidebook, *Oregon River Tours*. Thus, between *Oregon River Tours* and this book, river logs for some 99 miles of the Wallowa and Grande Ronde rivers are available to the boater who would like to make the whole trip, which takes 4–7 days. The rapids on the stretch above Troy are class 2 and 3, and the river canyon is even more remote, with fine campsites.

The Grande Ronde has been the subject of several dam proposals in the 1970s and 1980s. The narrow canyon attracts hydroelectric developers. While none of these proposals is active now, they will undoubtedly be revived in the future. Get to know the Grande Ronde, *before* it is destroyed.

Getting There

The take-out is at Heller's Bar on the Snake River, 23 miles south of Asotin, which is 5 miles south of Clarkston. The road south of Asotin is paved for 14 miles, becoming gravel for the last 9 miles. At high water, the Snake sometimes floods the road, requiring either a drive through shallow water or complete closure of the road.

Washington State Route 129 stretches southwest into Oregon (becoming Oregon State Route 3) from Asotin. It is paved all the way and crosses the Grande Ronde at about river mile 26. Because of the depth of the river canyon, Route 129 winds down the steep slopes in many hairpin turns to the river.

Just south of the State Route 129 bridge over the river is a small cafe called the Oasis. The Oasis can arrange to shuttle your car from Troy to the Snake for you. The fare for the first car is $90 and each additional car is about $50. It's best to make arrangements one week in advance. Call the Oasis at (509) 256-3372 or (509) 256-3375.

To reach Troy, take the gravel road that turns upstream off State Route 129 just north of the bridge over the river. It winds along the river bank some 29 miles to Troy.

Put-ins and Take-outs

The put-in is on the right bank, just downstream of the bridge across the river at Troy. Parking is scarce here; be sure that you don't block the access for others.

At the Oasis is another good put-in or take-out spot, to run either the easier upper part of the trip or the more difficult and remote lower part.

Besides the Heller's Bar take-out on the Snake, you can take out at a fishing access site on the left bank of the Grande Ronde at mile 2 or just above the bridge over the river at approximately mile 3. The lower access point is equipped with sanicans. An advantage of these upper take-outs is that there is less chance that your car will be flooded; the Heller's Bar parking can be inundated when the Salmon River (a tributary to the Snake) rises in the spring run-off. Remember that you need a Department of Wildlife Conservation License to park at fishing access sites.

Shuttling takes at least 1 hour, 45 minutes, of hard driving, 65 miles one way. The route is not well signed but generally follows the main roads in the area. From Heller's Bar, drive back downstream toward Asotin 10 miles, turn left on Asotin County Road No. 206, the Couse (pronounced "cows") Creek Road. This one-lane gravel road snakes up a draw and winds around several hairpin turns to the top of the plateau above the river canyon.

On top of the plateau, continue another 5 miles on Road 206, which is now called the Montgomery Ridge Road, to State Route 129. It is 15 miles from the Snake to State Route 129. Turn left on State Route 129 and you will shortly reach Rattlesnake Summit (nearly 4,000 feet high) and begin the descent to the Grande Ronde. After winding down to the Grande Ronde, continue to Troy by turning right just before the bridge over the river. To run the shuttle the other way, watch for Montgomery Ridge

Going into The Narrows

Road, Road 206, off State Route 129 a little less than 2 miles beyond the turn-off to Fields Spring State Park.

Water Level

The Grande Ronde is a nice trip between 1,500 and 9,000 cfs. Below 1,500 cfs you may run aground on some of the gravel bars, and over 9,000 cfs the river approaches flood stage, eliminating most of the nice camping beaches. The water is much clearer and more attractive below 6,000 cfs. You should realize that the trip will take nearly twice as long at 1,500 cfs as it does at 7,000 cfs, the logged level.

Grande Ronde
Troy Gauge
Recommend 1,500 to 9,000 cfs

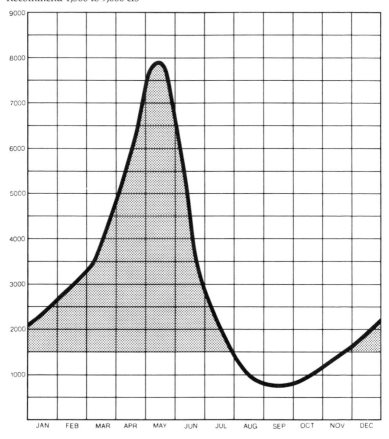

Special Hazards
None other than the **Narrows**.

Scenery
Fifteen million years ago several volcanoes in the area of the Grande Ronde produced numerous lava flows. These flows built up the present-day plateau through which the river has cut a canyon over 3,000 feet deep. On the sides of the canyon you can see the different lava lows that stand out as giant stairs separated by layers of soil. More recent molten rock has been injected into the early lava flows, forming a series of basalt dikes called the Grande Ronde Dike Swarm. The dikes appear as strong,

Coming out of The Narrows

dark, resistant vertical streaks of rock. In some places the dikes stand up in erosional relief like great ruined walls.

The basalt dikes make for many spectacular rock formations, including some natural stone arches. For 9 miles below the State Route 129 bridge, the canyon is particularly narrow and beautiful. There is no road access to this section of the river and it is wonderful for picnicking and camping.

The Grande Ronde valley is generally too dry to support trees, a contrast to the pine forests along State Route 129, 3,000 feet above the river. A few semi-open pine forests occur in draws along the upper part of this run, but there are no forests in the lower part of the run. Small, scrub oaks along the lower part of the trip provide shade for camping.

Cattle from the many ranches along the river graze on the banks. They

Cattle and abandoned cabins are frequently seen along the banks.

are particularly prevalent above the State Route 129 bridge and between river miles 12 and 16. Otherwise, the scenery is quite natural.

Camping

Along the Grande Ronde are many beautiful and excellent campsites. The campsites shown on the log are all on benches above the river and therefore are available at high or low water. At water levels below 7,000 cfs, many other beach campsites would be possible. Much of the land along the river is in private hands and you may not camp without the owner's permission. All of the campsites on the log are on U.S. Bureau of Land Management land as best as I can determine. Locating boundary lines is difficult, however, because many of the lines have no fences. If you see anyone in the area, ask permission to camp. Often ranchers will allow camping on private land, if you ask. If you don't, you may well be run off with a shotgun. Designation of the Grande Ronde as a Wild & Scenic river would provide money for purchasing more public access and camping sites.

Some planning in finding campsites is necessary because they are scarce in certain sections of the river. Generally, there are very few campsites away from the road in the section of the river above the State Route 129 bridge. Because of heavy ranching, campsites are also scarce between river miles 12 and 16 unless you get permission to camp on private land.

None of the water in the river or the tributaries is safe to drink. Bring your own water or purify the water with iodine or by sufficient boiling.

Rapids

The **Narrows** is the only significant rapid on this section of the Grande Ronde. This trip is rated advanced because of the Narrows and the isolation of the canyon below the State Route 129 bridge.

If you run your own shuttle, you can get a long-range look at the Narrows by driving up the road beyond the take-out. The road crosses from the north to the south side of the Grande Ronde at about river mile 3 and then winds over the ridge and up Joseph Creek (named for Chief Joseph of the Nez Perce). As the road starts up Joseph Creek, it is high above the river and, looking upstream, you can see the Narrows about a quarter of a mile away. Bring a pair of binoculars if you want to make much out.

The Narrows consists of three closely spaced class 3 drops around a gradual left bend in the river. At high water levels, you have to run all three drops at once because there is no place to eddy out between them. You can easily scout the drops from the left bank and portage light boats along the trail there (about 200 yards long).

There are numerous large waves and holes on the right side (outside of the bend) of the drops, but you can usually run down the middle as long as you meet the waves head on. At lower water levels, the river channel can narrow to a chute only 8–10 feet wide, forcing you to run right down the middle of the waves.

GRANDE RONDE RIVER

TROY (ORE.) TO CORRAL RIDGE

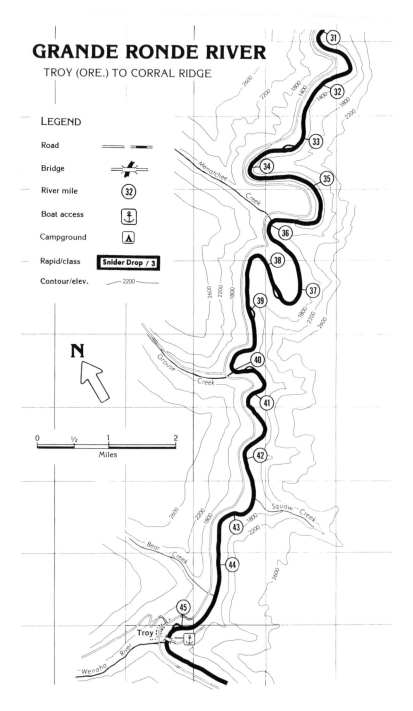

LEGEND

Road

Bridge

River mile

Boat access

Campground

Rapid/class   Snider Drop / 3

Contour/elev.   2200

N

0   ½   1   2
Miles

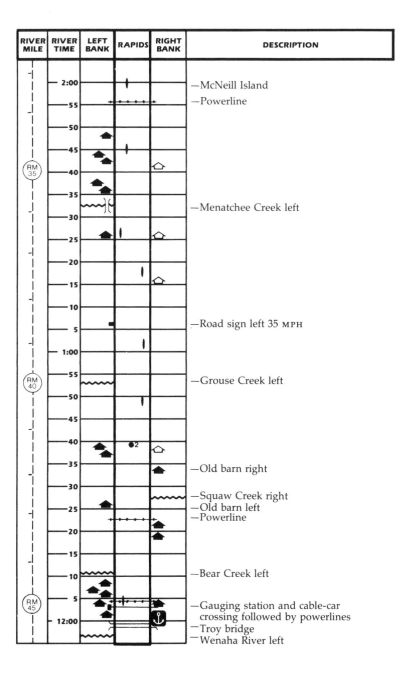

RIVER MILE	RIVER TIME	LEFT BANK	RAPIDS	RIGHT BANK	DESCRIPTION
	2:00				—McNeill Island
	55				—Powerline
	50				
	45				
RM 35	40				
	35				
	30				—Menatchee Creek left
	25				
	20				
	15				
	10				
	5				—Road sign left 35 MPH
	1:00				
	55				—Grouse Creek left
	50				
	45				
	40		2		
	35				—Old barn right
	30				—Squaw Creek right
	25				—Old barn left
	20				—Powerline
	15				
	10				—Bear Creek left
RM 45	5				—Gauging station and cable-car crossing followed by powerlines
	12:00				—Troy bridge
					—Wenaha River left

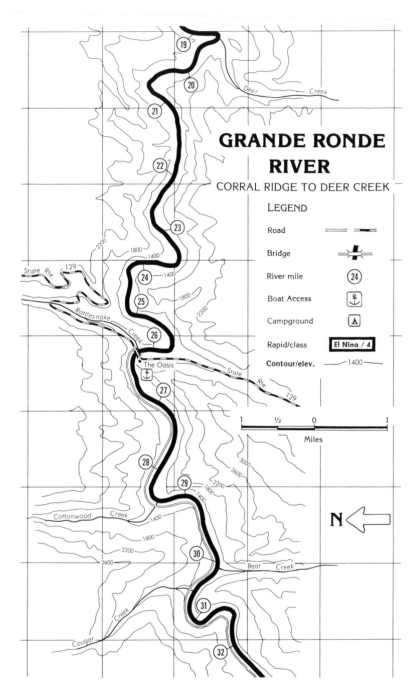

GRANDE RONDE RIVER

CORRAL RIDGE TO DEER CREEK

LEGEND

Road	
Bridge	
River mile	(24)
Boat Access	
Campground	
Rapid/class	El Nino / 4
Contour/elev.	1400

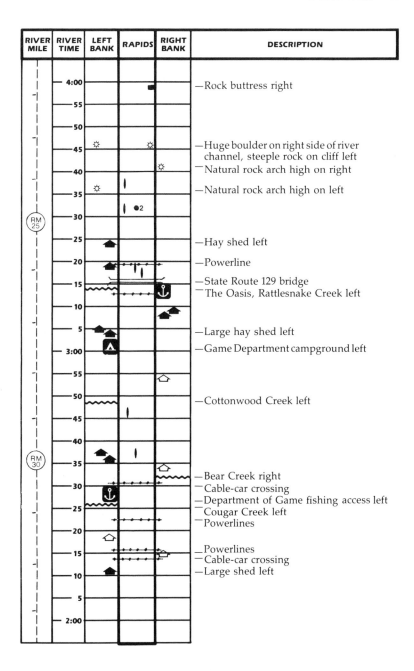

RIVER MILE	RIVER TIME	LEFT BANK	RAPIDS	RIGHT BANK	DESCRIPTION
	4:00				—Rock buttress right
	55				
	50				
	45	✿	✿		—Huge boulder on right side of river channel, steeple rock on cliff left
	40			✿	⁻Natural rock arch high on right
	35	✿			—Natural rock arch high on left
RM 25	30		●2		
	25				—Hay shed left
	20				—Powerline
	15			⚓	—State Route 129 bridge ⁻The Oasis, Rattlesnake Creek left
	10				
	5				—Large hay shed left
	3:00	⛺			—Game Department campground left
	55			⬦	
	50				—Cottonwood Creek left
	45				
	40				
RM 30	35			⬦	
	30	⚓			—Bear Creek right ⁻Cable-car crossing
	25				—Department of Game fishing access left ⁻Cougar Creek left ⁻Powerlines
	20	⬦			
	15				⁻⁻Powerlines ⁻Cable-car crossing
	10				—Large shed left
	5				
	2:00				

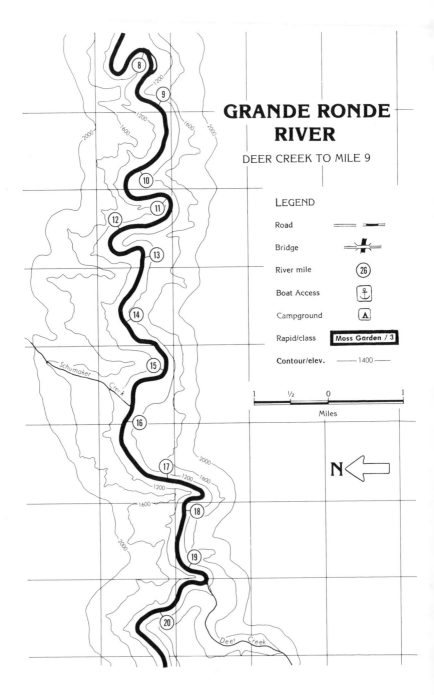

GRANDE RONDE RIVER

DEER CREEK TO MILE 9

LEGEND

Road	
Bridge	
River mile	26
Boat Access	
Campground	
Rapid/class	Moss Garden / 3
Contour/elev.	1400

Miles

N

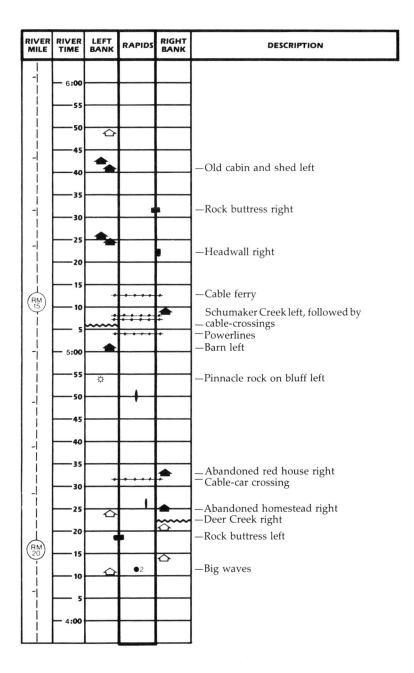

RIVER MILE	RIVER TIME	LEFT BANK	RAPIDS	RIGHT BANK	DESCRIPTION
	6:00				
	55				
	50				
	45				
	40				—Old cabin and shed left
	35				
	30				—Rock buttress right
	25				
	20				—Headwall right
	15				
RM 15	10				—Cable ferry
	5				Schumaker Creek left, followed by — cable-crossings ⁻Powerlines
	5:00				—Barn left
	55				—Pinnacle rock on bluff left
	50				
	45				
	40				
	35				—Abandoned red house right
	30				⁻Cable-car crossing
	25				—Abandoned homestead right
					—Deer Creek right
	20				—Rock buttress left
RM 20	15				
	10		●2		—Big waves
	5				
	4:00				

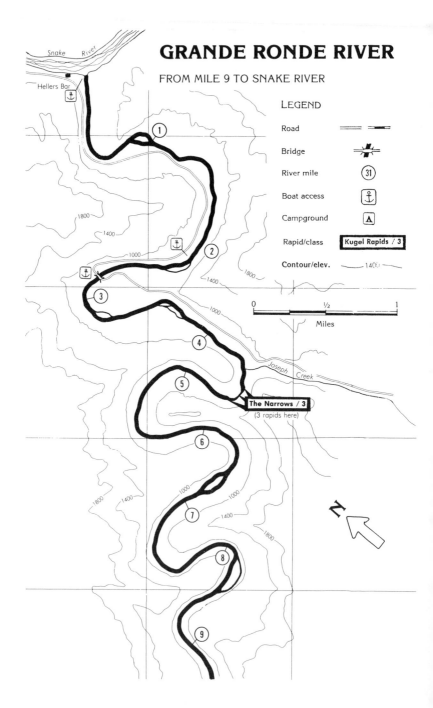

GRANDE RONDE RIVER

FROM MILE 9 TO SNAKE RIVER

Snake River

Hellers Bar

LEGEND

Road	
Bridge	
River mile	31
Boat access	⚓
Campground	A
Rapid/class	Kugel Rapids / 3
Contour/elev.	1400

0   ½   1
Miles

Joseph Creek

The Narrows / 3
(3 rapids here)

N

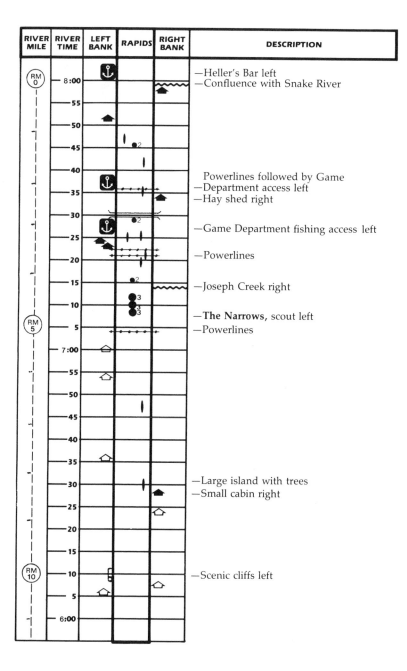

RIVER MILE	RIVER TIME	LEFT BANK	RAPIDS	RIGHT BANK	DESCRIPTION
RM 0	8:00				—Heller's Bar left
					—Confluence with Snake River
	55				
	50				
	45		2		
	40				
	35				Powerlines followed by Game
					—Department access left
	30				—Hay shed right
	25		2		—Game Department fishing access left
	20				—Powerlines
	15		2		—Joseph Creek right
	10		3		—**The Narrows,** scout left
			3 3		
RM 5	5				—Powerlines
	7:00				
	55				
	50				
	45				
	40				
	35				
	30				—Large island with trees
					—Small cabin right
	25				
	20				
	15				
RM 10	10				—Scenic cliffs left
	5				
	6:00				

12

Suiattle

Logged at - 5,700 cfs Sauk gauge
Recommended water level - 2,500 to 9,000 cfs
Best time - July and August
Rating - Advanced
Water level information - NOAA Tape (206) 526-8530
River mile - 11.7 to (Sauk River) 12.4; 12.7 miles
Time - 2 hours, 19 minutes; 5.5 mph
Elevation - 750' to 365'; 30' per mile

Rat Trap Bridge to Sauk River Bridge

The Suiattle River will provide you with a remote trip on a river with an undeveloped shoreline. Although there is evidence of logging on the surrounding ridges, the banks are thickly forested and there are no other signs of civilization until you reach the take-out. The river is protected as a scenic river under the national Wild & Scenic Rivers Act and is a good place to spot deer, waterfowl and even an occasional bear. It is the traditional home of the Suiattle Indian tribe, and there is an Indian cemetery not far from the river a few miles upstream from the put-in.

The river is largely fed by glaciers on the north and east sides of Glacier Peak. Its milky water is often runnable through August and early September, when other rivers are too low. The milky appearance of the Suiattle is the result of glacier flour. As the glacier grinds against rock formations, the ice wears the rock down to a fine powder. When the glacier melts, the rock powder flows into local streams and rivers.

Only expert open canoeists can run the Suiattle, and even they should wait for a warm day because they are likely to be swamped frequently.

Getting There

The Suiattle flows into the Sauk River a few miles north of the town of Darrington. Darrington is about 65 miles northeast of Seattle on State Route 530. To reach the river, drive north out of Darrington toward Rockport.

Put-ins and Take-outs

You'll reach the take-out first, so you may wish to drop a car off there.

It is on the right side of the bridge over the Sauk river, about 8 miles up the road from Darrington. (An alternative take-out is along the road just 0.5 mile south of the bridge, opposite the mouth of the Suiattle. There is a large dirt turn-out there.)

To reach the put-in, continue on the highway away from Darrington. About 200 yards from the east end of the bridge over the Sauk, the main road bends to the left while a smaller paved road continues straight ahead. Go straight ahead on this road about 12 miles to Rat Trap Bridge. The road is generally well away from the river through the forest. It is paved all the way to Rat Trap Bridge with the exception of a couple of short gravel sections.

Water Level

The only gauge from which you can get a current reading is on the Sauk River, below the confluence of the Sauk and Suiattle. The Suiattle is best run between 2,500 and 9,000 cfs on the Sauk gauge. It can be run at higher levels, but many of the rapids are washed out. Also, at higher levels you will find a considerable amount of debris floating down the river. At levels below 2,500 cfs it can be run in kayaks but is too low for rafts.

Suiattle
Sauk Gauge
Recommend 2,500 to 9,000 cfs

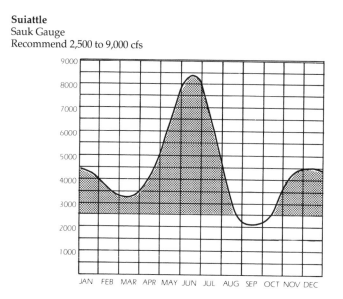

Special Hazards

The Suiattle is a young river that continually eats away at and changes its silt and clay banks. As the banks are eroded, trees and debris fall into the river, creating frequent **logjams**. The logjams can (and do) change

The middle section of the run has nearly constant whitewater action.

from year to year and can go completely across the river. They present a severe hazard to boaters. Being forced against and underneath a sweeper will likely kill you.

The other principal danger is the **metal remains** of a bridge pier at log time 23 minutes. Stay well left.

In some years, commercial rafters have put in above Rat Trap Bridge, about 3 miles farther up the river at approximately river mile 15.4. In many recent years, however, the river has been completely blocked below this put-in by logjams 200–300 feet long. This section of the river should be completely scouted prior to attempting to run it. It is reported to be about as hard as the section covered by the following log.

The river as been run all the way from the end of the road at Sulphur

Creek Campground down. The upper section is approximately 11 miles (Sulphur Creek Campground is near river mile 26.5) of very swift water. The rapids are not very difficult (class 3) but are nearly constant, with the water averaging about 12–15 miles per hour. There are lots of logjams (recently eight logjams completely blocked the river), and getting out of the river is difficult due to the speed of the water and lack of eddies. NO ONE should undertake a raft trip on this section of the river without first having it scouted by an expert kayaker. It is almost impossible to scout the river from the road because the two are usually separated by several hundred yards of thick forest and brush.

Scenery

You will have many beautiful views of natural forest with mountains in the background. There are almost no signs of civilization from the put-in to the take-out. If you turn around and look back a little below the mouth of Big Creek, you'll have a beautiful view of Big Creek falls.

Camping

There are three Forest Service campgrounds within a 12-mile drive up the Suiattle from the put-in. The campgrounds at Buck Creek and Sulphur Creek are good-sized, whereas the one at Downey Creek is quite small. No fee is charged.

Rapids

Hurricane rapid at log time 51 minutes is the most difficult stretch of rapids and demands both good river-reading skills and control of the boat to avoid the numerous holes in the rapid. You can scout it from a gravel bar on the left bank, but landing is difficult because there is no eddy. You will reach Hurricane not long after passing Big Creek—a very noticeable large creek of clear water entering on the right. After a couple of bends in the river, you will see a gray, clay wall on the outside of a left bend in the river. Following that is a class 2 rapid and, around the next bend, Hurricane. It begins at a right bend in the river and has two drops with about 100 feet of fast water between them.

The other rapids are straightforward and, though many are exciting, they can easily be read from the boat by any experienced river runner.

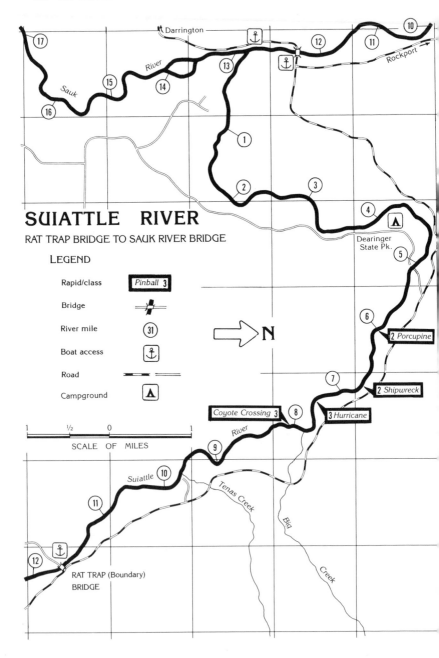

SUIATTLE RIVER

RAT TRAP BRIDGE TO SAUK RIVER BRIDGE

LEGEND

Rapid/class	*Pinball* 3
Bridge	
River mile	31
Boat access	⚓
Road	
Campground	▲

SCALE OF MILES
½   0

N

Darrington

Rockport

Sauk

River

Dearinger
State Pk.

2 *Porcupine*

2 *Shipwreck*

3 *Hurricane*

Coyote Crossing 3

River

Suiattle

Tenas Creek

Big

Creek

RAT TRAP (Boundary)
BRIDGE

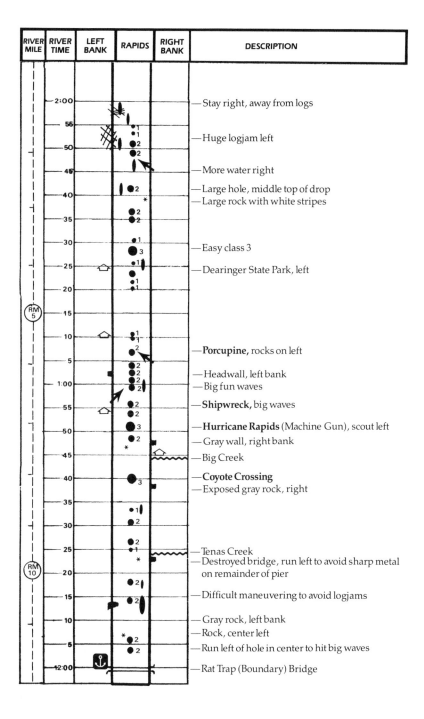

RIVER MILE	RIVER TIME	LEFT BANK	RAPIDS	RIGHT BANK	DESCRIPTION
	2:00				—Stay right, away from logs
	55		•1 •1		—Huge logjam left
	50		•2 •2		
	45				—More water right
	40		•2 *		—Large hole, middle top of drop —Large rock with white stripes
	35		•2 •2		
	30		•1		
			●3		—Easy class 3
	25		•1		—Dearinger State Park, left
	20		•1 •1		
RM 5	15				
	10		•1 •1		
	5		●2		—**Porcupine,** rocks on left
	1:00		●2 ●2 ●2 ●2		—Headwall, left bank —Big fun waves
	55		●2 ●2		—**Shipwreck,** big waves
	50		●3		—**Hurricane Rapids** (Machine Gun), scout left
	45		●2 *		—Gray wall, right bank —Big Creek
	40		●3		—**Coyote Crossing** —Exposed gray rock, right
	35				
	30		•1 ●2		
	25		●2 •1 *		—Tenas Creek —Destroyed bridge, run left to avoid sharp metal on remainder of pier
RM 10	20		●2		
	15		●2		—Difficult maneuvering to avoid logjams
	10				—Gray rock, left bank
	5		* ●2 ●2		—Rock, center left —Run left of hole in center to hit big waves
	12:00				—Rat Trap (Boundary) Bridge

RIVER MILE	RIVER TIME	LEFT BANK	RAPIDS	RIGHT BANK	DESCRIPTION
	4:00				
	55				
	50				
	45				
	40				
	35				
	30				
	25				
	20				
	15				
	10				
	5				
	3:00				
	55				
	50				
	45				
	40				
	35				
	30				
	25				
	20				— Sauk River Bridge
	15				— Confluence with Sauk River
	10				
	5				— Cut bank, right
	2:00				

Bouncing through the waves of Porcupine

13

Upper Soleduck

Logged at - 1,400 cfs McDonald Bridge gauge
Recommended water level - 1,200 to 3,000 cfs (varies)
Best time - April to mid-June
Rating - Advanced
Water level information - NOAA Tape (206) 526-8530
River mile - 53.8 to 29.9; 23.9 miles
Time - 7 hours, 19 minutes; 3.3 mph
Elevation - 1,020' to 330'; 29' per mile

Fibreboard Bridge to Salmon Hatchery

The Upper Soleduck provides interesting rapids on a rain forest odyssey. The rapids are not difficult at the moderate water levels found in spring and summer, but they enliven one of the most beautiful river trips in Washington. There are lush, moss-covered forests, abundant wildlife, breath-taking gorges and crystalline water in a boulder-studded channel. This trip is also long enough to provide a nice overnight for those who are not afraid to risk camping in the rain. The Soleduck has been found eligible by the Forest Service and Park Service to be a Wild & Scenic river.

Getting There
US 101 parallels the Soleduck about 30 miles west of Port Angeles.

Put-ins and Take-outs
To reach the upper put-in, turn off of US 101 on the South Fork Soleduck road (Forest Service 2918 road). The road leaves US 101 4.7 miles west of the west end of Lake Crescent or about 0.4 mile east of mile marker 216. The upper put-in is at the bridge (known as the Fibreboard Bridge) over the Soleduck about 3 miles up the South Fork Soleduck road.

For an alternative put-in, turn right off the South Fork Soleduck road about 0.95 mile from US 101 on an unmarked dirt road. Drive about 0.1 mile to the river where you start your trip at log time 39 minutes. This put-in has the advantage of being below two of the three spots where water may be insufficient because the river braids around several islands.

The next potential put-in or take-out is at Klahowya Forest Service Camp. From US 101 turn in at the campground and bear to the left around the one-way road. At the last campground (the farthest down-

Riding the waves at the bottom of Snider Drop

stream) you will find an unimproved boat ramp. This appears at log time 2 hours, 53 minutes.

The next potential put-in or take-out is at a place known locally as Riverside. It is just a rough spot over the bank next to a wide asphalt turn-out along US 101, just west of a sign (facing west) saying "Slow Vehicles Use Turnouts Next 15 miles." The sign is 0.8 mile west of the bridge over the river near Klahowya Campground or, coming from the west, 1.5 miles east of an Olympic National Forest sign. Riverside appears on the log at 3 hours, 8 minutes.

The Bear Creek boat ramp is a favorite put-in or take-out of fishermen for their drift boats. To reach the boat ramp, turn off US 101 on an unmarked dirt road opposite the Bear Creek Tavern. The turn-off is 0.3 mile east of the bridge on US 101 over Bear Creek. About 0.2 mile down the dirt road you will reach the boat ramp marked by a sign warning "Extreme Danger, Hazardous Rapids Downstream, Washington Game Department."

The last take-out on the run is at the salmon hatchery below Sappho. The turn-off to the hatchery leaves US 101 where the road cuts off a bend in the river, about 0.2 mile from a bridge from either direction. Immediately after taking the turn-off to the south, you should turn right, in the direction marked by a small white hatchery sign. Drive about 1.5 miles downriver to the hatchery; the boat ramp is to your right. There is a low dam just above the boat ramp, and you may wish to take out above it.

Water Level

No gauge has up-to-date reports on the Soleduck, so the water level must be judged by the gauge on the Elwha, the next basin over. The Elwha gauge provides a fairly good indication of conditions on the Soleduck, but certainly not an exact measurement. The Elwha gets more snow run-off than the Soleduck, so a higher reading is needed on the McDonald Bridge gauge later in the season than early on. What you are looking for is a somewhat greater than average flow in the spring. It is usually present after a good rain or after a couple days of hot weather that melts the snow. Recommended minimum and maximum levels for the Soleduck in spring are as follows:

	April	May 1–15	May 16–31	June 1–15	June 16–on
Min	1,200	1,500	1,800	2,100	2,400
Max	2,400	3,000	3,600	3,700	3,900

You have to use some good sense in making use of this table. It is based on average weather conditions. For example, in early May, if it has been colder and wetter than normal, look at the April figures. If it has been hotter and drier than normal, however, look at the May figures. Also note that these are the recommended boating levels; you can scrape down the river with a lot less. Fishermen regularly take their drift boats down the Soleduck at least through mid-June every year, but they're looking for good fishing, not good boating.

McDonald Bridge Gauge
Upper Soleduck
Recommend 1,200 to 3,000 cfs

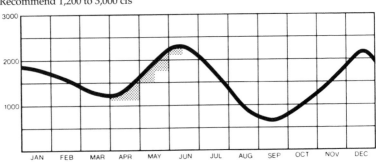

Hole-riding in Water Garden

Special Hazards

Fishermen are not really a special hazard, but remember that they were here first. Stay out of the way of their lines, particularly if they have a fish on. Fishing season usually lasts from winter through March and begins again in late May, continuing through July. The part of the river open to fishing can vary from year to year, but generally the Upper Soleduck is not open above Klahowya Campground, thus it's a good area to boat during fishing season.

A difficulty, though not much of a hazard, is that in the uppermost part of the river are several places where the river braids around islands leaving none of the several channels with enough water to boat. This problem requires a short portage over a boulder bar, or at least some pushing and sliding of your boat over the rocks. Using the put-in at log time 39 minutes avoids two of three particularly bad spots. They are located at log times 13 minutes, 28 minutes, and 52 minutes.

A lot of boulders stud the heavily forested path of the Soleduck.

The Washington State Department of Fisheries has constructed a dam across the river just above the boat ramp at the salmon hatchery in order to divert water for the hatchery. A boat slot cut in the dam, on the right side, is where you should go over the dam to avoid damage to your boat.

Scenery

Although paralleled by roads, the upper part of this run seems quite remote. It presents a fantasy of greenery: deep green ferns, luxuriant mosses and bright new shoots blend into a study of green, accentuated by the brown of the trees and rocks. Between the rapids are many deep, clear pools where salmon and steelhead can be seen. Bald eagles come to the Soleduck for the fish and I've seen them every time I've boated the upper part of the river.

The river has cut its own narrow channel, which lies about 30 feet below the level of the surrounding valley. Its heavily forested slopes screen out most evidence of civilization. A trip on the Soleduck is the best way to enjoy the rain forest.

Camping

Klahowya Campground, at log time 2 hours, 45–55 minutes, provides many beautiful campsites with views of the river. It's open year-round, and during the 1991 summer season the fee was $6.00.

The State DNR Wahlgren Memorial Campground, open throughout the year, is above the river on the right bank at log time 5 hours, 23–28 minutes. It is not visible from the river but provides campsites with picnic tables and fire pits. It is about 3 miles east of the turn-off to the salmon hatchery, just a little downriver from the turn-off to the Bear Creek boat ramp.

Campsites provided by ITT Rayonier are available in the Tumbling Rapids Recreation Area right across US 101 from the turn-off to the salmon hatchery. Tumbling Rapids is usually open only from Memorial Day weekend through Labor Day, however.

For those who would like to make this an overnight trip, potential campsites on public property are indicated on the log. Nearly all of the land on the left bank of the river is owned by government agencies, and you can camp there if you do a little scouting first to make sure that you are not near someone's house.

Rapids

Although this trip has a good number of class 2 and 3 rapids, its primary attraction is the scenery rather than the whitewater. The drops provide many good playspots and put a little excitement in the trip but are fairly widely spaced. The last part of this trip, known to fishermen as the Bear Creek stretch, offers the only sustained rapids of the trip. Most of the rapids are boulder gardens, requiring technical maneuvering, rather than big drops with large waves. The biggest rapid of the trip, **Snider Drop**, provides a long technical rock dodge, followed by a good drop at the end.

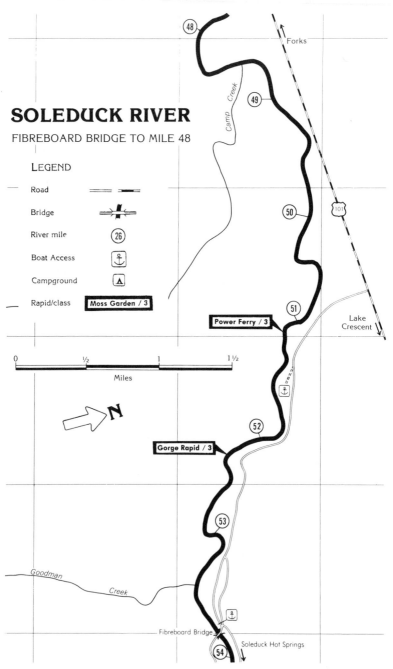

SOLEDUCK RIVER

FIBREBOARD BRIDGE TO MILE 48

LEGEND

Road

Bridge

River mile ㉖

Boat Access

Campground ▲

Rapid/class   Moss Garden / 3

Forks

Camp Creek

㊽

㊾

⑤⓪

101

⑤①

Power Ferry / 3

Lake Crescent

0   ½   1   1½

Miles

N

⑤②

Gorge Rapid / 3

⑤③

Goodman Creek

Fibreboard Bridge

Soleduck Hot Springs

⑤④

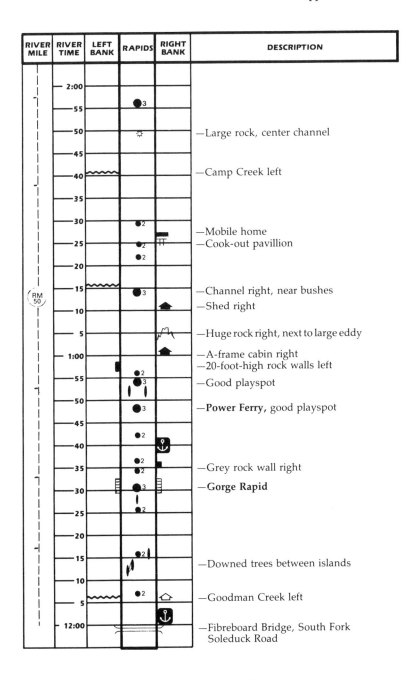

RIVER MILE	RIVER TIME	LEFT BANK	RAPIDS	RIGHT BANK	DESCRIPTION
	2:00				
	55		●3		
	50		☼		—Large rock, center channel
	45				
	40				—Camp Creek left
	35				
	30		●2		
	25		●2		—Mobile home
					—Cook-out pavillion
	20		●2		
	15		●3		—Channel right, near bushes
RM 50	10				—Shed right
	5				—Huge rock right, next to large eddy
	1:00				—A-frame cabin right
					—20-foot-high rock walls left
	55		●2		
			●3		—Good playspot
	50		●3		—**Power Ferry,** good playspot
	45				
	40		●2		
	35		●2		
			●2		—Grey rock wall right
	30		●3		—**Gorge Rapid**
	25		●2		
	20				
	15		●2		
	10				—Downed trees between islands
	5		●2		—Goodman Creek left
	12:00				—Fibreboard Bridge, South Fork Soleduck Road

SOLEDUCK RIVER

MILE 48 TO MILE 39

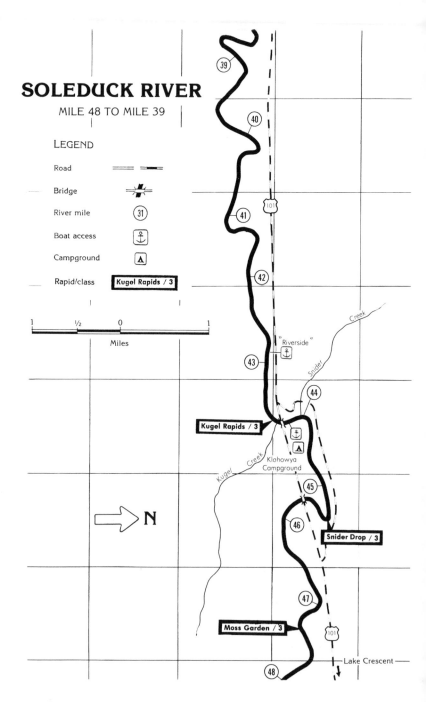

LEGEND

Road	
Bridge	
River mile	31
Boat access	
Campground	
Rapid/class	Kugel Rapids / 3

Miles

N

Kugel Rapids / 3

Snider Drop / 3

Moss Garden / 3

"Riverside"

Klahowya Campground

Lake Crescent

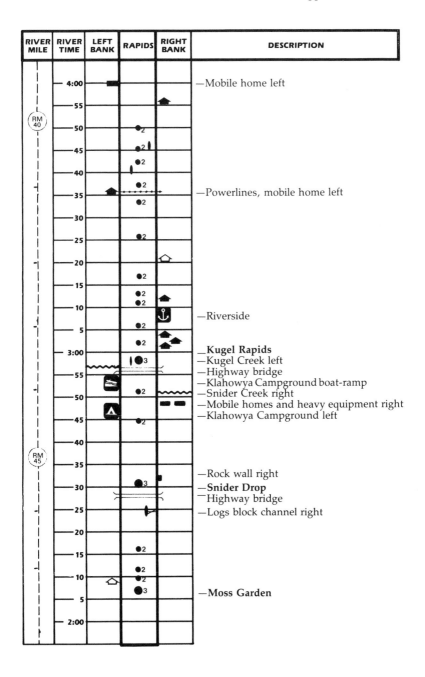

RIVER MILE	RIVER TIME	LEFT BANK	RAPIDS	RIGHT BANK	DESCRIPTION
	4:00				—Mobile home left
	55				
RM 40	50		●2		
	45		●2		
	40		●2		
	35		●2		—Powerlines, mobile home left
	30		●2		
	25		●2		
	20				
	15		●2		
	10		●2 ●2		
					—Riverside
	5		●2		
	3:00		●2		**Kugel Rapids**
			●3		—Kugel Creek left
	55				—Highway bridge
					—Klahowya Campground boat-ramp
	50		●2		—Snider Creek right
					—Mobile homes and heavy equipment right
	45		●2		—Klahowya Campground left
	40				
RM 45	35				—Rock wall right
	30		●3		—**Snider Drop**
					—Highway bridge
	25				—Logs block channel right
	20				
	15		●2		
	10		●2 ●2 ●3		
	5				—**Moss Garden**
	2:00				

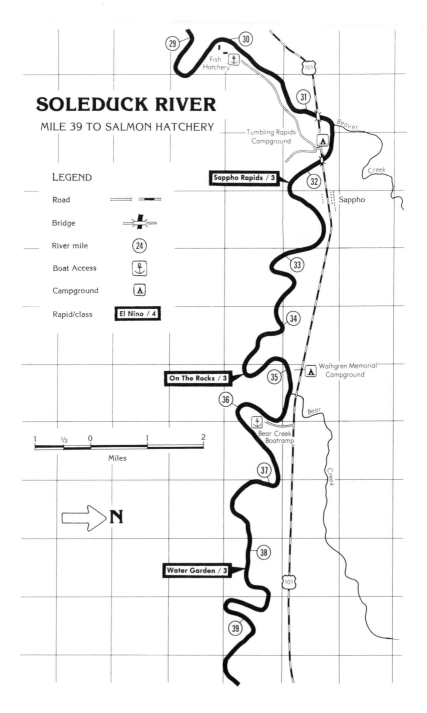

SOLEDUCK RIVER

MILE 39 TO SALMON HATCHERY

Fish Hatchery

Tumbling Rapids Campground

Beaver Creek

Sappho Rapids / 3

Sappho

LEGEND

Road	
Bridge	
River mile	24
Boat Access	
Campground	
Rapid/class	El Nino / 4

On The Rocks / 3

Walhgren Memorial Campground

Bear Creek Boatramp

Bear Creek

Miles

⇨ N

Water Garden / 3

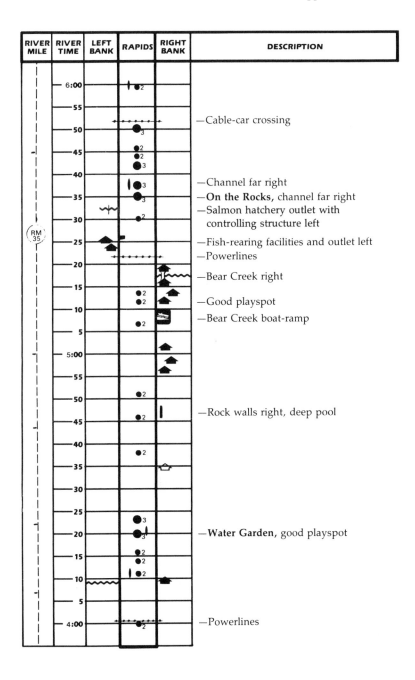

RIVER MILE	RIVER TIME	LEFT BANK	RAPIDS	RIGHT BANK	DESCRIPTION
	6:00		●2		
	55				
	50		●3		—Cable-car crossing
	45		●2 ●2 ●3		
	40				
	35		●3 ●3		—Channel far right —**On the Rocks,** channel far right
	30		●2		—Salmon hatchery outlet with controlling structure left
RM 35	25				—Fish-rearing facilities and outlet left
	20				—Powerlines
	15				—Bear Creek right
	10		●2 ●2		—Good playspot
	5		●2		—Bear Creek boat-ramp
	5:00				
	55				
	50		●2		
	45		●2		—Rock walls right, deep pool
	40				
	35		●2		
	30				
	25				
	20		●3 ●3		—**Water Garden,** good playspot
	15		●2 ●2		
	10		●2		
	5				
	4:00		●2		—Powerlines

There's a lot of rock dodging on the Soleduck.

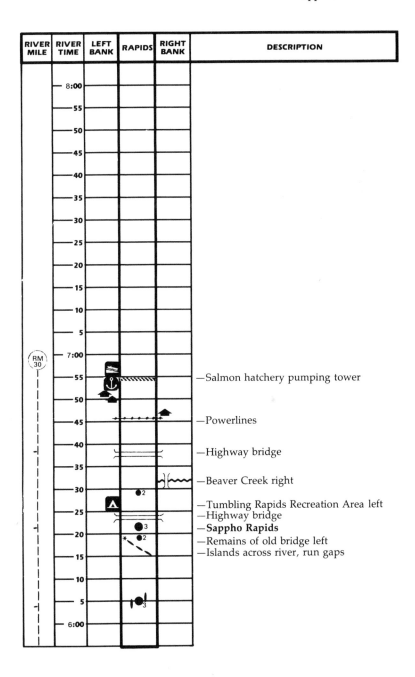

RIVER MILE	RIVER TIME	LEFT BANK	RAPIDS	RIGHT BANK	DESCRIPTION
	8:00				
	55				
	50				
	45				
	40				
	35				
	30				
	25				
	20				
	15				
	10				
	5				
RM 30	7:00				
	55				—Salmon hatchery pumping tower
	50				
	45				—Powerlines
	40				—Highway bridge
	35				
	30		●2		—Beaver Creek right
	25				—Tumbling Rapids Recreation Area left
					—Highway bridge
	20		●3		—**Sappho Rapids**
			* ●2		—Remains of old bridge left
	15				—Islands across river, run gaps
	10				
	5		●3		
	6:00				

14

Wenatchee

Logged at - 6,700 cfs Peshastin gauge
Recommended water level - 4,000 to 13,000 cfs
Best time - May to mid-July
Rating - Advanced
Water level information - NOAA Tape (206) 526-8530
River mile - 24.6 to 5.8; 18.8 miles
Time - 3 hours, 30 minutes; 5.4 mph
Elevation - 1,100' to 680'; 22' per mile

Leavenworth to Monitor

The Wenatchee is a snow-fed river running off the east side of the North Cascades. It is probably the most popular and frequently run river in Washington. After the winter snowpack has melted and pooled in Lake Wenatchee, the river thunders through Tumwater Canyon and exits near Leavenworth. The Indians fished for salmon and steelhead near present-day Leavenworth, and "Wenatchee" comes from their name for the river, which means "river flowing from canyon." Boaters with an instinct for survival pass up the class 4 to 6 rapids of Tumwater Canyon and put in at Leavenworth.

Getting There

US 2 parallels the Wenatchee from Leavenworth to Monitor.

Put-ins and Take-outs

The old put-in near the Icicle Creek Road bridge has been closed because boaters using the riverbank as a restroom posed a health hazard to Leavenworth, which has its water supply intake near there. The log still starts at the bridge to orient those who are familiar with that area, but the first put-in is downstream, opposite Leavenworth at log time 28 minutes.

To get to the new put-in, turn off US 2 just east of the bridge over the river, east of Leavenworth. The road goes west, up the Wenatchee. In about 0.8 mile, turn right (off the outside of a bend in the road) onto a dirt road 0.1 mile to the river. This unimproved boat ramp gives you barely 12 minutes to warm up before you are into Boulder Bend—the most difficult rapid on this stretch of river.

There is an access site in the Peshastin area. The state Department of

In years past, a rodeo with a hole-riding competition has been held on the Wenatchee.

Wildlife has a rough boat ramp on School Street in Peshastin. Cross the bridge from US 2 to Peshastin and turn right on School Street. Go 0.3 mile to the ramp on the north side of the river at log time 1 hour, 36 minutes. A Department of Wildlife conservation license is needed to use this access site (see Introduction).

The upper take-out is provided by Cashmere, just below the Division Street Bridge. Parking, sanicans and a changing area are available; you can reach it by turning off Division Street, which intersects US 2. Note that to reach the take-out, you have to go to the right of a gravel bar, which is to the right of the center of the river.

The City of Cashmere also allows noncommercial boaters to use a dirt boat ramp just below the downstream bridge in Cashmere. There are no facilities here but it is an easier take-out than the one off Division Street.

The lower take-out is at Monitor (named for the Union ironclad in the Civil War) at the Department of Wildlife's river access site (conservation license required). To reach the access site, turn off US 2 at the Monitor Bridge. The take-out is just upstream from the bridge on the right bank.

Water Level

The Wenatchee is runnable at a wide range of water levels. About 3,000 cfs is needed for larger rafts (though the recommended 4,000 cfs is more enjoyable), but small rafts and kayaks can run it on as little as 1,500 cfs. It can be run in open canoes at levels below 3,000 cfs, although only experts are likely to avoid swamping at levels above 1,800 cfs in Boulder Bend, Rock 'n Roll and Drunkard's Drop.

Above 10,000 cfs many rocks are covered and the river channel becomes less interesting, but the powerful hydraulics can make for a very exciting ride. Above 13,000 cfs, Boulder Bend and Rock 'n Roll should be considered class 4 rapids. The run is slower and distinctly less exciting below 6,000 cfs, and you may wish to use the lower put-in at Peshastin at these levels.

Wenatchee
Peshastin Gauge
Recommend 4,000 to 13,000 cfs

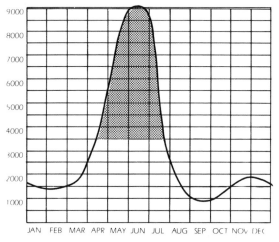

Special Hazards

PORTAGE the irrigation **dam** at Dryden, a little below Rock 'n Roll. The dam forms a small pool, and it is easy to take out on the right bank and carry around on the path cleared for portaging. The dam used to be runnable at moderate water levels but was reconstructed over the 1986–87 winter and is now a drowning machine. It creates a uniform wave breaking upstream all the way across the river. The water on the surface moves upstream toward the face of the dam. It is very difficult for people caught in this hydraulic to escape; they will likely recirculate until they drown. When putting back into the river below the dam, be sure to get well below the boil line. The current is stronger than it looks and can pull a boat back upriver into the dam.

Scenery

There are some nice bluffs and apple orchards along the Wenatchee, but other than the view of the mountains at the beginning of the trip, you're here for the whitewater, not the scenery. Civilization is much in evidence on this trip, and in many places junk is scattered along the riverbank.

Camping

Nearly all the land along the river is privately owned, so don't camp along the river except at Wenatchee County Park (just below the lower take-out) or the KOA campground near Leavenworth. A fee is charged for the use of these campgrounds. About 8 miles up Icicle Creek Road is the first of a series of Forest Service campgrounds (fees charged also).

Rapids

The first significant rapid you will reach after the put-in and also the most difficult on the Wenatchee is Boulder Bend. Often called Boulder Garden, the rapid is upon you soon after the highway bridge. **Boulder Bend** consists of a right bend that shelves to the left (or outside) of the bend with a large rock formation in the middle. The formation is an ob-

There's big water on the Wenatchee during spring runoff. (Kevin O'Brien photo)

stacle below 8,000–9,000 cfs and a large hole above that level.

Scouting Boulder Bend is difficult. The only good landing places are on the left bank. Once a boat has landed on the left bank, however, the force of the water pushing toward the outside of the bend makes it almost impossible to ferry and run the right side of the rock formation. To preserve the option of running the right side (or inside of the bend) scout right. Scouting right is difficult, because there are no real eddies or landing places on the right bank; you must simply jump out and grab a boulder. Once you are into the rapid, you cannot scout it.

At water levels over 5,000 cfs, it is possible to ferry to the right of the rock formation, running the inside of the bend, then dodging the rocks and running the waves below. You must run to the left of the rock formation at lower water levels because there will be insufficient water on the right; this run is very difficult due to the shelving to the left. The shelving forces the water to pour in from the right, carrying you left toward the outside of the bend and many large rocks and holes. Thus, stay well right where possible.

The next major and longest (200-yard) rapid on the Wenatchee is **Rock 'n Roll**. This rapid contains Satan's Eyeball, a large hole that forms in the right center of the river at water levels from about 2,500 cfs up to about 12,000 cfs. You should scout by landing at the head of the island on the left (watch for a small flow of the river that goes off through boulders and brush on the left side of the island). It is necessary to push through brush, but by working your way down the island, the whole rapid can be scouted. Above 3,500 cfs, in addition to the Eyeball and another hole downstream to the left (Son of Satan), the rapid consists of big waves, great fun for paddlers. Below 3,500 cfs rocks become increasingly evident, and below 2,500 cfs the rapid becomes a rock garden. Ferrying left of Satan's Eyeball becomes difficult over about 9,000 cfs because most of the water flows across the river toward the hole. The conservative run from 9,000 to 12,000 cfs is to hug the right shore. Above 12,000 cfs Satan's Eyeball disappears and is replaced by an immense wave that can stand a 10-man raft on end. Hard paddling or rowing is necessary to avoid stalling on the wave.

Below the dam, you'll reach the third class 3 rapid, **Gorilla Falls**, under the highway bridge. The best run is near the right pier, away from rocks on the left.

Kayakers will find great surfing on the ledges at river mile 14.

Drunkard's Drop is the fourth significant rapid on the Wenatchee. It involves a substantial 3–4-foot drop but no other real obstacle other than its shallowness at lower water levels. The drop, however, is at an angle to the flow of the river, so you will encounter waves hitting you at an angle from the right.

The rapid occurs right where the river turns upon encountering a sheer dirt bluff on the left side. At levels between 4,000 and 10,000 cfs, a power-

Paddle rafts frequently lose passengers in the big waves. (Kevin O'Brien photo)

ful eddy forms next to the bluffs on river left. Scouting can be done either right or left. Scouting the river right allows you to walk downstream of the drop for additional inspection but is difficult at high water because the gravel bar on the right side is covered. When scouting, land far enough upriver to allow time for a ferry, if necessary, prior to entering the rapid.

The best raft approach is to swing left, just above the drop, and go straight down the drop and toward the center of the river, hitting the waves head on. Attempting to cheat the drop on the right is often unsuccessful. Avoid the far left, where there is often a nasty, swirling wave.

For smaller boats, the drop is actually most difficult at about 2,000 cfs because the first wave becomes a back-curler, creating a hole that extends all the way across the river. The back-curler is 2–3 feet high and will easily stop a small raft or flip a poorly handled kayak. At 2,500 cfs the back-curler turns into a smooth wave, whereas at 1,500 cfs the back-curler is too small to be a problem.

The last significant rapid on the river is Snowblind. The river tumbles over several rocks and ledges, creating waves and holes. Generally, it can be run down the center or left by threading around the holes. It has become more interesting as a result of the 1990 floods and a large hole now forms at the bottom center left at flows from 5,000 to 8,000 cfs.

Granny's Rapid is not considered class 3, because you can avoid it. The large waves can provide a lot of fun, however.

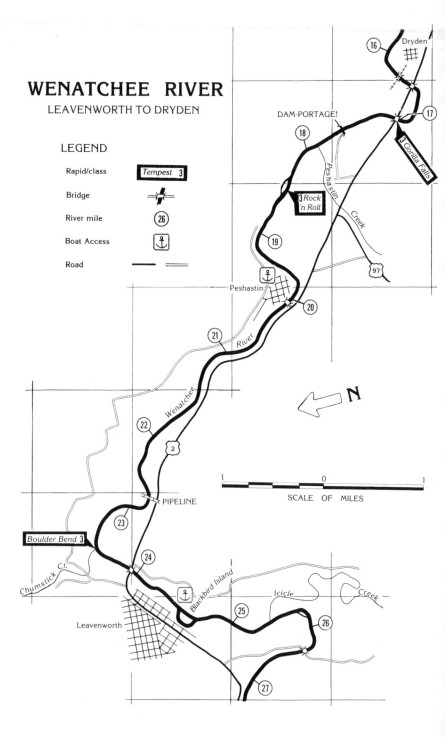

WENATCHEE RIVER

LEAVENWORTH TO DRYDEN

LEGEND

Rapid/class	Tempest 3
Bridge	
River mile	26
Boat Access	⚓
Road	

DAM-PORTAGE!

3 Rock 'n Roll

3 Gorilla Falls

Dryden

Peshastin

Creek

97

Peshastin

Wenatchee   River

Wenatchee

2

PIPELINE

Boulder Bend 3

Chumstick Cr.

Blackbird Island

Icicle   Creek

Leavenworth

N

SCALE OF MILES

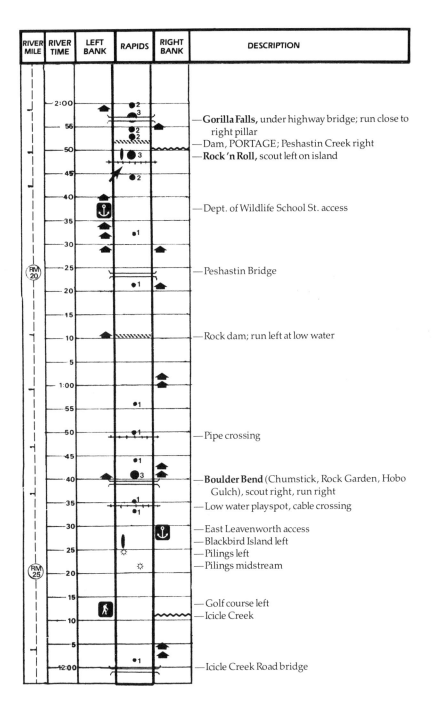

RIVER MILE	RIVER TIME	LEFT BANK	RAPIDS	RIGHT BANK	DESCRIPTION
	2:00		● 2 ● 3		
	56		● 2 ● 2		—**Gorilla Falls,** under highway bridge; run close to right pillar
	50				—Dam, PORTAGE; Peshastin Creek right
			● 3		—**Rock 'n Roll,** scout left on island
	45		● 2		
	40				
	35	⚓			—Dept. of Wildlife School St. access
	30		● 1		
RM 20	25				—Peshastin Bridge
	20		● 1		
	15				
	10				—Rock dam; run left at low water
	5				
	1:00				
	55		● 1		
	50		● 1		—Pipe crossing
	45		● 1		
	40		● 3		—**Boulder Bend** (Chumstick, Rock Garden, Hobo Gulch), scout right, run right
	35		● 1 ● 1		—Low water playspot, cable crossing
	30			⚓	—East Leavenworth access
	25				—Blackbird Island left —Pilings left
RM 25	20				—Pilings midstream
	15				
	10	🚶			—Golf course left —Icicle Creek
	5				
	12:00		● 1		—Icicle Creek Road bridge

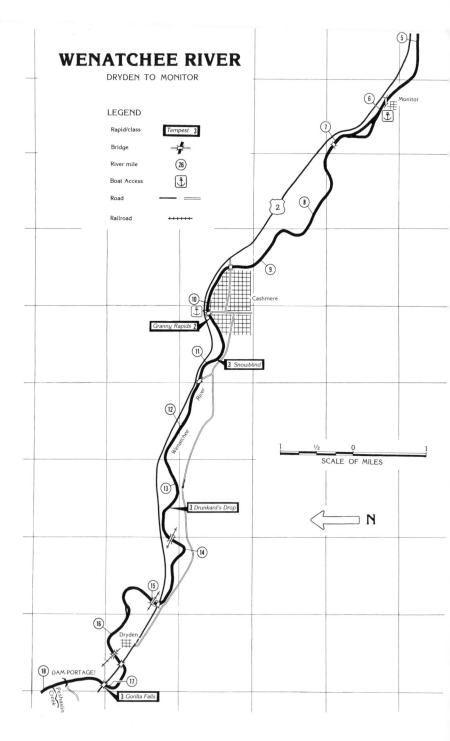

WENATCHEE RIVER
DRYDEN TO MONITOR

LEGEND

Rapid/class	Tempest 3
Bridge	
River mile	26
Boat Access	
Road	
Railroad	+++++

Monitor

Cashmere

Granny Rapids 2

3 Snowblind

Wenatchee River

3 Drunkard's Drop

SCALE OF MILES

N

Dryden

DAM-PORTAGE!

Peshastin Creek

3 Gorilla Falls

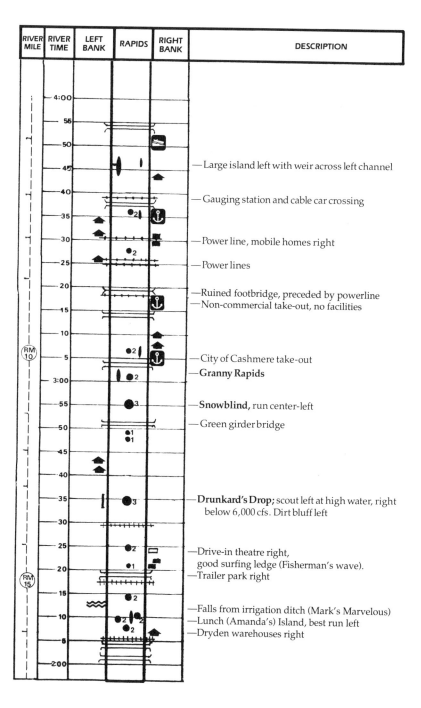

RIVER MILE	RIVER TIME	LEFT BANK	RAPIDS	RIGHT BANK	DESCRIPTION
	4:00				
	55				
	50				
	45				—Large island left with weir across left channel
	40				—Gauging station and cable car crossing
	35		●2		
	30				—Power line, mobile homes right
	25		●2		—Power lines
	20				—Ruined footbridge, preceded by powerline
	15				—Non-commercial take-out, no facilities
	10				
RM 10	5		●2		—City of Cashmere take-out
	3:00		●2		—**Granny Rapids**
	55		●3		—**Snowblind,** run center-left
	50				—Green girder bridge
	45		●1 ●1		
	40				
	35		●3		—**Drunkard's Drop;** scout left at high water, right below 6,000 cfs. Dirt bluff left
	30				
	25		●2		—Drive-in theatre right,
	20		●1		good surfing ledge (Fisherman's wave).
RM 15	15				—Trailer park right
	10		●2		—Falls from irrigation ditch (Mark's Marvelous)
			●2		—Lunch (Amanda's) Island, best run left
	5		●2		—Dryden warehouses right
	2:00				

Roller Coaster *on the Lower Cispus*

15

Lower Cispus

Logged at - 1,500 cfs on Randle gauge
Recommended water level - 1,400 to 4,000 cfs
Best time - April to early July
Rating - Advanced
Water level information - NOAA Tape (206) 526-8530
U.S. Geological Survey
(206) 593-6510
River mile - 17.6 to 1.6; 16.0 miles
Time - 3 hours, 22 minutes; 4.8 mph
Elevation - 1,265' to 815'; 26' per mile

Road 28 Bridge to Reservoir

The Cispus is a relatively little-known whitewater run in Gifford Pinchot National Forest. It has very enjoyable class 2 to 3 rapids at moderate water levels, pretty scenery and a fairly long season. If you connect this lower run with the upper part of the river, it provides the longest whitewater run in Washington State: nearly 30 miles of excitement. As mentioned in the chapter on the Upper Cispus, it would make a great overnight trip with a camp along the river, if the channel between runs could be kept free of logs.

The Army Corps of Engineers would like to study the feasibility of building a large hydroelectric dam on the Cispus. Called the Greenhorn Creek Project, this dam would inundate all of this trip above Iron Creek. If you would like to save the Cispus, contact the Rivers Council of Washington (see the Preface) and help make the Cispus a federally protected Wild & Scenic river.

Getting There

The Cispus is usually approached through the town of Randle on US 12. Randle is about 54 miles east of I-5 and has a Forest Service Ranger Station. From the Puget Sound area north of Tacoma, the fastest way to Randle is on State Route 7, south through Spanaway, LaGrande and Morton to US 12.

Put-ins and Take-outs

To reach the put-in from Randle, take the Forest Service 23 road south toward Trout Lake. You'll cross the Cowlitz just after leaving Randle and, in about 1 mile, bear left toward the Cispus Environmental Center and Trout Lake. After driving about 10 miles through beautiful forest, turn right onto the 28 road, which crosses the Cispus toward the Environmental Center. Put-in on the left bank, downstream from the bridge.

A put-in or take-out can also be made at Tower Rock Campground at river mile 15.7 or at Iron Creek Campground at river mile 8. An alternative to the Iron Creek Campground is about 1 mile upriver at the beach marked on the log at time 1 hour, 52 minutes. The river guides refer to this place as the "twin cedars" due to the two large trees there.

Another possible put-in or take-out point is at the mouth of Greenhorn Creek, reached at the end of the Forest Service 044 road. This 0.2-mile-long gravel road is not well marked but turns off of the Greenhorn 76 road that runs along the south side of the Cispus, a little downriver from where the 77 road turns off.

A put-in or take-out could also be made at Huffaker Bridge at river mile 7 or at the bridge near river mile 4.5, though the bank is quite steep in both places. The bridges, the mouth of Greenhorn Creek, and both Tower Rock and Iron Creek campgrounds can be reached along the south side of the river. From the put-in, head south on the 28 road. Just beyond where the road crosses Yellowjacket Creek Bridge (0.9 mile from the put-in), turn right onto the Greenhorn 76 road. In 0.7 mile, bear right toward the Trout Farm. In 0.3 mile, a right turn will take you to Tower Rock Campground and a left will allow you to continue on the 76 road on the

There are a lot of logs along the banks for the first few miles.

south bank of the Cispus. About 3 miles farther (just beyond the intersection with the 77 road), the pavement ends and the road becomes gravel. The gravel road continues about another 3.5 miles until the bridge over Iron Creek.

To get to the lower take-outs, cross the river on the Huffaker Bridge on the 25 road at about river mile 7. Drive north a little over 1 mile and make a sharp left on an unmarked dirt road and continue down the north bank. This will take you to the bridge at river mile 4.5 and to the new take-out just above the reservoir behind the Cowlitz Falls dam. The Rivers Council of Washington intervened in the dam-licensing proceeding to ensure that a boat ramp at the head of the reservoir was provided. As of 1995 the road is blocked by a locked gate just below the Crystal Creek bridge at river mile 4.5. The Rivers Council is working to get access to the take-out opened at the head of the reservoir.

Water Level

The Cispus is an enjoyable class 2 to 3 run at a wide variety of water levels. Above 3,000 cfs some of the class 3 rapids can develop powerful

Tower Rock *dominates the view at the put-in.*

hydraulics, approaching class 4. You can bump your way down the river with as little as 1,000 cfs, but the ride is much more enjoyable with at least 1,400 cfs.

Lower Cispus
Randle Gauge
Recommend 1,400 to 4,000 cfs

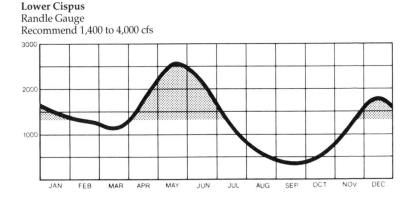

Much of the Lower Cispus is heavily forested.

Special Hazards

A number of logs on this part of the Cispus can form jams along the outside of river bends. Rarely, however, will they block the main river channel, but keep alert!

Scenery

The trip begins with a nice view of Tower Rock, but for the next 3.5 miles it is not very pretty, with many logjams on the gravel bars. The run between log time 55 minutes and 2 hours, 5 minutes, however, is exceptionally beautiful. Evergreen trees reach for the heavens straight up from the banks of the river, creating a cathedral-like effect. The clear water winds through a very rocky channel that alternates between gently flowing pools and fast, easy rapids. A number of cabins appear along the river in two stretches near the beginning of the trip, but below river mile 14 you see few signs of civilization. Several clearcuts become painfully evident once you emerge from the National Forest, but the more exciting whitewater takes your attention away from that "scenery."

Camping

Forest Service campgrounds are available at Tower Rock near river mile 15.7 and at Iron Creek near river mile 8. Check with the Randle Ranger Station, (206) 497-7565, on when these campgrounds will be open; they may not open until well into May.

Rapids

The first part of the run has many gravel bars that make for fun little class 2 rapids, but the river channel really becomes interesting just above Iron Creek. Big boulders begin to appear in the riverbed creating obstacles and rapids. Let's Make a Deal and Roller Coaster involve quick drops down chutes studded with huge boulders. Because of its relatively small water volume, the Cispus produces more technical rapids than big holes or waves, but some large holes and waves can form where the water gathers and goes over a good drop particularly at higher water levels.

In early 1992, Barrish and Sorenson Hydro applied for a license to build a hydroelectric project on the Lower Cispus. The proposed project would divert nearly all of the river's water a little below Huffaker Bridge and run it through a canal and penstocks and into the reservoir behind the Cowlitz Falls dam. The project would end boating on the Lower Cispus just below Huffaker Bridge, destroying about half of the major whitewater of the run. To help stop this ill-conceived project, contact the Northwest Rivers Council (see Preface).

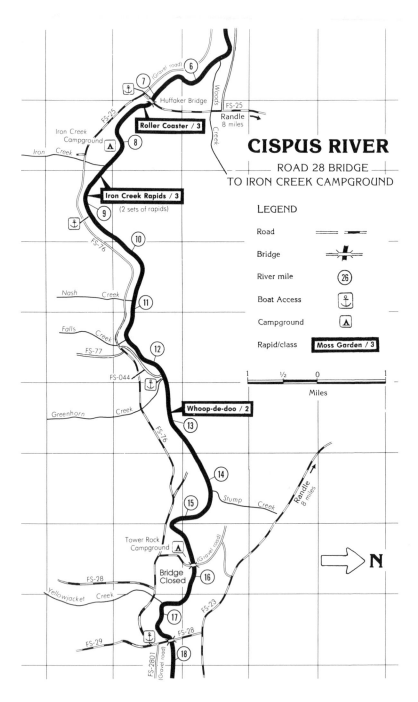

CISPUS RIVER

ROAD 28 BRIDGE
TO IRON CREEK CAMPGROUND

LEGEND

Road	
Bridge	
River mile	26
Boat Access	
Campground	
Rapid/class	Moss Garden / 3

Roller Coaster / 3

Iron Creek Rapids / 3
(2 sets of rapids)

Whoop-de-doo / 2

Huffaker Bridge

FS-25

Randle
8 miles

Iron Creek
Campground

Iron Creek

FS-25

FS-76

Nash Creek

Falls Creek

FS-77

FS-044

Greenhorn Creek

FS-76

Stump Creek

Randle
8 miles

Tower Rock
Campground

Bridge
Closed

FS-28

Yellowjacket Creek

FS-29

FS-2801
(Gravel road)

FS-23

FS-28

Woods Creek

(Gravel road)

Miles

N

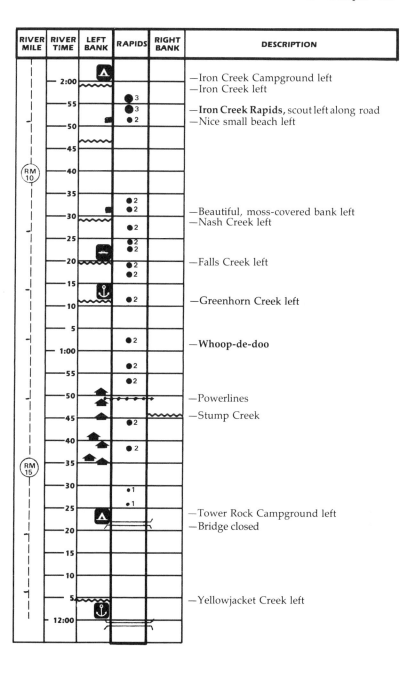

RIVER MILE	RIVER TIME	LEFT BANK	RAPIDS	RIGHT BANK	DESCRIPTION
	2:00	⛺			—Iron Creek Campground left
		〜			—Iron Creek left
	55		●3		**Iron Creek Rapids,** scout left along road
			●3		—Nice small beach left
	50		●2		
	45		〜		
RM 10	40				
	35		●2		
			●2		—Beautiful, moss-covered bank left
	30	〜			—Nash Creek left
	25		●2		
			●2		
	20	⬅	●2		—Falls Creek left
		〜	●2		
	15		●2		
		⚓			
	10	〜	●2		—Greenhorn Creek left
	5				
			●2		—**Whoop-de-doo**
	1:00				
	55		●2		
			●2		
	50	⬆	●●●●		—Powerlines
	45	⬆	〜		—Stump Creek
		⬆	●2		
	40	⬆			
		⬆	●2		
	35	⬆			
	30		●1		
	25		●1		—Tower Rock Campground left
		⛺			—Bridge closed
	20				
	15				
	10				
	5	〜			—Yellowjacket Creek left
		⚓			
	12:00				

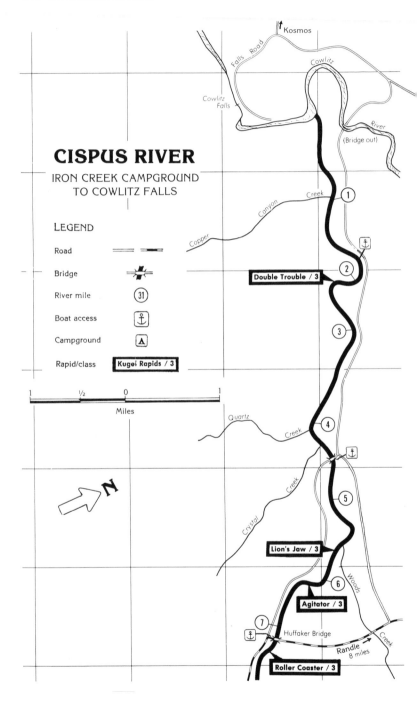

CISPUS RIVER

IRON CREEK CAMPGROUND TO COWLITZ FALLS

LEGEND

Road	
Bridge	
River mile	(31)
Boat access	
Campground	A
Rapid/class	Kugel Rapids / 3

Miles

N

Kosmos

Cowlitz

Falls Road

Cowlitz

Cowlitz Falls

River

(Bridge out)

Creek

Canyon

Copper

Double Trouble / 3

Quartz

Creek

Crystal

Creek

Lion's Jaw / 3

Woods

Agitator / 3

Huffaker Bridge

Randle
8 miles

Creek

Roller Coaster / 3

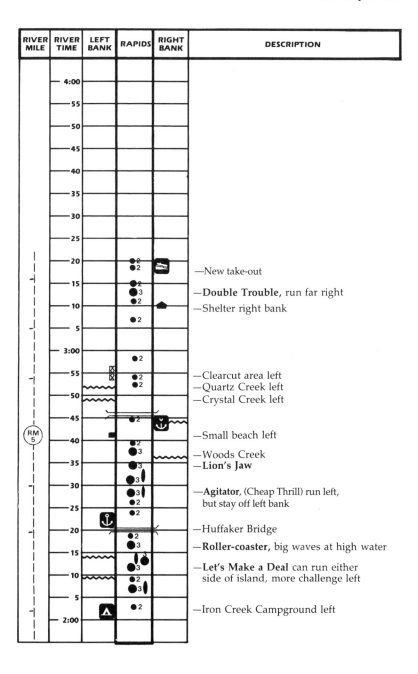

RIVER MILE	RIVER TIME	LEFT BANK	RAPIDS	RIGHT BANK	DESCRIPTION
	4:00				
	55				
	50				
	45				
	40				
	35				
	30				
	25				
	20		●2 ●2		—New take-out
	15		●2 ●3		—**Double Trouble,** run far right
	10		●2		—Shelter right bank
	5		●2		
	3:00		●2		
	55		●2 ●2		—Clearcut area left —Quartz Creek left
	50				—Crystal Creek left
	45		●2		
RM 5	40		●2		—Small beach left
	35		●3 ●3		—Woods Creek —**Lion's Jaw**
	30		●3		
	25		●3 ●2		—**Agitator,** (Cheap Thrill) run left, but stay off left bank
	20		●2		—Huffaker Bridge
	15		●2 ●3		—**Roller-coaster,** big waves at high water
	10		●3 ●2 ●3		—**Let's Make a Deal** can run either side of island, more challenge left
	5				
	2:00		●2		—Iron Creek Campground left

16

Entiat

Logged at -	10,200 cfs Peshastin gauge
Recommended water level -	5,500 to 11,000 cfs
Best time -	May to mid-July
Rating -	Advanced
Water level information -	NOAA Tape (206) 526-8530
River mile -	12.6 to 0.4; 12.2 miles
Time -	2 hours, 4 minutes; 6.1 mph
Elevation -	1,345' to 720'; 51' per mile

Ardenvoir to Columbia River

The Entiat provides a fast ride on a small river in the eastern Washington sunshine. The Indian meaning of Entiat is "rapid water." There are no big rapids here, but nearly constant class 2 water, with occasional class 3 drops. Although signs of civilization are nearly always present, the scenery is generally pleasant, mainly farms and orchards. The Entiat is less crowded and more intimate than the other east slope rivers that empty into the Columbia.

Getting There

The turn-off to the Entiat River Road is just south of the town of Entiat on US 97 about 16 miles north of Wenatchee.

Put-ins and Take-outs

About 0.1 mile up the Entiat River Road, you will see a portion of the old highway leaving the new road and going downriver closer to the river than the new road. This old highway provides access to the take-out. The take-out shown on the log as a light boat take-out is down a steep, short path to the river just downstream of a gate on the old highway. If the gate is closed, this is the best take-out to use.

If the gate is open, an easier take-out is farther down the old road and straight ahead for another 150 yards on the dirt road it becomes. Here you'll find an easy beach take-out. To reach it by river, go right around the final island and then come back up to the take-out on the slack water (backed up by Rocky Reach dam on the Columbia).

Finding a put-in on the Entiat is difficult because nearly all the land is

Constrictions in the river produce some big waves at high water.

privately owned. A small strip of Forest Service land provides access to the river 1.4 miles above a sign Wenatchee National Forest, Steliko Unit on your right (as you drive upriver). This sign is about 10 miles from the turn-off from US 97 on the Entiat River Road. The put-in is just upriver of a left bend in the river (right bend in the road as you drive upriver) and a turn-out provides a parking area about 50 feet upstream on the side of the road away from the river. Since the shoulder of the road next to the put-in is narrow, it is not a very good place to rig a raft.

There is more enjoyable class 2 to 3 boating for another 3 miles above this point (readily scouted from the road), but no public property on which to put in. So this is the uppermost put-in point unless you wish to knock on the door of a local resident and ask permission to put in.

Another potential small put-in is about 1.5 miles downriver, at the confluence with the Mad River, at log time 22 minutes. You can reach this spot by turning left off the Entiat River Road onto the Mad River Road about 9.5 miles from US 97. There is very little parking here, but it is easy access for kayaks.

Water Level

No gauge reports are available on the Entiat. The Entiat flows in a pattern very similar to the Wenatchee, however, so the gauge on the Wenatchee at Peshastin provides a good indication of water level on the Entiat. The Entiat is a good trip between 5,500 and 11,000 cfs on the Peshastin gauge. Below 5,500 it becomes quite rocky, whereas above 11,000 many of the rapids begin to wash-out and eddies become scarce.

Entiat
Peshastin Gauge
Recommend 5,500 to 11,000 cfs

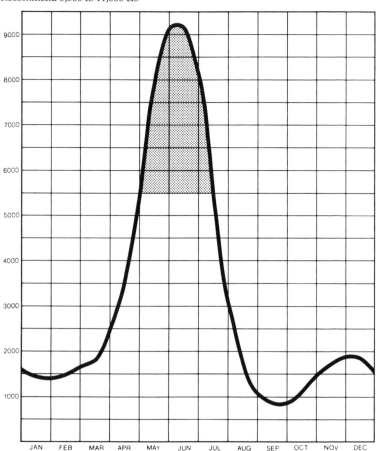

Special Hazards

The weir at log time 1 hour deserves special attention. While it is not a big drop and not difficult to run, it does present a perfect hydraulic that can hold a swimmer. At most water levels a tongue cuts through the hydraulic just to the right of center, but the tongue may be weak at flows under 8,000 cfs. Scout the weir from the road by turning down a dirt road with dense trees on both sides just under 1 mile past the turn-off to the fish hatchery. The old weir at log time 1 hour, 27 minutes, has been breached on the right and presents no difficulties as long as it is run on the right.

At high water, finding an eddy can be difficult on the Entiat.

Scenery

Orchards, ranches and summer cabins line the Entiat. The mountain slopes in the distance are tree-covered at the put-in, sage-covered at the take-out. The water of the Entiat is clear when low and muddy-brown when high. It flows through a pleasant, narrow, dead-end valley, without many people or much junk on the banks.

Camping

There is a nice, small Forest Service campground at Pine Flat, about 4 miles up the Mad River Road. It is not well signed; when the road turns to gravel and starts to climb up the ridge away from the river, take the unmarked turn-off down to the campground by the river. A short hike up the trail from the campground will bring you to the beautiful Mad River canyon. The Mad River provides the longest trail uninterrupted by roads along a river, outside of wilderness, on the east side of the Cascades. It is a prime candidate to become a Wild & Scenic river.

There are numerous Forest Service campgrounds on up the Entiat itself. The first of these, Fox Creek, is about 28 miles from the Columbia and 14 miles above the put-in. The upper part of the river near these campgrounds provides a beautiful class 4 to 5 run for expert kayakers, but care should be taken to scout the dangerous and beautiful Box Canyon near Lake Creek Campground. Another scenic attraction is Entiat Falls on the main river, just below where the North Fork joins it some 34 miles above the Columbia. The upper Entiat and its North Fork have good fishing and beautiful scenery and would make a fine addition to our national Wild & Scenic Rivers system.

Rapids

The Entiat flows swiftly throughout the logged run; class 1 fast water quickly blends into class 2 waves and back again. The class 3 rapids are not much larger than the class 2s, but some large holes in them demand care. Particularly large waves occur in the section just above **Powerline Rapids**.

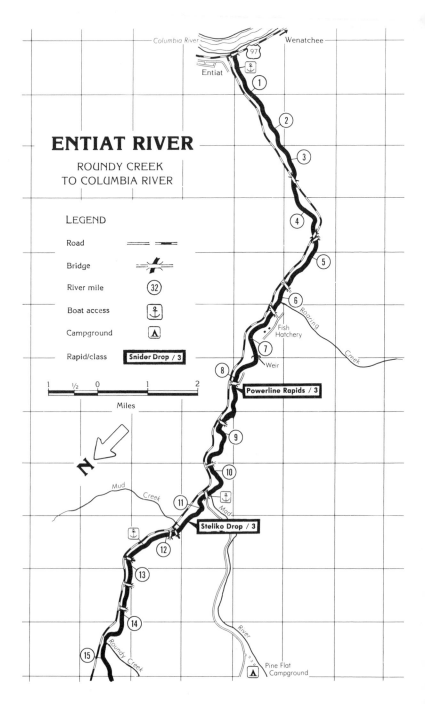

ENTIAT RIVER

ROUNDY CREEK
TO COLUMBIA RIVER

LEGEND

Road	
Bridge	
River mile	32
Boat access	
Campground	▲
Rapid/class	Snider Drop / 3

1 ½ 0 1 2

Miles

N

Columbia River
Wenatchee
97
Entiat

Fish Hatchery
Roaring Creek

Weir

Powerline Rapids / 3

Mud Creek

Steliko Drop / 3

Mud

Roundy Creek

River

Pine Flat Campground

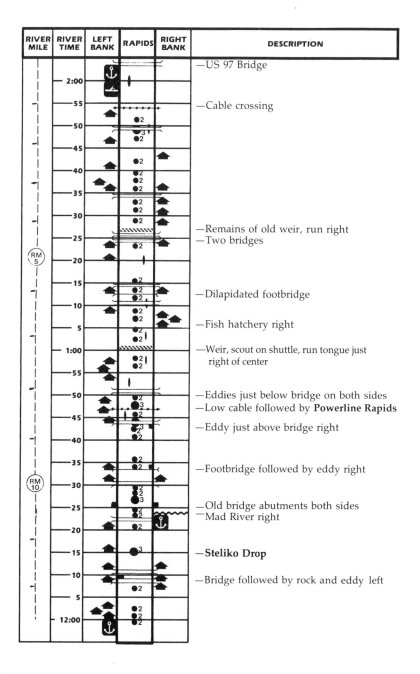

RIVER MILE	RIVER TIME	LEFT BANK	RAPIDS	RIGHT BANK	DESCRIPTION
	2:00				—US 97 Bridge
	55				—Cable crossing
	50		●2		
	45		●2		
	40		●2		
	35		●2 ●2		
	30		●2 ●2		
	25				—Remains of old weir, run right
			●2		—Two bridges
RM 5	20				
	15		●2		
	10		●2 ●2		—Dilapidated footbridge
	5		●2 ●2		—Fish hatchery right
	1:00				—Weir, scout on shuttle, run tongue just right of center
			●2 ●2		
	55				
	50				—Eddies just below bridge on both sides
			●2 ●3 ●2		—Low cable followed by **Powerline Rapids**
	45		●3 ●2 ●2		—Eddy just above bridge right
	40				
	35		●2 ●2		—Footbridge followed by eddy right
RM 10	30				
			●2 ●2 ●3		—Old bridge abutments both sides
	25		●2 ●2		—Mad River right
	20		●2		
	15		●3		—**Steliko Drop**
	10				—Bridge followed by rock and eddy left
			●2		
	5				
	12:00		●2 ●2 ●2		

17

White

Logged at -	2,300 cfs Buckley gauge
Recommended water level -	1,000 to 3,400 cfs
Best time -	May to late July
Rating -	Advanced
Water level information -	NOAA Tape (206) 526-8530
	Army Corps (206) 764-6702
River mile -	51.5 to 38.0; 13.5 miles
Time -	2 hours, 3 minutes; 6.6 mph
Elevation -	1,925' to 1,330'; 44' per mile

West Fork Road to Bridge Camp

The White River is a hole-hog's delight. There are good holes to crash in rafts and to play in kayaks at all water levels. It's a quick trip from the Puget Sound area, and the glaciers on Mt. Rainier provide water through the end of July. The White runs nearly clear in the spring and becomes milky in the summer, finally turning chocolate brown in late summer because of glacial silt.

Getting There
State Route 410 east of Enumclaw, some 35 miles southeast of Seattle, parallels the White. Enumclaw, named after a local mountain, means "home of the evil spirits."

Put-ins and Take-outs
To reach the take-out, head out of Enumclaw on State Route 410 toward Cayuse and Chinook passes. About 5 miles out of town, turn right at the Weyerhaeuser road where there is a gate, called Grass Mountain, staffed on weekends 7:00 A.M. to 5:00 P.M. An annual $50 vehicle permit, bearing the vehicle license number, is required. Call 1(800) 433-3911 for a recording with the latest regulations and a list of stores where the permit may be purchased.

From the gate, proceed south about 0.25 mile to a T intersection. Turn left on Weyerhaeuser 3700 road (the "mainline") and drive about 6 miles east to a bridge on your right. Cross the bridge and turn right into the unimproved Bridge Camp. It's also possible to take-out just downstream of the bridge on river right.

Splashing through the milky waters of the White River.

About 3 miles farther upriver, the Weyerhaeuser road crosses the river on a concrete bridge visible from the highway. This bridge is on the log at 1 hour, 29 minutes, and provides an alternate, though steep, put-in or take-out.

The town of Greenwater is about 5 miles farther upriver. Two miles beyond the Greenwater General Store is a log overpass. Turning right just before the overpass, you'll reach another alternate put-in or take-out point at a bridge over the river at log time 20 minutes.

The put-in on the West Fork White River Road is on Forest Service 74 road. The turn-off to the 74 road is 0.4 mile beyond milepost 46 which is 3.2 miles beyond the Greenwater General Store.

Water Level

The Army Corps (which operates the Mud Mountain Dam) maintains a gauge on the river, which measures flow in the area of the dam. It is called the White River above Buckley. The White is a good run for rafts and kayaks from 1,000 to 3,400 cfs. Above 3,400, there are very few eddies, the water is very swift and rescue is difficult. Below 1,000, several gravel bars are exposed, making it difficult for rafts, but kayakers who don't mind scraping a bit will find good holes to play in down to 700 cfs.

White
Buckley Gauge
Recommend 1,000 to 3,400 cfs

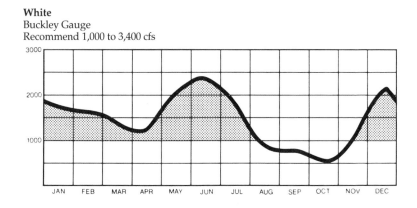

Bridges across the river are the major landmarks.

Special Hazards

The Osceola Mudflow, one of the largest mudflows in the world, filled the valley of the White 150 years ago. As a result, the valley is full of loose soil and rocks; bedrock is buried hundreds of feet below. The soft banks are constantly being eroded and the river channel frequently shifts, dropping many trees into the river and creating frequent logjams. Stay alert!

Scenery

Nice views of Mt. Rainier appear at several points along the river, but the immediate river shore is not very pretty. Although there are not many man-made structures for most of the trip, many of the surrounding banks have been recently clearcut and frequent logjams occur on the gravel bars.

The section of the White River just above this run still has considerable old-growth forest along it. This section, which has a nice trail running along its west bank, has been recommended by the Forest Service for designation as a Scenic River in our national Wild and Scenic Rivers system.

Camping

Campsites are available at the State's Federation Forest Campground a little below Greenwater and at the Forest Service's Dalles Campground about 4 miles above the put-in.

Rapids

The White provides a lot of waves and easily crashable holes, which make for a fun trip. **Cyclone Drop** begins a series of rapids and an exciting end to the run. These are rocky ledge drops with few obstacles. The only rapid with many exposed boulders is at log time 1 hour, 33 minutes.

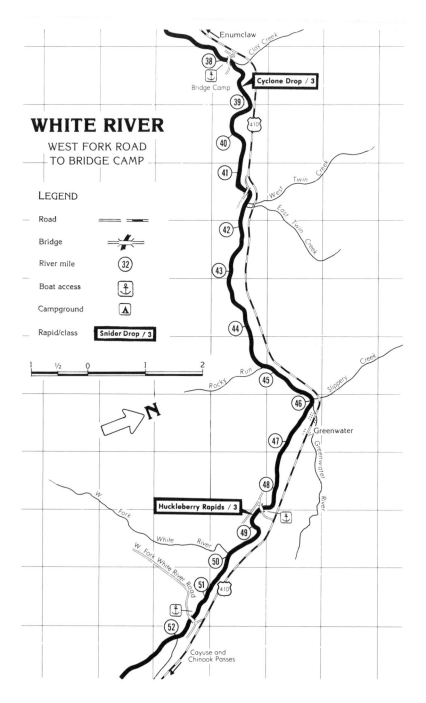

WHITE RIVER

WEST FORK ROAD
TO BRIDGE CAMP

LEGEND

Road

Bridge

River mile

Boat access

Campground

Rapid/class

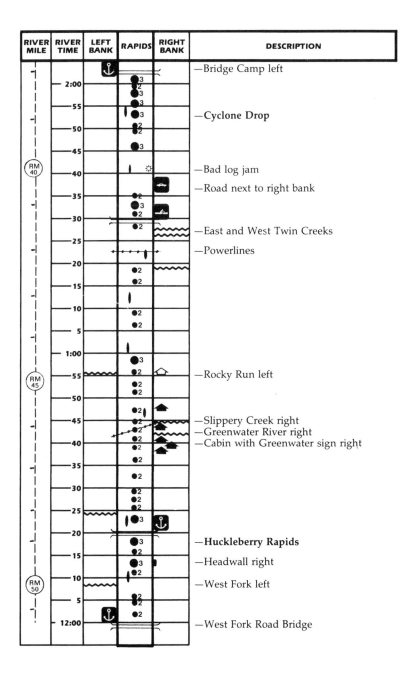

RIVER MILE	RIVER TIME	LEFT BANK	RAPIDS	RIGHT BANK	DESCRIPTION
		⚓			—Bridge Camp left
	2:00		●3 ●2 ●3		
	55		●3 ●3		—Cyclone Drop
	50		●2 ●2		
	45		●3		
RM 40	40			☀	—Bad log jam
	35			🚗	—Road next to right bank
	30		●3 ●2	🚗	
	25		●2	〰️	—East and West Twin Creeks
	20		┼•••┼		—Powerlines
	15		●2 ●2	〰️	
	10				
	5		●2 ●2		
	1:00				
RM 45	55	〰️	●3 ●2	⌂	—Rocky Run left
	50		●2 ●2		
	45		●2	▲	—Slippery Creek right
	40		●2 ●2 ●2 ●2	▲ 〰️ ▲ ▲	—Greenwater River right —Cabin with Greenwater sign right
	35		●2		
	30		●2		
	25	〰️	●2 ●2 ●2		
	20		❘●3	⚓	
	15		●3 ●2		—**Huckleberry Rapids**
RM 50	10		●3 ❘●2	▪	—Headwall right
	5		●2 ●2		—West Fork left
	12:00	⚓	●2		—West Fork Road Bridge

Looking back upriver at Bowl & Pitcher

18

Lower Spokane

Logged at	-	12,000 cfs Spokane gauge
Recommended water level	-	4,000 to 19,000 cfs
Best time	-	April to June
Rating	-	Advanced
Water level information	-	Washington Water Power (509) 489-0500 (Ext. 2141)
River mile	-	69.8 to 63.5; 6.3 miles
Time	-	1 hour, 13 minutes; 4.8 mph
Elevation	-	1,675' to 1,605'; 11' per mile

T. J. Meenach Bridge to Plese Flat

In spite of the fact that this run starts right within the city of Spokane, the heavily forested, steep river valley is quite pretty. There are numerous signs of civilization, including a sewage plant, but the broad river and spectacular rock formations make you forget that this trip is so near to town. The trip is largely class 1 and 2, but there are two serious class 3 rapids. Even though there are not many difficult rapids, the volume of water in the river creates strong hydraulics and the river demands respect.

Getting There

From I-90, take the Maple Toll Bridge exit 280 and follow the signs to the Maple Toll Bridge (25 cents for cars to cross). Continue north on Maple 1.3 miles past the toll bridge and turn left on Northwest Boulevard. Go approximately 0.7 mile on Northwest Boulevard and make another left at a stop light on T. J. Meenach Drive. A short distance down the drive, you will reach the bridge.

Put-ins and Take-outs

Take a right just before the T. J. Meenach Bridge and turn into the turnout area to park. From here you can carry your boat down to the water. Excessive use of the area by four-wheel-drive vehicles has torn up the hillside so much that two-wheel-drive vehicles can rarely negotiate it.

To reach an easier put-in, drive downriver on Downriver Drive approximately 1 mile from the Fort Wright Bridge to where a dirt road turns off the main road downriver. The main road cuts across a bend in the river while the dirt road follows the riverbank in front of a nursing home. The dirt road continues downriver and reconnects with Downriver Drive about 0.3 mile below where it left the Drive.

To reach the take-out, continue downstream on Downriver Drive, past the entrance to Riverside State Park. About 2 miles below the entrance to the park, you'll pass under a set of powerlines; 0.5 mile below that is the take-out. There is a small, paved turn-out road on the river side of the main road. Running upriver from this turn-out is an unused dirt road that provides a convenient path to the water.

Note that park regulations prohibit putting in or taking out in the main part of Riverside State Park where the camping and picnicking facilities are near **Bowl & Pitcher**. The state doesn't want to give ideas to anyone using these public facilities, who might try running the river with inadequate equipment and no understanding of the potentially dangerous hydraulics in a large river. People are killed on this stretch of the Spokane nearly every year simply because it is accessible to so many people who have no idea what dangers they face.

Approaching the dramatic rocks of Bowl & Pitcher

Water Level

The Lower Spokane provides an exciting run from 4,000 to 19,000 cfs on the Spokane gauge. Below 4,000 cfs the run is a real bottom scraper.

Spokane Gauge
Recommend 4,000 to 19,000 cfs

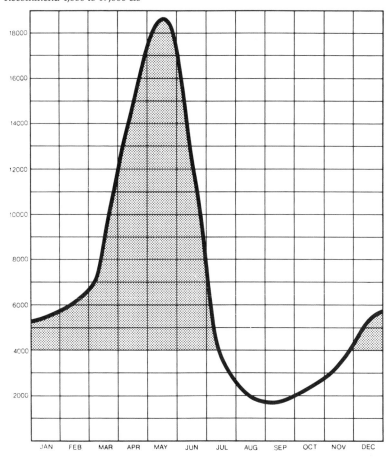

Special Hazards

The great volume of water in the Lower Spokane can make for very powerful hydraulics. You shouldn't run the river above 19,000 cfs unless you are already familiar with its currents and power from making runs at lower water levels.

Sun and whitewater just below the capitol of the Inland Empire.

Scenery

The steep sides of the river valley, covered with a pretty, semi-open pine forest, make the trip very pleasant. Not many buildings are visible, but you get several reminders of civilization, such as the sewage treatment plant. The spectacular volcanic rock outcroppings make **Bowl & Pitcher** one of the most interesting class 3 rapids in the state. The water surges through several passages between huge pillars of volcanic rock.

Camping

Many campsites are available in Riverside State Park near **Bowl & Pitcher**. A fee is charged.

Rapids

The big rapids of the trip are **Bowl & Pitcher** and **Devil's Toenail**. Because of the large volume of water in the Spokane, these rapids can provide some powerful hydraulics. The best way to scout them is on the shuttle.

To take a look at Bowl & Pitcher, turn in the main entrance to Riverside State Park, take the third spur road to the right, and park in the parking area. From here you can see the footbridge that crosses the river. Walk out on the footbridge to scout the rapid. It begins above the footbridge and continues another 100 yards below it through the dramatic rock formations that give Bowl & Pitcher its name. Avoid the dangerous pour-over on river left below the footbridge. There are several good play waves right below the footbridge, and kayakers usually eddy out on the right just below the bridge to try their luck on the waves.

To scout the Devil's Toenail, continue downriver 0.9 mile from the entrance of the park to Bowl & Pitcher (or 1.6 miles above the take-out, going the other direction) and park on the paved turn-out on the outside of a bend along the river. Scramble down the slope to the river's edge for a look. The run is near the right bank where you are standing. Some large rocks here on the right bank provide a good place to take pictures.

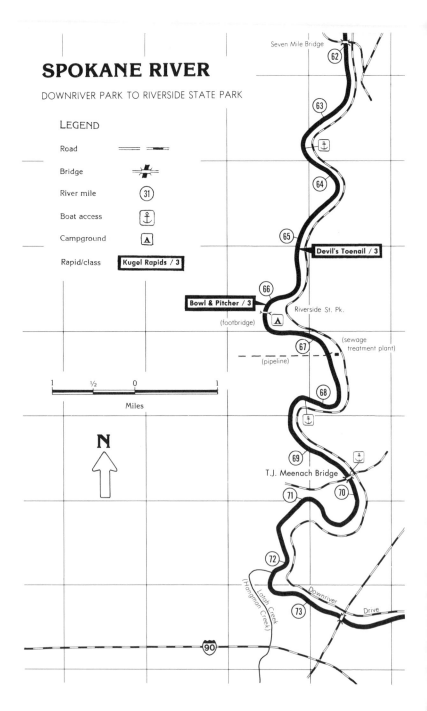

SPOKANE RIVER

DOWNRIVER PARK TO RIVERSIDE STATE PARK

LEGEND

Road	
Bridge	
River mile	(31)
Boat access	
Campground	A
Rapid/class	Kugel Rapids / 3

Miles

N

Seven Mile Bridge

62
63
64
65   Devil's Toenail / 3
66
Bowl & Pitcher / 3
Riverside St. Pk.
(footbridge)
(sewage treatment plant)
67
(pipeline)
68
69
T.J. Meenach Bridge
71   70
72
Lolah Creek (Hangman Creek)
73   Downriver   Drive
90

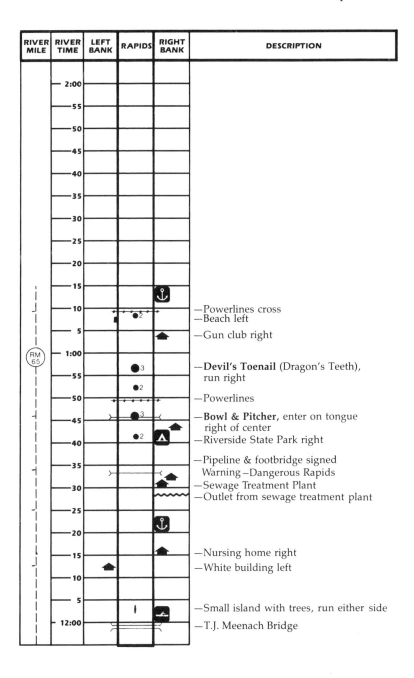

RIVER MILE	RIVER TIME	LEFT BANK	RAPIDS	RIGHT BANK	DESCRIPTION
	2:00				
	55				
	50				
	45				
	40				
	35				
	30				
	25				
	20				
	15				
	10		●2		—Powerlines cross —Beach left
	5				—Gun club right
RM 65	1:00				
	55		●3		—**Devil's Toenail** (Dragon's Teeth), run right
	50		●2		—Powerlines
	45		●3		—**Bowl & Pitcher,** enter on tongue right of center
	40		●2		—Riverside State Park right
	35				—Pipeline & footbridge signed Warning—Dangerous Rapids
	30				—Sewage Treatment Plant —Outlet from sewage treatment plant
	25				
	20				
	15				—Nursing home right
	10				—White building left
	5				
	12:00				—Small island with trees, run either side —T.J. Meenach Bridge

19

Chiwawa

Logged at - 7,000 cfs Peshastin gauge
Recommended water level - 4,000 to 10,000 cfs
Best time - May to mid-July
Rating - Advanced
Water level information - NOAA Tape (206) 526-8530
River mile - 12.8 to Wenatchee mile 46.5;
14.7 miles
Time - 2 hours, 53 minutes; 5.1 mph
Elevation - 2,380' to 1,810'; 39' per mile

Huckleberry Ford to Plain

The Chiwawa provides a fast and exciting ride through largely un-touched eastern Washington forest. The rapids are nearly constant in the three gorge stretches and you only have time to catch your breath in the sections between. This is the closest river trip to the Puget Sound area where you can enjoy beautiful scenery in the sunny skies of eastern Washington.

Getting There
State Route 207 turns off US 2 at Coles Corner about 21 miles east of Stevens Pass or 16 miles west of Leavenworth. If you go 5 miles north on 207, you'll come to its intersection with State Route 209. A right turn on 209 will take you, in about 5 miles, to the take-out at the bridge over the Wenatchee. Traveling straight ahead on 207 will take you to the put-in.

Put-ins and Take-outs
The take-out is just north of the bridge over the Wenatchee on the east side of the river near the town of Plain. An alternative take-out for those who wish to avoid the quieter water at the end of the trip (or a put-in for those seeking a less exciting trip) is at the bridge over the Chiwawa at about river mile 2. It can be reached by continuing north from the 207–209 intersection and bearing right after crossing the Wenatchee in the direc-tion of signs pointing to Fish Lake and the Chiwawa River Road. If you continue straight ahead (and not up the Chiwawa River Road) for a little more than 4 miles, you'll reach the bridge.

To reach the put-in, follow State Route 207 across the Wenatchee River,

Hotdogging the Chiwawa

then turn right. About 1.5 miles farther, turn left on the road toward Chiwawa River and Trinity. This road will take you by Fish Lake and then cross the Chiwawa on the bridge that is at log time 1 hour, 10 minutes. This could serve as either a put-in or take-out for shorter runs.

To reach the upper put-in, turn left on the Chiwawa River Road (toward Trinity) about 0.5 mile after crossing the bridge. Approximately 6 miles up this road, Huckleberry Ford is reached by turning left and going 0.2 mile onto an unmarked dirt road. This turn-off is 0.1 mile beyond a sign for Upper Grouse Creek Campground.

Another potential intermediate put-in or take-out point is at Meadow Creek Campground at log-time 45 minutes. You can reach Meadow Creek Campground by turning off the main Chiwawa road about a quarter of a mile before the bridge over the river. Turn north on the one-lane (paved) Forest Service 6300 road. In about 3 miles you will come to the signed turn-off to Meadow Creek Campground.

Huckleberry Ford could be used as a take-out point for those who would like to go for a river canoeing trip. The river is nearly flat from Schaefer Creek Campground to here, about 12 miles. There are many logjams in the river, though, requiring numerous portages. Canoeing skill is also needed to avoid the many rocks that stud the slow-moving current. Only expert whitewater canoeists should attempt the river below Huckleberry Ford in a canoe; the nearly continuous whitewater found in many stretches would swamp any but the most perfectly handled canoes.

Water Level

There is no gauge operating on the Chiwawa River, but historical water records reveal that the Chiwawa normally contributes about 20 percent of the water in the Wenatchee River at Peshastin. The Chiwawa should provide you with an exciting first run at levels between 4,000 and 10,000 cfs on the Peshastin gauge. I wouldn't recommend the river above 10,000 cfs until you are familiar with it, because its steep slope makes for nearly continuous whitewater at higher levels.

Special Hazards

The Chiwawa is a fast run, which increases the danger posed by the frequent logjams, particularly in the Gate Creek Gorge. There is a low cable across the river at log time 22 minutes (river mile 11) that requires moving far right or left at high water. Care should also be taken in determining which side of an island you choose to go around because some passages are completely blocked by logs. The islands are small enough, however, that the jams can always be seen before you commit yourself.

Just above the mouth of the Chiwawa, the Department of Fisheries has placed a fish barrier across the river. It is designed for boats to pass over it at high water, but take care in doing so. At medium- and low-water levels, watch for the portage route, marked by signs, on the right bank after the second long string of cabins on the right bank below the bridge at mile 2.2.

Chiwawa
Peshastin Gauge
Recommend 4,000 to 10,000 cfs

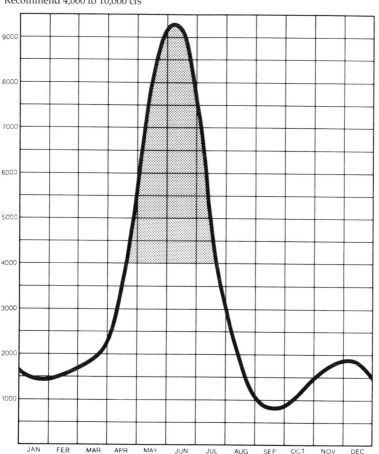

Scenery

The Chiwawa will treat you to nearly unspoiled eastern Washington forested riverbanks. The river channel is fairly narrow with few islands. The largely fir forest is interspersed with numerous cedars in the lower end around Goose Creek Gorge. There are a few gravel beaches for nice lunch stops. Watch for the beaches just around the inside of river bends; if you aren't ready to pull in before you see them, you'll never make it.

The Forest Service has recommended that the Chiwawa be added to the national Wild & Scenic Rivers system. If you enjoy boating the

The banks of the Chiwawa are heavily forested.

Chiwawa, write your Congressman and help preserve this beautiful river for us all to enjoy.

Camping

There are numerous Forest Service campgrounds around the Chiwawa. Meadow Creek and Goose Creek campgrounds along the river are shown on the map. It would be easy to even pull your boat up at Big Meadow Creek Campground if you were inclined to stop on your way down the river and continue the next day. Grouse Creek Campground is a Group Reservation Site and you must obtain permission from the Forest Service before camping there. Check with the Lake Wenatchee Ranger Station at (509) 763-3103 or 763-3211. In addition, Lake Wenatchee State Park has campsites available at the east end of the lake.

Rapids

The rapids on this trip come in distinct sets that I have labeled as gorges, even though they don't have the sort of narrow defiles often associated with gorges. Each gorge is named after the creek which comes into the river at its beginning. Each gorge presents you with nearly continuous whitewater that demands constant attention until you are hurled out of it by the swift current.

The water does not slow down very much even in the sections between the gorges, but the lack of obstacles and little waves there give you a chance to relax and bail. Eddies are few and landing a raft requires that you anticipate where an eddy is likely to be found and start pulling for it even before you see whether it is there or not.

The whitewater in Gate Creek and Big Meadow Creek gorges mostly consists of waves with few obstacles. The drops in Goose Creek Gorge present you with more obstacles and are more interesting challenges. The bulk of the whitewater is over after Goose Creek Gorge, but you still have a pleasant float to the bridge near Plain. The easier whitewater of the lower portion of the run provides good training for those graduating from beginning to intermediate boaters. The big difference between the size of the Chiwawa and the Wenatchee is dramatically revealed when you drift out of the narrow Chiwawa onto the broad Wenatchee.

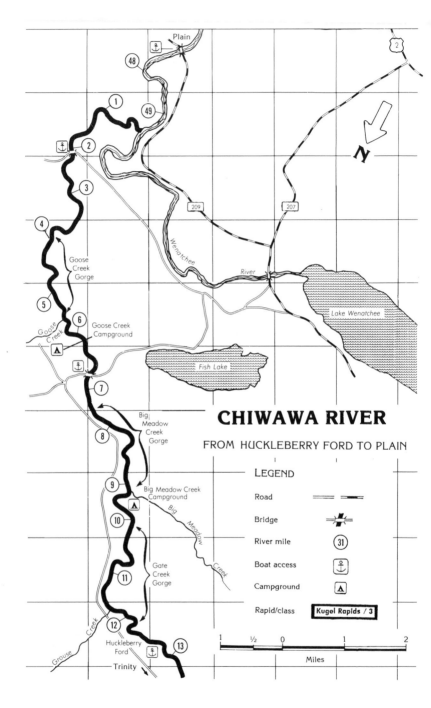

CHIWAWA RIVER

FROM HUCKLEBERRY FORD TO PLAIN

LEGEND

Road	
Bridge	
River mile	(31)
Boat access	⚓
Campground	◮
Rapid/class	Kugel Rapids / 3

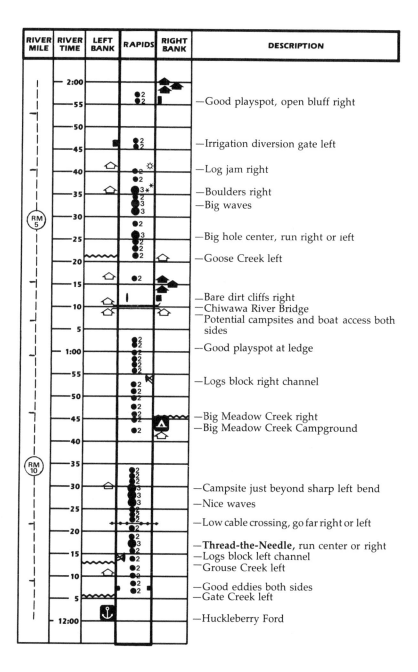

RIVER MILE	RIVER TIME	LEFT BANK	RAPIDS	RIGHT BANK	DESCRIPTION
	2:00				
	55				—Good playspot, open bluff right
	50				
	45				—Irrigation diversion gate left
	40				—Log jam right
	35				—Boulders right
					—Big waves
RM 5	30				
	25				—Big hole center, run right or left
	20				—Goose Creek left
	15				
	10				—Bare dirt cliffs right
					—Chiwawa River Bridge
	5				—Potential campsites and boat access both sides
	1:00				—Good playspot at ledge
	55				
	50				—Logs block right channel
	45				—Big Meadow Creek right
					—Big Meadow Creek Campground
	40				
RM 10	35				
	30				—Campsite just beyond sharp left bend
	25				—Nice waves
	20				—Low cable crossing, go far right or left
					—**Thread-the-Needle,** run center or right
	15				—Logs block left channel
					—Grouse Creek left
	10				—Good eddies both sides
	5				—Gate Creek left
	12:00				—Huckleberry Ford

Top: *Nose-plugs come in handy when the action gets heavy.*

Bottom: *There are few eddies for all those playspots; catch them on your way down.*

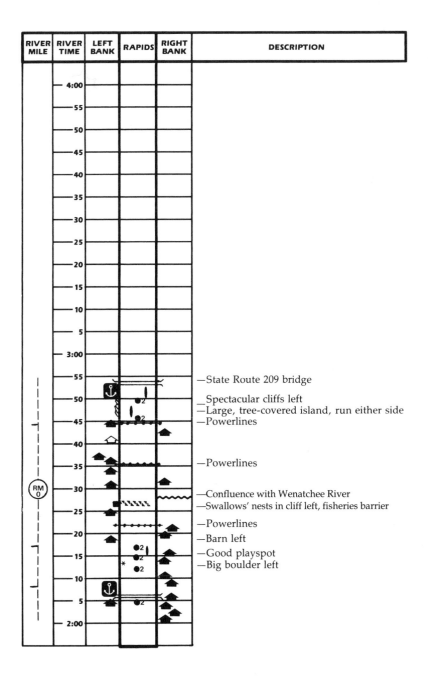

RIVER MILE	RIVER TIME	LEFT BANK	RAPIDS	RIGHT BANK	DESCRIPTION
	4:00				
	55				
	50				
	45				
	40				
	35				
	30				
	25				
	20				
	15				
	10				
	5				
	3:00				
	55				—State Route 209 bridge
	50				_Spectacular cliffs left
					—Large, tree-covered island, run either side
	45				—Powerlines
	40				
	35				—Powerlines
	30				—Confluence with Wenatchee River
RM 0	25				—Swallows' nests in cliff left, fisheries barrier
	20				—Powerlines
					—Barn left
	15				—Good playspot
					—Big boulder left
	10				
	5				
	2:00				

20

Tieton

Logged at - 1,700 cfs Rimrock gauge
Recommended water level - 1,000 to 2,500 cfs
Best time - September
Rating - Advanced
Water level information - NOAA Tape (206) 526-8530
Bureau of Reclamation
(509) 575-5854
River mile - 20.1 to 8.5; 11.6 miles
Time - 1 hour, 57 minutes; 5.9 mph
Elevation - 2,640' to 2,015'; 54' per mile

Rimrock to Windy Point

A pleasant way to cap a season of paddling is to make a September run of the high waters of the Tieton in sunny eastern Washington. The Tieton takes its name from an Indian word meaning "roaring water." A trip on the river will convince you that it's an appropriate name. The Tieton would make a fine addition to our national Wild & Scenic Rivers system as a recreational river.

During most of the spring and summer, the federal Bureau of Reclamation, which operates Rimrock Dam, holds back the water of the Tieton. Irrigation water for the lower Yakima Valley is drawn from the Keechelus, Kachess and Cle Elum reservoirs farther up the Yakima River. In September, salmon and steelhead return to the Yakima to spawn, and the water level in the upper river has to be reduced so that the fish do not spawn in a portion of the riverbed that will be exposed when the water level is low during the winter.

To accommodate the fish, the water in the upper Yakima is dropped to winter levels in September, and the irrigation water needed in the lower Yakima Valley is drawn from the Tieton, which flows into the Naches and then into the Yakima near the City of Yakima, below the spawning beds. Thus, when the river comes up is determined by the fish, who are watched by fisheries biologists. In wet years, the Tieton will reach runnable levels in June, when excess water is spilled into the river after the reservoir has been filled. But in most years, the Tieton only comes alive in September, when the fish spawn and the irrigation water roars down the river.

A lot of rocks stud the steep descent of the Tieton. (Alyce Daniels photo)

Getting There

US 12 runs along the Tieton between White Pass and Yakima, just west of prime apple orchard country.

Put-ins and Take-outs

Because the river is so swift, both putting in and taking out are difficult, as is rescue in the event of an upset. The run starts in a steep, pine-forested valley just below Tieton Dam. The upper put-in shown on the log is reached by turning off US 12 on an unmarked dirt road 0.65 mile below the Rimrock grocery. It is not easy to put in here because the river is lined with bushes.

An easier put-in is found at Hause Creek Campground at log time 18 minutes. The other campgrounds shown on the map and log can also be used for put-ins and take-outs, but landing is not easy because there are very few eddies.

Water Level

You can run the Tieton on 1,000 to 2,500 cfs on the Rimrock gauge. Be cautious at the higher levels, however, because lack of eddies makes rescues difficult. Kayaks and small inflatables can scrape down the river on about 700 cfs.

Tieton
Rimrock Gauge
Recommend 1,000 to 2,500 cfs

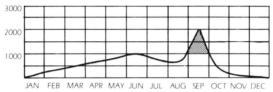

Special Hazards

The **dam** at log time 53 minutes is now runnable. It has been reconfigured so it can be run on either the right or left side: left for those who are conservative, right for the big yahoos! At higher water levels, there are still the remnants of a reversal in the center. The dam is hidden 20 feet past a sharp left bend in the river. An alternative route at flows above 2,000 cfs is to take the creek bypass route on the left bank. To get to the creek, take the small channel between the two islands on the left. Then paddle hard to make the entry to the creek, which is often hidden in the shadows on the left bank. A scout on the shore can help locate the creek, allowing you to float more easily around the dam. The gatekeeper and his family live right by the dam and this is their backyard. Do not relieve yourself in the bushes; there are facilities at the campgrounds.

There are often frequent **logjams** on the portion of the Tieton below the logged run and always the possibility of one on this section. Stay alert!

Scenery

The plant life changes dramatically as the river descends from approximately 2,650 feet at the put-in to 2,000 feet at the take-out. The valley becomes drier, and pine forests disappear, replaced by sage-covered hills and stark rock formations. In September, the only green remaining near the end of the run is right along the riverbed.

Camping

The Tieton is lined with U.S. Forest Service campgrounds, so camping is easy. But as always, the drive-in camps may be crowded and noisy. You will avoid the crowds, however, by camping after Labor Day. Hause

The dam has now been altered so that it is runnable. (Alyce Daniels photo)

Creek Campground is particularly large, but much of it is closed after September 15. You'll have to pay a fee to use any of the campsites along the river.

Rapids

The Tieton is rated a class 2 to class 3 river. However, this run is actually more difficult than the class ranking indicates. The first 6 miles are very steep and the water moves very fast. The rapids are all short drops, and the class 3s earn their ratings more because rescues are difficult in those areas than because they're technically challenging. The rapids are nearly constant, the water swift with almost no eddies.

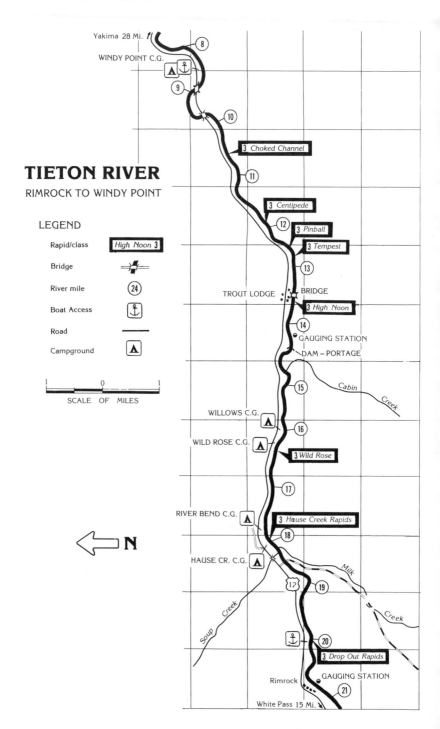

TIETON RIVER

RIMROCK TO WINDY POINT

Yakima 28 Mi.

WINDY POINT C.G.

LEGEND

Rapid/class	High Noon 3
Bridge	
River mile	24
Boat Access	
Road	
Campground	

SCALE OF MILES

3 Choked Channel

3 Centipede

3 Pinball

3 Tempest

TROUT LODGE   BRIDGE

3 High Noon

GAUGING STATION

DAM — PORTAGE

Cabin Creek

WILLOWS C.G.

WILD ROSE C.G.

3 Wild Rose

RIVER BEND C.G.

3 Hause Creek Rapids

HAUSE CR. C.G.

Milk Creek

Soup Creek

3 Drop Out Rapids

Rimrock   GAUGING STATION

White Pass 15 Mi.

N

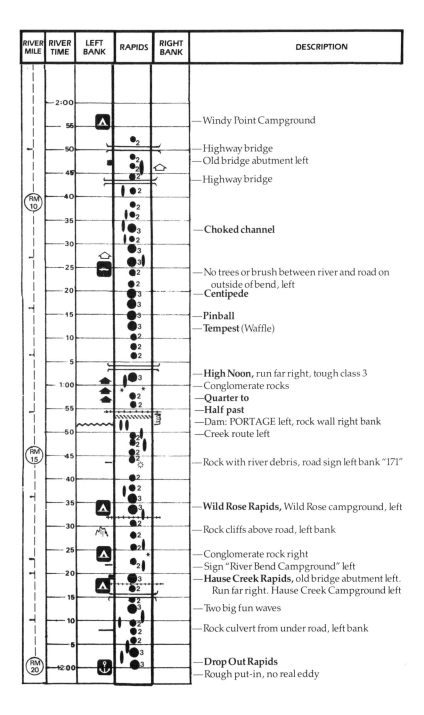

RIVER MILE	RIVER TIME	LEFT BANK	RAPIDS	RIGHT BANK	DESCRIPTION
	2:00				
	55				—Windy Point Campground
	50		2		—Highway bridge
	45		2 2 2		—Old bridge abutment left
					—Highway bridge
RM 10	40		2		
	35		2 2		
	30		3 2		—**Choked channel**
	25		3 3 3		
	20		2 2		—No trees or brush between river and road on outside of bend, left
			3		—**Centipede**
	15		3 3		—**Pinball**
	10		3 2		—**Tempest** (Waffle)
	5		2 2		
	1:00		3		—**High Noon,** run far right, tough class 3
			* *		—Conglomerate rocks
	55		2 2		—**Quarter to**
					—**Half past**
	50				—Dam: PORTAGE left, rock wall right bank
					—Creek route left
RM 15	45		2 2 ✧		—Rock with river debris, road sign left bank "171"
	40		2		
	35		2 3 3		—**Wild Rose Rapids,** Wild Rose campground, left
	30		2		—Rock cliffs above road, left bank
	25		2 *		—Conglomerate rock right
	20		2		—Sign "River Bend Campground" left
			3 2		—**Hause Creek Rapids,** old bridge abutment left. Run far right. Hause Creek Campground left
	15		2 3		—Two big fun waves
	10		2 2		—Rock culvert from under road, left bank
	5		3		
RM 20	12:00		3		—**Drop Out Rapids**
					—Rough put-in, no real eddy

21

North Fork Nooksack

Logged at - 700 cfs on North Fork gauge
Recommended water level - 600 to 1,300 cfs
Best time - May through October
Rating - Advanced
Water level information - NOAA Tape (206) 526-8530
River mile - 59.3 to 51.5; 7.8 miles
Time - 1 hour, 40 minutes; 4.7 mph
Elevation - 970' to 555'; 53' per mile

Douglas Fir Campground to Maple Falls

The North Fork of the Nooksack is fed by snow and ice from Mt. Baker and the North Cascades. It is named after the Indians who lived in the area and were known as the "mountain men." On clear days, there are spectacular views of Mt. Baker and the surrounding mountains. The trip begins in a narrow gorge with many class 3 rapids in quick succession.

Just above the put-in, across the highway from Douglas Fir Campground, is the Horseshoe Bend Interpretive Trail. If you take a short walk up this trail, you will see very intense whitewater in a beautiful gorge. The most difficult of the drops are probably unrunnable in a raft and could be run only by a very skillful kayaker. The North Fork was recommended by the Forest Service for designation as a scenic river as part of our national Wild & Scenic Rivers system.

Getting There

State Route 542, the Mt. Baker Highway, parallels the North Fork of the Nooksack. Take exit 255 from I-5, the Sunset Drive exit. Turn right and head first for Deming and then Maple Falls.

Put-ins and Take-outs

You may wish to drop a car off at the take-out. The lower one is at the end of a very short dirt road just beyond mile marker 27, about 1.5 miles above Maple Falls. It is on private land and the owners have been kind enough to allow boaters to take out here. Don't leave any litter behind; if the property is abused, the owners may close it to boaters. You may want to tie a flag to a tree so you don't miss the take-out.

Another mile upriver is the take-out used by all the commercial raft trips. It is on a broad gravel bar reached by turning toward the river on a poor dirt road just upstream of the bridge over Boulder Creek.

An intermediate put-in or take-out point is reached at the highway bridge over the river, about 2.5 miles below Glacier. A short dirt road turns off the downstream side of State Route 542, 50 yards northwest of the bridge over the river. The dirt road is steep, and often four-wheel drive is required in wet weather. Recently, the main channel of the river shifted away from the right bank in this area, and boats have to be dragged over a gravel bar to get them to and from the river.

The main put-in is at Douglas Fir Campground, about 2 miles upriver from Glacier and clearly marked on the highway. You should put in as far upstream in the campground as possible in order to have a short warm-up before hitting the class 3 rapids of the gorge. You may want to put in on the upstream (east) side of the highway on the right bank to avoid disturbing campers in the campground.

Milky glacial water will challenge your river-reading skills.

Water Level

Because of the large amount of glacial melt from Mt. Baker flowing into the North Fork, it is one of the few free-flowing rivers that is normally runnable in late August and September. Radio telemetry has recently been installed on the North Fork gauge, making current river-level readings available, so it is usually not necessary to calculate the North Fork's flow from the Deming gauge. The North Fork can be run from 600 cfs to 1,300 cfs, though care should be taken in the gorge at higher levels due to the swiftness of the water.

If only the gauge reading from the main Nooksack at Deming is available, the recommended flows vary throughout the year. Because of its snow and glacier melt, the North Fork provides a greater portion of the main Nooksack flow in the summer. The approximate percentages of the main Nooksack flow that are coming from the North Fork vary by month as follows: May 25 percent, June 33 percent, July 39 percent, August 41 percent, September 33 percent, October 25 percent, November and April 17 percent, December to March 14 percent. Because the percentage is so low in the winter, and the river would only be runnable on floodwaters, these guidelines would be very inaccurate from November to April, and the river should not be run then. Recommended minimum and maximum levels for the North Fork for the remainder of the year are as follows:

The beginning of the Nooksack run is in a very steep and narrow gorge.

	May	June	July	Aug	Sept	Oct
Minimum	2,400	1,800	1,500	1,400	1,800	2,400
Maximum	4,800	3,600	3,000	2,800	3,600	4,800

Nooksack
North Fork Gauge
Recommend 600 to 1,300 cfs

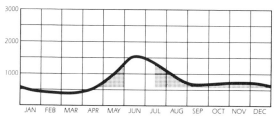

Special Hazards

Logs are a great hazard on the Nooksack and occasionally have completely blocked the channel; stay alert! Watch the water level closely, it can rise rapidly with rain or hot weather.

Scenery

The gorge that makes up the first part of this run is dark, narrow and dramatic. It is rock-choked and very scenic, with moss covering the banks and hanging from the trees. The end of the gorge is reached near the mouth of Glacier Creek, where the boater trades the beauty of the gorge for the wider view of the broadened river valley and the surrounding mountains. The channel begins to braid but still contains some interesting rapids, at least as far as the highway bridge. The whole trip is through a natural valley with few signs of civilization.

Camping

Campsites are available at Douglas Fir Campground—the put-in. There are other Forest Service campgrounds farther up State Route 542.

Rapids

The rapids at the beginning of the trip come fast and furious. You must be prepared to read and run many successive class 3 rapids without scouting. After Glacier Creek, the pace slackens, but you should watch carefully for logs across the river.

NORTH FORK, NOOKSACK RIVER

DOUGLAS FIR CAMP TO MAPLE FALLS

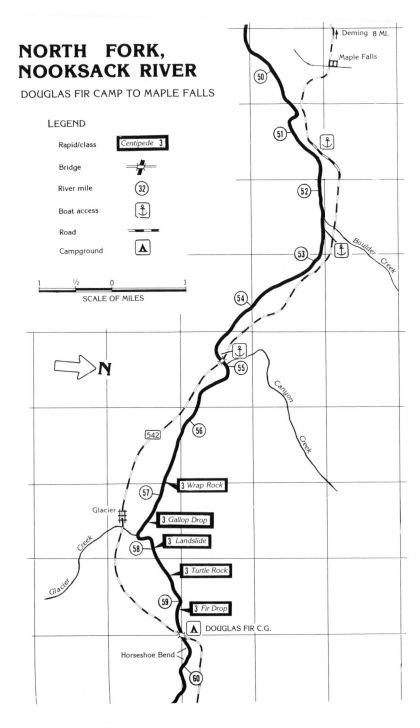

LEGEND

Rapid/class	Centipede 3
Bridge	
River mile	32
Boat access	
Road	
Campground	A

SCALE OF MILES

Deming 8 MI.

Maple Falls

50

51

52

Boulder Creek

53

54

55

Canyon

56

542

Creek

57 — 3 Wrap Rock

Glacier

3 Gallop Drop

3 Landslide

58

Glacier Creek

3 Turtle Rock

59 — 3 Fir Drop

A DOUGLAS FIR C.G.

Horseshoe Bend

60

RIVER MILE	RIVER TIME	LEFT BANK	RAPIDS	RIGHT BANK	DESCRIPTION
	2:00				
	55				
	50				
	45				
	40			⚓	—Take-out on right of small right channel
	35				
	30				—Farm just visible over bar
	25		●2	⚓	—Boulder Creek, bridge visible in distance
	20				
	15				
	10		●2		—Fun waves
					—Beaver area right
	5		●2		—Fun waves
	1:00		●2		—Fun waves
	55		●2	⚓	—Small beach left
RM 55	50		●2 ●2 ●2		—Highway bridge, preceded by Canyon Creek right
					—Shallow drop between islands
	45		●2		
	40		●2		—Large islands with trees, Cornell Creek left
	35		●2		—Small beach left
	30		●2 ●3 ●2	■	—**Wrap Rock,** stay left of large rock below
					—Large gravel bar right, shallow, stay left
	25		●2 ●2 ●3		—Bare bluff right
					—**Gallop Drop,** big hole bottom right, Gallop Creek
	20		●2		—Glacier Creek left
	15		●3	■	—**Landslide,** landslide area right
			●3		—Good playspot
	10		●2 ●3 ●3 ●2		—**Turtle Rock,** run left around huge boulder
	5	▲	●3		—Camp shelters & house left
		▲	●3		—**Fir Drop**
	12:00			▲	—Douglas Fir Campground

Kayakers go into orbit over the North Fork.

22

Snoqualmie, North Fork

Logged at -	1,050 cfs North Fork gauge
Recommended water level -	600 to 1,600 cfs
Best time -	Late April through June
Rating -	Advanced
Water level information -	NOAA Tape (206) 526-8530
	King County (206) 296-8100
River mile -	11.7 to 5.4; 6.3 miles
Time -	1 hour, 30 minutes; 4.2 mph
Elevation -	1,270' to 1,020'; 40' per mile

Deep Creek to Swinging Bridge

The North Fork of the Snoqualmie has one of the most interesting river channels to be found in Washington. Its narrow streambed—large boulders in the channel and wide variety of pools, drops, ledges, chutes, rock gardens and gravel bars—provides the greatest diversity of challenges on any 6-mile stretch of river in the state.

This run has been one of the favorite runs of the Washington Kayak Club and the University of Washington Canoe Club for many years, but it is not well known outside of western Washington. It has recently been threatened with destruction by dams for a variety of ill-considered water supply projects. Instead of implementing aggressive water conservation programs, Puget Sound municipalities have been looking for new sources of water for the region's rapidly expanding population. If you would like to help stop this avoidable destruction, contact the Rivers Council of Washington (see the Preface).

This trip is difficult for rafts; there are several obstacles to rafting the river: (1) Rafts need 800 cfs to run the river, which it rarely has, (2) the trip is only 1 hour, 30 minutes long and the shuttle takes nearly 1 hour to drive round-trip (not a problem for kayakers due to the number of great playspots), (3) because of the small water volume, there is a good chance of the channel being completely blocked by fallen trees, and (4) the put-in and take-out are 50-yard carries through the woods.

Getting There

The North Fork lies within Weyerhaeuser's Snoqualmie Tree Farm. For access to the tree farm, each vehicle must obtain a $50 annual access permit. Permits may be purchased starting May 1; they are good through May 31 of the following year. Call 1(800) 433-3911 for a recording with the latest regulations and a list of stores where a permit may be purchased.

To reach the Spur 10 gate, which is staffed from 7:00 A.M. to 5:00 P.M. on weekends, take exit 31 from I-90 and go west on State Route 202 about 0.5 mile into the town of North Bend. Turn right on North Bend Way. In about one block turn left immediately after Loveland Chevrolet and Olds on Ballarat Avenue North. Ballarat turns and twists; stay on it. After 0.5 mile it ceases to be called Ballarat and becomes 108th Street, then NE 12th Street, then 428th Street NE.

Stay on the main road and cross a new concrete bridge over the Middle Fork of the Snoqualmie. You then cross an older bridge over the North Fork. One and one-half miles after crossing the North Fork, the road divides. There are dead end signs at both forks. Take the left fork, which has signs saying "Dead End" and "For 24 Miles."

Put-ins and Take-outs

About 0.5 mile up the road, the pavement ends. Continue up the road about 3.0 miles to an intersection at the Spur 10 gate, the only access to the take-out areas. Unfortunately, the road from the Spur 10 gate does not connect with the Swinging Bridge road, the traditional take-out. You can either take-out at the Spur 10 bridge and miss some of the run or take out on a 100-yard carry just below Hancock Drop. For one, go about 0.8 mile from the Spur 10 gate toward the river (about 0.2 mile beyond the Weyerhaeuser 33900 road) and turn right on an unmarked spur road. Follow its longest branch (on the right) and find the faint trail from the end of the road to the river.

Alternatively, you can cross the river on the Spur 10 bridge and turn right (south) on the Weyerhaeuser 32000 road just over 0.1 mile from the bridge. About 0.6 mile down this road, shortly after crossing Hancock Creek, turn right on the Weyerhaeuser 32970 road. This road runs south along the east side of the river and has several rather steep places where the river can be accessed.

To get to the put-in, return to the Spur 10 gate and turn right on the North Fork county road. In 5.5 miles, you'll cross a bridge over Deep Creek (not signed). At 0.6 mile later, park along the main road to scramble down the bank to the river. Do not boat above the put-in. Between Wagner Bridge (just upstream 0.3 mile) and the put-in is class 6 water.

Water Level

From 600 to 1,600 cfs on the North Fork gauge, the North Fork is a great run for kayaks. Above 1,600 many of the drops begin to wash out. Rafts need a minimum of 800 cfs to avoid scraping on gravel bars.

Snoqualmie, North Fork
North Fork Gauge
Recommend 600 to 1,600 cfs

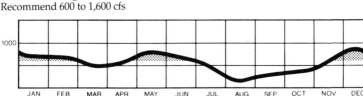

Special Hazards

Because of the small water volume of this river, it is quite easy for trees to fall all the way across the channel; watch out for sweepers.

Scenery

Although the surrounding forest has been heavily clearcut, the scenery from the river is superb. A strip of trees along the river screens out most evidence of logging, and other than one bridge and a couple of cables, there are no signs of civilization. A fascinating feature of the North Fork is the number of very large boulders in the middle of the channel. They highlight the scenery and provide interesting obstacles. There are also beautiful rock walls and nice small beaches.

Camping

There are no developed campgrounds near the North Fork; the nearest is Tinkham, 11 miles farther east on I-90. All of the land in this area belongs to the Weyerhaeuser Company, and no overnight camping is allowed below Lennox Creek, 7 miles farther up the North Fork county road, where the National Forest boundary is reached.

Rapids

Deep Creek Drop provides a good place to play and a warm up for what's ahead. It sweeps over a gravel bar and then around a right bend to a good drop at the end. The most difficult rapids are the series of class 3 drops at log time 21–27 minutes and a second series near the end at log time 1 hour, 18–27 minutes. Both series of rapids involve four or five drops coming so close together that they become one long rapid approaching class 4 in difficulty because of its length. About two-thirds of the way through the first series, you'll encounter an exciting 3-foot-ledge drop. The biggest hydraulics of the trip are found in the rapid at log time 53 minutes and in **Hancock**, where passage is found between the right bank and a large boulder near the right shore.

Play until you drop.

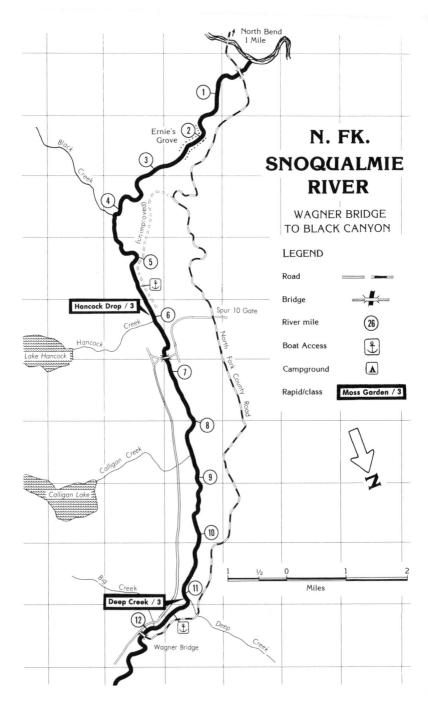

N. FK. SNOQUALMIE RIVER

WAGNER BRIDGE TO BLACK CANYON

LEGEND

Road	
Bridge	
River mile	26
Boat Access	
Campground	A
Rapid/class	Moss Garden / 3

North Bend
1 Mile

Ernie's Grove

Black Creek

(unimproved)

Hancock Drop / 3

Creek

Hancock

Lake Hancock

Spur 10 Gate

North Fork County Road

Calligan Creek

Calligan Lake

Big Creek

Deep Creek / 3

Wagner Bridge

Deep Creek

1 ½ 0 1 2
Miles

N

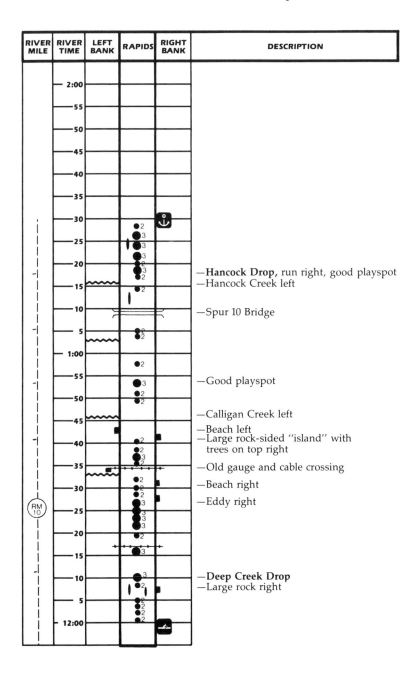

RIVER MILE	RIVER TIME	LEFT BANK	RAPIDS	RIGHT BANK	DESCRIPTION
	2:00				
	55				
	50				
	45				
	40				
	35				
	30			⚓	
	25		2 3 3		
	20		3 2 3 2		—**Hancock Drop,** run right, good playspot
	15		2		—Hancock Creek left
	10				—Spur 10 Bridge
	5		2 2		
	1:00				
	55		2		
			3		—Good playspot
	50		2 2		
	45				—Calligan Creek left
					—Beach left
	40		2		—Large rock-sided "island" with trees on top right
	35		2 3 2		—Old gauge and cable crossing
	30		2 2		—Beach right
	25		2 3 3 3 3		—Eddy right
	20		2		
	15		3		
RM 10	10		3 2		—**Deep Creek Drop**
					—Large rock right
	5		2 2		
	12:00		2		

23

Kalama

Logged at - 1,850 cfs Kalama gauge
Recommended water level - 1,100 to 3,200 cfs
Best time - April to early May
Rating - Advanced
Water level information - NOAA Tape (206) 526-8530
River mile - 20.4 to 10.9; 9.5 miles
Time - 2 hours, 14 minutes; 4.2 mph
Elevation - 450' to 170'; 29' per mile

Pigeon Springs to Lower Kalama Falls

The Kalama is my favorite early-season run. It combines beautiful scenery with fun whitewater. Having just a couple of challenging drops, it gets the season off to a good start on a small, intimate river. The Indian meaning of Kalama is "fair maiden." Others praise the river as well. Fly fishermen revere the upper part of the river as the "holy water" and salmon and steelhead fishermen flock to the river below the falls for the perfect fishing trip.

Getting There

The Kalama is about 30 miles north of Portland on I-5. Turn off at the Kalama River Road exit and drive east some 9 beautiful miles to the Washington State Salmon Hatchery, the take-out.

Put-ins and Take-outs

The take-out at the salmon hatchery is just beyond the parking lot and to the left, behind some houses. It is an excellent take-out, with a broad, fairly level, gravel beach. Leave your vehicles in the parking lot and take them down to the bank only for loading.

About 0.5 mile above the hatchery, the road divides. The upper road is in better condition and will get you to the upper put-in.

The upper put-in is just above a concrete bridge over the river next to a very broad dirt turn-out. The surrounding area has been completely logged. The put-in is steep and rugged, but it's the only one on this section of the river.

To reach the intermediate access point, take the lower road 0.5 mile above the hatchery. About 1.8 miles above the fork in the road, you will

A narrow, rock-walled gorge highlights the Kalama scenery.

pass a suspension bridge (designed for cars, but I wouldn't want to test it) over the river. About 0.9 mile beyond the suspension bridge is a steep, short path to an eddy through a stand of evergreens. It is a good place to take out for those who want to avoid the flatwater and a good place to put in for those seeking a class 1 canoe trip.

Water Level

Although the Kalama drains the west side of Mt. St. Helens, most of its drainage is under 3,000 feet in elevation so it does not have enough snow run-off to provide good water levels in late spring or summer. Some recent rain is usually necessary to have enough water for boating, and the river is usually only at runnable levels in the late fall, winter and early spring.

I recommend 1,100 cfs minimum for a good trip, though kayaks could probably sneak down the river on 800 cfs. Because the gauge is quite a way farther downriver, it probably shows a third again as much water as is in the logged run.

Now, was it right or left of the gray rock?

Kalama
Kalama Gauge
Recommend 1,100 to 3,200 cfs

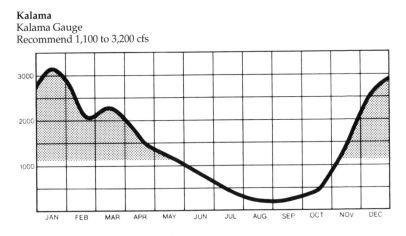

Special Hazards

Avoid **Lower Kalama Falls**. The principal drop is about 15 feet and has been subjected to man-made "improvements" that create a perfect hydraulic. At most water levels a boater would be lucky to survive a trip over the falls. The falls are only about 500 feet below the take-out at the salmon hatchery, so don't miss it! The hatchery take-out is easy to spot, but don't day-dream.

Scenery

There is near rain forest beauty on this small river. Much of the banks are lined with thick forest and moss-covered rock outcroppings. A couple hundred yards of the river, at log time 58 minutes, flow through solid rock walls like a miniature Mule Creek Canyon. The creek at log time 1 hour, 4 minutes, enters the river over a series of beautiful little falls. The lower portion of the run provides some of the most unspoiled scenery of the trip, but almost no whitewater.

Camping

A campsite is not easy to come by near the Kalama. The nearest public campground is Speelyai, operated by Pacific Power and Light at the lower end of Lake Merwin on the Lewis River. To get there, travel south some 10 miles on I-5 to Woodland and take State Route 503 east toward Cougar about 12 miles.

Rapids

Most of the rapids on the Kalama are very enjoyable class 2s that have an abundance of good playspots. The two rapids that may deserve a scout are **What's That? Falls** and **Leader Rapids**. You may also wish to take a look at **Summers Creek Drop**, right under the concrete Summers Creek bridge, on the drive to the put-in. It is easily run right down the middle, however.

What's That? Falls acquired its name from our reaction to seeing a horizon line and boiling whitewater below, when we first ran the river based on some sketchy reports. It's quite a straightforward drop, but much more easily run if you scout the correct line for the tongue rather than try to pick it out as you bear down on it. You should land just around a left bend in the river, above a short class 2 rapid. Once you enter the class 2, you're committed to What's That? Falls.

Leader Rapids is only marginally class 4 at most of the recommended water levels, but it definitely requires a scout on the right bank before running it. None of the moves required is very difficult, but there are so many boulders staggered down the drop that it is essential to have a route planned in advance. Above 1,600 cfs, Leader Rapids can be run either on the right or on the left. Below 1,600 cfs, rocks exposed on the right suggest the left-hand route.

Kayakers may wish to consider running a very exciting, but short, part of the river below the section logged and below the Lower Kalama Falls. Because the road is some distance above the river at this point, a put-in requires a steep carry down some 120 vertical feet of rough hillside to the river. Make sure that you put in *below* **Lower Kalama Falls**! You'll be rewarded with a 2.5-mile canyon run having two class 4 and a half dozen class 3 rapids before the road returns to the river bank at Indian Creek. From here on down, the river is very pretty, but all class 1.

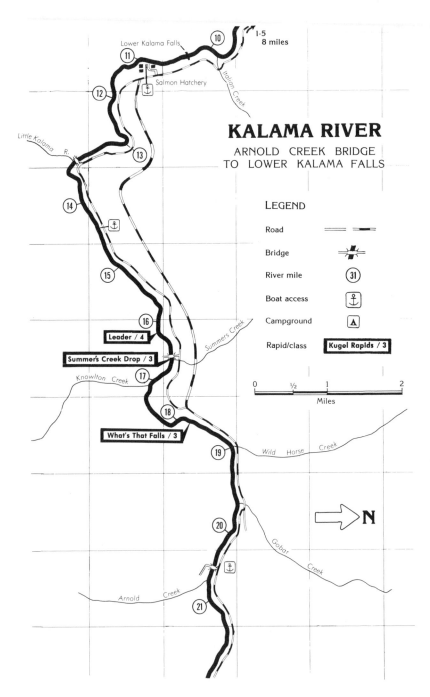

KALAMA RIVER
ARNOLD CREEK BRIDGE
TO LOWER KALAMA FALLS

Lower Kalama Falls
Salmon Hatchery
I-5
8 miles
Italian Creek
Little Kalama R.
Summers Creek
Knowlton Creek
Wild Horse Creek
Gobar Creek
Arnold Creek

Leader / 4
Summer's Creek Drop / 3
What's That Falls / 3

LEGEND

Road	
Bridge	
River mile	31
Boat access	
Campground	
Rapid/class	**Kugel Rapids / 3**

0   ½   1   2
Miles

N

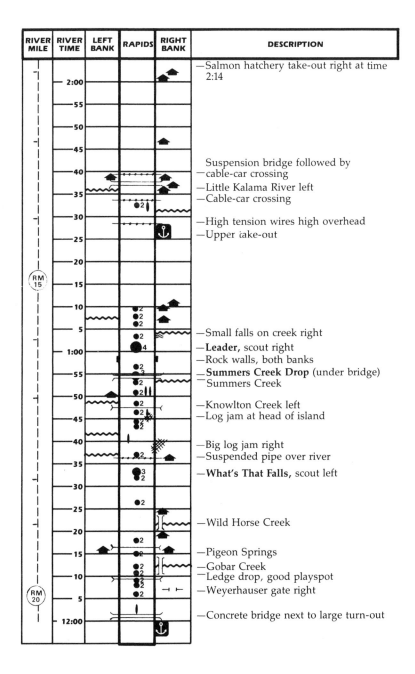

RIVER MILE	RIVER TIME	LEFT BANK	RAPIDS	RIGHT BANK	DESCRIPTION
	2:00				—Salmon hatchery take-out right at time 2:14
	55				
	50				
	45				
	40				Suspension bridge followed by cable-car crossing
	35		●2		—Little Kalama River left / —Cable-car crossing
	30				—High tension wires high overhead
	25		⚓		—Upper take-out
	20				
RM 15	15				
	10		●2 ●2 ●2		
	5		●2		—Small falls on creek right
	1:00		●4		—Leader, scout right
					—Rock walls, both banks
	55		●2 3		—Summers Creek Drop (under bridge)
	50		●2 ●2		—Summers Creek
	45		●2 ●2		—Knowlton Creek left / —Log jam at head of island
	40				
	35		●2		—Big log jam right / —Suspended pipe over river
	30		●3 2		—What's That Falls, scout left
	25		●2		
	20				—Wild Horse Creek
	15		●2 ●2		—Pigeon Springs
	10		●2 ●2 ●2		—Gobar Creek / —Ledge drop, good playspot
RM 20	5		●2		—Weyerhauser gate right
	12:00			⚓	—Concrete bridge next to large turn-out

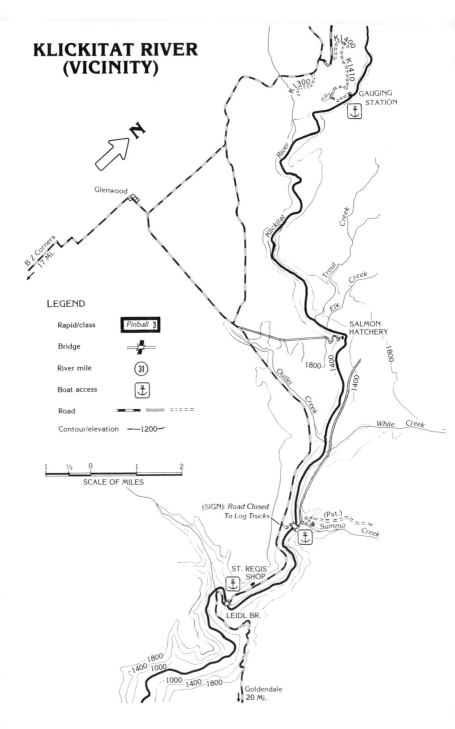

KLICKITAT RIVER (VICINITY)

LEGEND

Rapid/class — Pinball 3

Bridge

River mile — 31

Boat access

Road

Contour/elevation — 1200

SCALE OF MILES

24

Klickitat

Logged at	-	3,400 cfs Pitt gauge (May)
Recommended water level	-	1,400 to 3,500 cfs
Best time	-	Late April to late June
Rating	-	Advanced
Water level information	-	NOAA Tape (206) 526-8530
River mile	-	50.2 to 32.0; 18.2 miles
Time	-	2 hours, 40 minutes; 6.8 mph
Elevation	-	1,705' to 860'; 46' per mile

Gauging Station to Leidl Bridge

The Klickitat flows through a narrow canyon cut 400–800 feet into a pine-forested plateau in eastern Washington. The geography is dramatically revealed by a short side trip to "viewpoint" between Leidl and Glenwood. The river scenery is punctuated by beautiful 200-foot-high head-walls of columnar basalt. Because the Klickitat is so far east, it has the hot, dry climate of eastern Washington in May and June when the water levels are good. The surroundings are almost completely natural until you reach the fish hatchery, and even below this there are few signs of civilization.

Through the Columbia Gorge National Scenic Area Bill, Congress ordered the Forest Service to study the Klickitat above the mouth of the Little Klickitat for Wild & Scenic River designation. This is one of the most outstanding rivers in eastern Washington and richly deserves this protection.

A local citizens advisory committee has recommended that the whole river be added to the state scenic rivers program. Whether added to the national or state program, the Klickitat deserves careful management as one of Washington's finest rivers.

Getting There

From BZ Corner on State Route 141, follow the county road across the White Salmon, about 20 miles to Glenwood. From there, it is a short drive to either the put-in or the take-out at Leidl Bridge. Glenwood can also be reached by turning off State Route 142 about 11 miles west of Goldendale and driving about 30 miles on the county road to Glenwood. Note that snow can close the road to the put-in into May.

There are many spectacular basalt headwalls on the Klickitat. (Jeanne Martin photo)

Put-ins and Take-outs

The put-in is reached on a number of roads best explained by the vicinity map. You can make the turn-off just east of Glenwood or 3.5 miles east, just 100 yards west of the road that turns off to the fish hatchery (labeled with a sign). The road is largely paved, although there are some gravel stretches. You go about 6.5 miles until a turn-off is made on the dirt road labeled K1400, approximately 0.5 mile after the road labeled K1300. Three-fourths of a mile down K1400 an intersection is reached, at which point you should bear right on K1410 (unsigned). About 1.5 miles later, bearing left will take you 0.5 mile to an old gauging station at the river. The last 100 yards of the road are in bad condition. The equipment could be carried for this stretch.

There is a very good take-out or put-in about 100 yards below the Summit Creek bridge on the right. It is reached by turning off on a dirt road about 2.75 miles north of the St. Regis buildings above Leidl. A sign at the entrance to the road says "Road Closed to Log Trucks." A short, but steep, descent brings you to an intersection with a paved road used by the logging trucks. Turn left and in 100 yards the boat access site is on the right.

The take-out is on a good boat ramp at Leidl Campground. This is a Department of Wildlife site, requiring a license (see the Introduction).

Water Level

The gauging station at the put-in is abandoned. Readings must be taken from the gauge at Pitt, which is many miles below the portion of the river covered by this log. Numerous tributaries enter the river below the logged run but above the gauging station. Since these tributaries are largely rain-fed, they constitute a greater percentage of the water on the Pitt gauge early in the season than they do later. The approximate percentages of water on the Pitt gauge that are present in the logged portion of the river are as follows: January–March 32 percent, April 50 percent, May 70 percent, June and July 75 percent, August 65 percent, September–November 58 percent and December 43 percent. For normal running times, this produces recommended minimum and maximum discharge levels as follows:

	April	May	June	July	August
Min	2,000	1,500	1,400	1,400	1,700
Max	4,800	3,500	3,200	3,200	3,800

The log and description in this chapter are of the river at the higher end of the recommended water level. At low levels, the trip is less demanding, many of the rapids decline one class in difficulty and only about a half-dozen of the rapids remain class 3, but much rock-dodging is necessary. The water clears up at low levels, however, and the trip is so beautiful that it is almost preferable then.

Klickitat
Pitt Gauge
Recommend 1,400 to 3,500 cfs

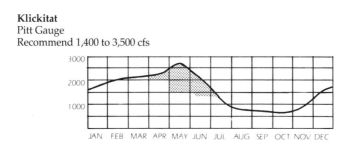

Special Hazards

The high gradient makes for nearly constant whitewater in the upper portion of the run. A bailer is essential for every raft that isn't self-bailing. At **higher water levels**, this section should be run only by very experienced boaters, as the lack of eddies could make for a very long swim in the event of an upset.

The water is melted snow and ice and very cold. It is always somewhat turbid due to glacial flour and becomes brown at the height of the spring run-off.

Logs are a great danger on the Klickitat. In some years, **logjams** have completely blocked the river channel.

The **dam** at the fish hatchery should be scouted on the left. It can be run on the left, but many boaters may wish to line it because of the ever-present debris.

Scenery

This is the most beautiful run in eastern Washington. There are no signs of civilization as the boat drifts through fragrant semi-open pine forests and by many spectacular basalt cliffs.

The river below the Summit Creek bridge is very beautiful and swift, with few eddies, but little whitewater. There is a good boat ramp take-out at Leidl Campground. The river canyon from Leidl down to Wahkiacus is very pretty and remote, the only road access being on St. Regis logging roads from which the public is excluded. The river channel is often braided, however, and many logs clog it in places. It has all class 1 water except for a nice class 2 drop just above Wahkiacus.

Camping

There is a lovely campsite at the put-in. There are also many beautiful semi-open meadows dotted with pine trees in the upper section which invite an overnight trip. An overnight trip is desirable at lower flows when boating time could approach 4 hours. Overnight camping is also attractive because of the few signs of civilization visible from the river.

Rapids

You will face continuous class 3 water from log time 35 to 51 minutes. This section is very demanding. The river surges and rolls over rocks and races between head-walls. There are almost no eddies. Past the fish hatchery, the difficulty eases, but the river is still very lively to Summit Creek bridge.

The Klickitat has cut deeply into the surrounding plateau.

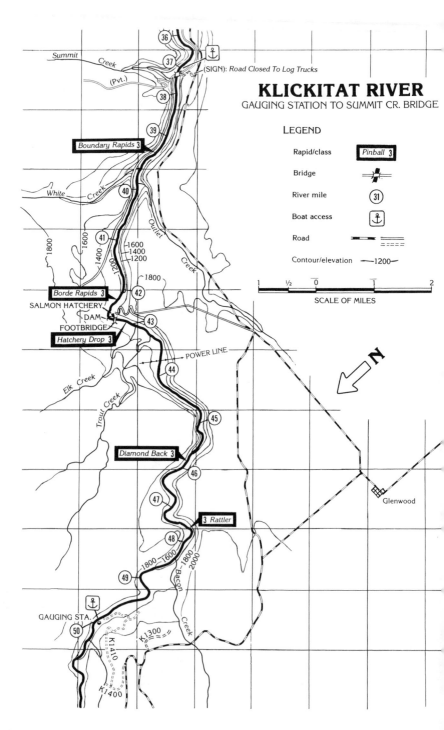

KLICKITAT RIVER
GAUGING STATION TO SUMMIT CR. BRIDGE

Summit Creek

(Pvt.)

(SIGN): Road Closed To Log Trucks

Boundary Rapids **3**

White Creek

Outlet Creek

1800

1600

1400

1200

—1600
—1400
—1200

1800

Borde Rapids **3**

SALMON HATCHERY

DAM

FOOTBRIDGE

Hatchery Drop **3**

Elk Creek

Trout Creek

POWER LINE

Diamond Back **3**

3 Rattler

1800 1600 1800 2000

Bacon Creek

GAUGING STA.

K1300

K1410

K1400

Glenwood

N

LEGEND

Rapid/class	Pinball **3**
Bridge	
River mile	③①
Boat access	
Road	
Contour/elevation	—1200—

1   ½   0   1   2

SCALE OF MILES

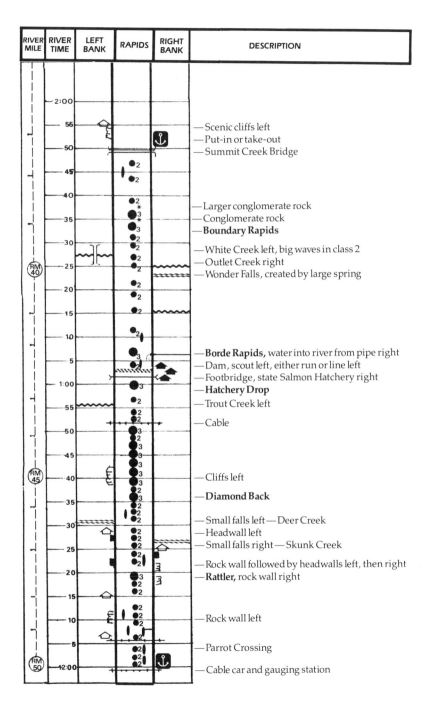

RIVER MILE	RIVER TIME	LEFT BANK	RAPIDS	RIGHT BANK	DESCRIPTION
	2:00				
	55				—Scenic cliffs left
					—Put-in or take-out
	50				—Summit Creek Bridge
	45		●2 ●2		
	40				
	35		●2 * ●3 * ●3		—Larger conglomerate rock —Conglomerate rock —**Boundary Rapids**
	30		●2 ●2		—White Creek left, big waves in class 2
RM 40	25		●2 ●2		—Outlet Creek right —Wonder Falls, created by large spring
	20		●2 ●2		
	15		●2		
	10		●2		
	5		●3 ●2		—**Borde Rapids,** water into river from pipe right —Dam, scout left, either run or line left —Footbridge, state Salmon Hatchery right
	1:00		●3		—**Hatchery Drop**
	55		●2		—Trout Creek left
			●2 ●2		—Cable
	50		●3 ●2 ●3		
	45		●3 ●3 ●3		
RM 45	40		●3 ●2		—Cliffs left
	35		●3 ●2 ●2		—**Diamond Back**
	30		●2 ●2		—Small falls left—Deer Creek —Headwall left
	25		●2 ●2 ●2		—Small falls right—Skunk Creek
	20		●2 ●2 ●3 ●2		—Rock wall followed by headwalls left, then right —**Rattler,** rock wall right
	15		●2		
	10		●2 ●2 ●2		—Rock wall left
	5		●2		—Parrot Crossing
RM 50	12:00		●2 ●2		—Cable car and gauging station

At high water, class 3 rapids are nearly constant for 2 miles. (Jeanne Martin photo)

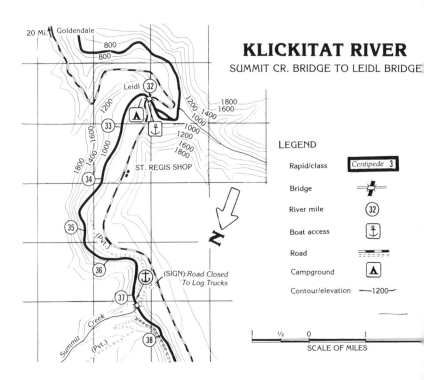

KLICKITAT RIVER
SUMMIT CR. BRIDGE TO LEIDL BRIDGE

20 Mi. Goldendale
800
800
Leidl 32
1200
1200 1400
1800
1600
1000
33
1000
1200
1600 1800 1400 1000
1600
1800
34
ST. REGIS SHOP
35
(Pvt.)
36
(SIGN):Road Closed To Log Trucks
37
Summit Creek
(Pvt.)
38

LEGEND

Rapid/class	Centipede 3
Bridge	
River mile	32
Boat access	⚓
Road	
Campground	🏕
Contour/elevation	—1200—

N

SCALE OF MILES
1 ½ 0 1

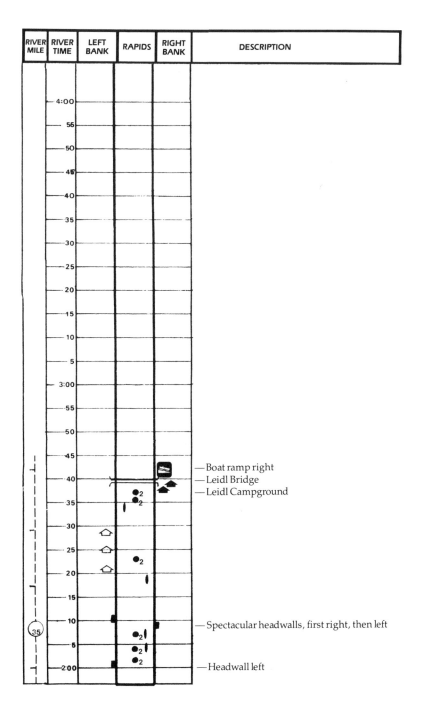

- Boat ramp right
- Leidl Bridge
- Leidl Campground
- Spectacular headwalls, first right, then left
- Headwall left

25

Middle Middle Fork Snoqualmie

Logged at - 1,500 cfs Middle Fork gauge
Recommended water level - 1,500 to 3,000 cfs
Best time - May and June
Rating - Advanced
Water level information - NOAA Tape (206) 526-8530
King County (206) 296-8100
River mile - 57.1 to 49.5; 7.6 miles
Time - 2 hours, 2 minutes; 3.7 mph
Elevation - 850' to 530'; 42' per mile

Concrete Bridge to Tanner

Although the Middle Fork of the Snoqualmie is only 30 miles from Seattle and close to the town of North Bend, it seems remote. The river, fed by run-off from the snowfields on the west side of the Cascades, flows through a heavily forested area, and few man-made structures are visible through the trees. You'll encounter a wide variety of rapids as the water winds past the numerous granite boulders in its path. There are drops, narrow chutes, islands and deep pools, as well as the swirls around the boulders. In the lower stretch, difficult rapids are closely spaced and the boating is challenging.

This log covers a run known as the Middle Middle. Chapter 5 covers the upper Middle and the two can be combined for an overnight trip. You can also run the 4-mile stretch from the take-out of this run down to the bridge at North Bend. It's known as the Club Stretch and has class 1 and 2 water and much visible development. The Middle Fork of the Snoqualmie has been recommended by the Forest Service for designation as a Wild & Scenic river.

Getting There

To reach the Middle Middle, take exit 34 (Edgewick Road) from I-90 and drive north about 200 yards to Ken's Truck Stop. Since Ken's is near the take-out, most groups will want to drop off a car at the take-out before going on upriver.

Put-ins and Take-outs

You can get to the take-out by taking a left just before Ken's and driv-

At lower water levels, many of the rapids are very rocky.

ing 1.5 miles west on the road that parallels I-90. Turn right just past a lumber mill onto SE Tanner Road. You can see the river from the turn-off. Go 0.5 mile on SE Tanner. There is now a locked gate across the head of the 200-yard-long dirt road on the left that leads to the take-out. This causes a very tough carry for rafts. There is room to park three or four cars in a gravel area along SE Tanner near the start of the dirt road. The Rivers Council of Washington is working on a new take-out. Call them at (206) 283-4988 for information about it.

To get to the put-in, drive north from Ken's approximately 200 yards and take a right at the T intersection. In about 0.9 mile, the road divides and then joins in another 1.2 miles.

Just after the two branches of the road rejoin, the pavement ends. Continue on the gravel road to the concrete bridge spanning the river. You can put in on the river-left side of the bridge. The access just downstream of the bridge may be blocked, so you may have to put in on the upstream side of the bridge, which is very steep.

The Middle Fork has many chutes dropping into pools at low to moderate water levels.

You can also put in on a gravel bar on the left bank at log time 20 minutes. The bar is about 25 feet below the road, and you'll be able to see it through the trees as you drive in. To reach it, continue past the point where you can see the gravel bar until you come to a sharp left bend in the road. About 0.1 mile beyond the bend, turn off onto the very poor dirt road and take it to the put-in.

It's also possible to put in or take out at Mine Creek Campground, either to reach or avoid the significantly more difficult whitewater below the campground.

Water Level

You'll need a water level of 1,500 cfs to run the Middle Middle in a raft without scraping a lot of rocks. Kayaks will find good playspots at levels over 1,100 cfs. At water levels over 2,500 cfs, there's much less danger of scraping on the rocks, but the hydraulics become quite powerful because the drop is so great. Be very careful if you're boating the section at over 4,000 cfs, as the holes become very large. I compiled this log at 1,500 cfs when the water was quite technical and rocky but still very enjoyable. The river generally flows above 1,500 cfs only in May and June during the spring run-off.

For first trips, I recommend a level of less than 3,000 cfs; above that level, many of the rapids merge and the hydraulics are too powerful to be run safely by a boater who's not familiar with the section.

Middle Middle Fork Snoqualmie
Middle Middle Fork Gauge
Recommend 1,500 to 3,000 cfs

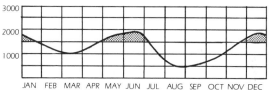

Special Hazards

None.

Scenery

Forested banks drop to a boulder-strewn channel. The scenery's quite beautiful.

Camping

You can camp at Mine Creek Campground along the run.

Rapids

Since there are very few clear landmarks on the Middle Middle, you should be prepared to run difficult water at all times. Despite the unusual house-sized boulders in midchannel, you probably won't recognize **House Rocks Drop** until it's too late to scout. You'll probably want to run it starting left of center, directly toward the largest boulder (to avoid the large hole on the right top), then use a strong ferry to go right of the largest boulder.

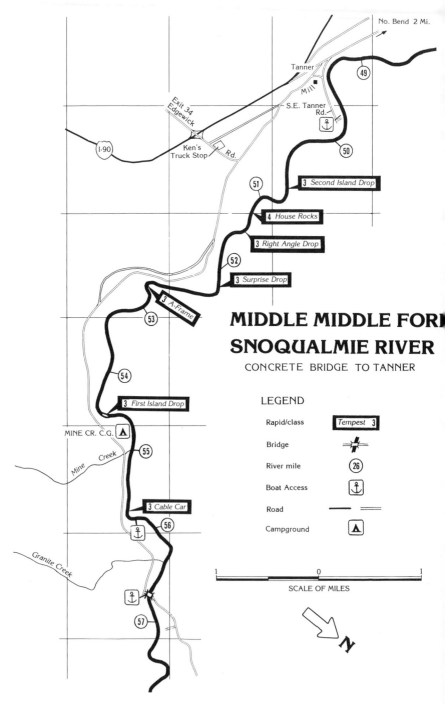

MIDDLE MIDDLE FORK

SNOQUALMIE RIVER

CONCRETE BRIDGE TO TANNER

No. Bend 2 Mi.

Tanner

Exit 34
Edgewick

I-90

Ken's
Truck Stop

S.E. Tanner Rd.

Mill

Rd.

3 Second Island Drop

4 House Rocks

3 Right Angle Drop

3 Surprise Drop

3 A-Frame

3 First Island Drop

MINE CR. C.G.

Mine   Creek

3 Cable Car

Granite Creek

LEGEND

Rapid/class   Tempest 3

Bridge

River mile   26

Boat Access

Road

Campground

1   0   1

SCALE OF MILES

N

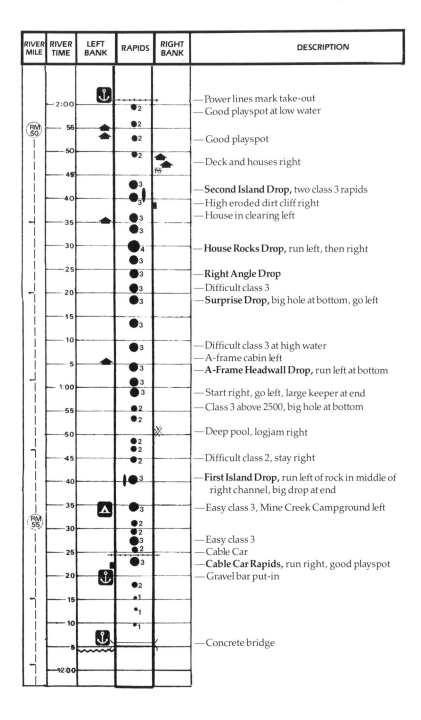

RIVER MILE	RIVER TIME	LEFT BANK	RAPIDS	RIGHT BANK	DESCRIPTION
	2:00				—Power lines mark take-out
			●2		—Good playspot at low water
RM 50	55		●2		
			●2		—Good playspot
	50		●2		—Deck and houses right
	45				
			●3		—**Second Island Drop,** two class 3 rapids
	40		●3		—High eroded dirt cliff right
	35		●3		—House in clearing left
			●3		
	30		●4		—**House Rocks Drop,** run left, then right
			●3		
	25		●3		—**Right Angle Drop**
	20		●3		—Difficult class 3
			●3		—**Surprise Drop,** big hole at bottom, go left
	15				
			●3		
	10				
			●3		—Difficult class 3 at high water
	5		●3		—A-frame cabin left
			●3		—**A-Frame Headwall Drop,** run left at bottom
			●3		
	1:00		●3		—Start right, go left, large keeper at end
	55		●2		—Class 3 above 2500, big hole at bottom
			●2		
	50				—Deep pool, logjam right
			●2		
	45		●2		
			●2		—Difficult class 2, stay right
	40		●3		—**First Island Drop,** run left of rock in middle of right channel, big drop at end
RM 55	35		●3		—Easy class 3, Mine Creek Campground left
	30		●2		
			●2		
			●3		—Easy class 3
	25		●2		—Cable Car
			●3		—**Cable Car Rapids,** run right, good playspot
	20				—Gravel bar put-in
			●2		
	15		●1		
			●1		
	10		●1		
	5				—Concrete bridge
	12:00				

26

White Salmon

Logged at	-	1,300 cfs Underwood gauge
Recommended water level	-	600 to 1,300 cfs
Best time	-	June through August
Rating	-	Advanced
Water level information	-	NOAA Tape (206) 526-8530
River mile	-	12.3 to 5.0; 7.3 miles
Time	-	1 hour, 37 minutes; 4.5 mph
Elevation	-	630' to 300'; 45' per mile

BZ Corner to Northwestern Lake

The White Salmon flows off the south side of Mt. Adams on the eastern side of the Cascade mountains and runs about 35 miles south to the Columbia River. Mount Adams glacial water is joined by water from numerous springs so that you can run the river throughout most of the summer. The numerous springs also promote lush vegetation along the banks, including maidenhair ferns and flowering plants. The White Salmon offers you the unique opportunity to enjoy simultaneously the beauty of near rain forest vegetation and the generally drier weather east of the crest of the mountains.

There is no such thing as a "white salmon," but many salmon take on a whitish cast when they head upriver to spawn. The great number of spawning salmon seen at the mouth of the river led to its name.

The run covered by this log is from just above the bridge at BZ Corner to the headwaters of Northwestern Lake, formed by Pacific Power and Light's Condit Dam. In the early 1980s this section of river was threatened by a proposed hydroelectric project that would have diverted most of the flow of the river through a long pipe, discharging it into Northwestern Lake. Friends of the White Salmon fought the project, and its permit expired in 1983. In 1986 this section of the river became a Scenic river under the national Wild & Scenic Rivers Act as part of the Columbia Gorge National Scenic Area Bill. The same bill authorized the Forest Service to study, for possible Wild & Scenic designation, the section of the river upstream of Gilmer Creek.

Getting There

State Route 141 parallels the White Salmon, which is just over an hour's drive east of Portland.

Put-ins and Take-outs

The put-in is just off State Route 141 two blocks north of the road that turns off to the bridge over the river at BZ Corner. You may want to walk out on the bridge (some 135 feet over the river) to get a look at the whitewater in the gorge below. The put-in is owned by Bill Gross, and he has marked it with a sign by the highway that reads "White Salmon River Launch Point." He has provided a trail down to the river and a cable system for lowering rafts down to the river. In 1995 he charged $9.00 per private raft, $3.00 per person on commercial raft trips and $1.50 per kayaker using the trail. There is always someone there to help with launching, but Bill asks that you call ahead if you have a group larger than 25 people launching on a weekday. His phone number is (509) 493-2054.

The take-out is on a boat ramp owned by Pacific Power and Light at the head of Northwestern Lake. To get to the boat ramp, turn off State Route 141 about 5 miles from the town of White Salmon or 2 miles from Husum on a paved road marked by signs to Northwestern Lake and Buck Creek Trail. Just beyond the bridge over the river, a left turn will lead you to the boat ramp.

Water Level

Because the White Salmon canyon is so narrow, water level is critical. A change of 300 cfs makes a big difference in the power of the river. I recommend between 600 and 1,300 cfs for a first trip. Above 1,500 cfs many of the rapids become one class higher, peppering this trip with class 4 rapids in Grasshopper, Corkscrew Falls, Water Spout and Stairstep Falls. Several of these are around blind corners in the canyon and are impossible to scout at higher water levels.

White Salmon
Underwood Gauge
Recommend 600 to 1,300 cfs

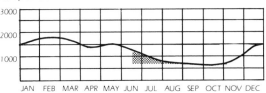

Special Hazards

Two-thirds of the way down the river is the town of Husum, where you should stop and look at **Husum Falls,** an 8-foot drop at the bridge which is run by many kayakers but not often run by rafters. Kayakers submarine and rafters go nose-down and are likely to flip end over end.

The land around the falls is owned by the Forest Service and is open to those who wish to portage or line their boats around the falls.

Scenery

The upper part of this trip is in a spectacular, narrow canyon. The river is close to the highway, but due to the steep rock walls, varying from 50 to 100 feet high, it is isolated from the farms and road. In the last mile before reaching Husum, the river slope diminishes and you come out of the canyon into farm areas. You can get out on the right bank as soon as Husum bridge is sighted, in order to avoid running the falls, or you can line the falls on the left. Below Husum Falls, there are lively rapids for the first mile and then more quiet drifting through beautiful forest, with much evidence of beavers, to Northwestern Lake.

Camping

Camping is available west in Gifford Pinchot National Forest or east at the Horsethief Lake recreation area near the Dalles Dam.

Rapids

The trip begins with a bang in **Maytag Drop**. This class 4 involves some maneuvering and a substantial drop into a hole at the end. Less aggressive boaters may want to portage or line it.

Between Maytag and **Husum Falls** there are several class 3 rapids. Four of these are larger than the others and have been named: Grasshopper, Corkscrew Falls, Water Spout and Stairstep. The average river slope is about 50 feet per mile, making the river velocity high. The river should be exciting for boaters with class 3 ability.

Grasshopper is fairly straightforward and can be read from the boat. **Corkscrew Falls** is the most difficult rapid at low water—stay well right to avoid the rocks and holes.

Waterspout is probably the most difficult rapid at high water because of the enormous spout created by large water flows. At high water, small rafts are well advised to carry a fair amount of water into Waterspout to avoid being thrown over by the force of the hydraulics.

Stairstep Falls consists of four drops. The first two and the last are good-sized while the third is more moderate. Run the first drop right of center and then pull left for the second drop. The third and fourth drops are straightforward.

The White Salmon is a cold river with its Mt. Adams glacial and spring water origins. The deep canyon also tends to screen out sun. Cold-water gear is nearly always necessary.

For "Husum Days" (the weekend following the 4th of July weekend) there is a slalom race on the White Salmon. (Dave Welch photo)

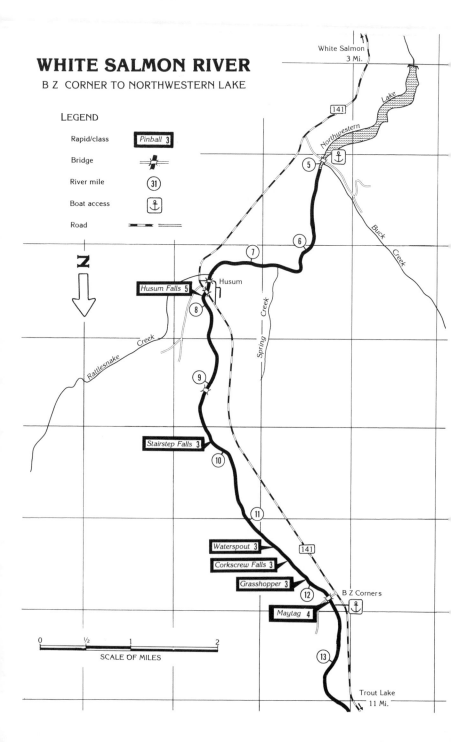

WHITE SALMON RIVER

B Z CORNER TO NORTHWESTERN LAKE

LEGEND

Rapid/class   Pinball 3

Bridge

River mile   31

Boat access

Road

White Salmon
3 Mi.

141

Lake

Northwestern

5

6

Buck Creek

7

Husum Falls 5   Husum

8

Spring Creek

Rattlesnake Creek

9

Stairstep Falls 3

10

11

Waterspout 3

Corkscrew Falls 3

Grasshopper 3   B Z Corners

12

Maylag 4

13

0   ½   1   2
SCALE OF MILES

141

Trout Lake
11 Mi.

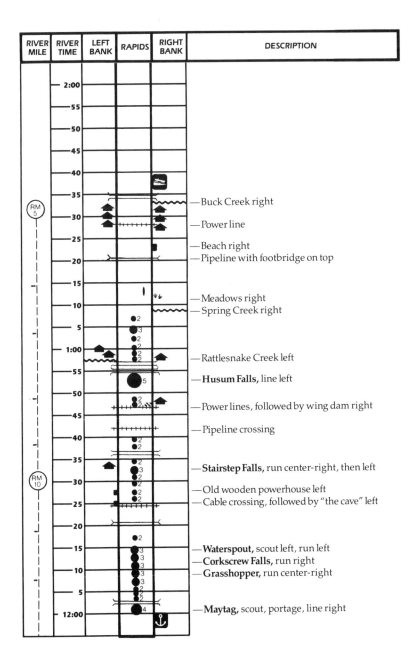

RIVER MILE	RIVER TIME	LEFT BANK	RAPIDS	RIGHT BANK	DESCRIPTION
	2:00				
	55				
	50				
	45				
	40				
	35				
RM 5	30				—Buck Creek right
	30				—Power line
	25				—Beach right
	20				—Pipeline with footbridge on top
	15				
	10				—Meadows right
					—Spring Creek right
	5		●2		
			●3		
			●2		
	1:00		●2		
			●2		—Rattlesnake Creek left
			●2		
	55				
			●5		**Husum Falls,** line left
	50		●2		
			●2		—Power lines, followed by wing dam right
	45				
					—Pipeline crossing
	40		●2		
			●2		
	35		●2		
RM 10			●3		**Stairstep Falls,** run center-right, then left
	30		●2		
			●2		—Old wooden powerhouse left
	25		●2		—Cable crossing, followed by "the cave" left
	20				
	15		●2		**Waterspout,** scout left, run left
			●3		**Corkscrew Falls,** run right
	10		●3		**Grasshopper,** run center-right
			●3		
			●3		
	5		●2		
			●2		
	12:00		●4		**Maytag,** scout, portage, line right

There are good waves next to the cliff in Black Canyon.

27

Methow

Logged at	-	7,200 cfs Pateros gauge
Recommended water level	-	3,000 to 11,000 cfs
Best time	-	May to mid-July
Rating	-	Advanced
Water level information	-	NOAA Tape (206) 526-8530
River mile	-	27.2 to 1.4; 25.8 miles
Time	-	3 hours, 48 minutes; 6.8 mph
Elevation	-	1,390' to 770'; 24' per mile

Carlton to Pateros

The Methow (pronounced Met' ow) originates high in the North Cascades and runs with melting snow into the lake formed on the Columbia River by Wells Dam. The Indian name for the river means "salmon falls river." It's a good description. The river has a lot of whitewater and fine runs of salmon. The valley through which it flows is surrounded by dray, sagebrush-covered hills that look like the setting for a Hollywood western. In fact, Owen Wister wrote *The Virginian* while he was living in Winthrop, where the Chewuch joins the Methow.

Most boating on the Methow takes place below the confluence of the Chewuch and Methow at Winthrop. The run from Winthrop to Carlton is mostly of class 1 difficulty but is punctuated by numerous diversion dams and logjams. The diversion dams can have very dangerous hydraulics and be life threatening; they should be portaged. The logjams rarely block the river completely, but they must be avoided; two rafters were killed on this section of the river in 1983 when their raft was swept into a logjam.

This chapter focuses on the lower portion of the river from Carlton to Pateros. At flows over 6,000 cfs, the Methow provides one of the best "big water" trips in Washington, with few exposed rocks but numerous big waves and holes. Because there is no federal land along this portion of the river, it is unlikely to become part of our national Wild & Scenic Rivers system, but it would make a fine addition to our state scenic rivers system. The state program has no impact on private land but could acquire more access and camping sites for fishermen and boaters and provide a management plan to reduce conflicts between local landowners and recreational users of the river.

Getting There

State Route 153, which can be reached on State Route 20 (the North Cascades Highway) at Winthrop or on US 97 at Pateros, parallels the Methow.

Put-ins and Take-outs

The upper put-in is at the Department of Wildlife's fishing access at Carlton (conservation license needed—see the Introduction). The access is just upstream of the bridge over the river at Carlton.

A put-in can also be made at log time 1 hour, 9 minutes, from the Gold Creek Road. Turn off the highway about 7 miles north of the town of Methow on the Gold Creek Road and put in on your right about 200 yards up the road.

The most popular put-in for the big water in the lower part of the run is at the McFarland Creek fishing access (conservation license required). The fishing access is just above the bridge 3 miles upstream from the town of Methow. The trail down to the river is fairly steep.

The take-out near Pateros is along the north side of the highway at the upper end of the reservoir formed by Wells Dam. There is a large parking area along the old, abandoned highway here.

Water Level

Because the Methow is snow-fed, it is a spring run-off river, generally only boatable from May through mid-July. The river is at its best with at least 3,000 cfs, but rafts can get down the river on 2,500 cfs and kayaks on 1,500 cfs.

Methow
Pateros Gauge
Recommend 3,000 to 11,000 cfs

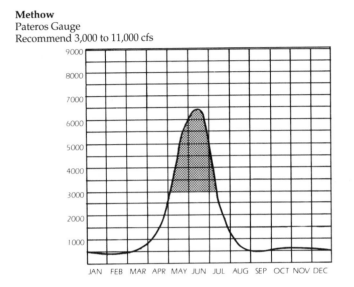

Special Hazards

A maximum flow of 11,000 cfs on the Pateros gauge is recommended for a first trip. Above that level the water becomes very dirty, and there are very few eddies. The river often flows through trees along its bank. Above 9,000 cfs there is likely to be **driftwood** in the river. Many consider 9,000 cfs the ideal water level for fast boating on big water, but the water becomes much clearer below 7,500 cfs.

Scenery

Between Winthrop and Carlton there are many farms and ranches along the riverbank. The valley narrows at Carlton, and the orchards and alfalfa fields are fewer. Natural scenery becomes more prevalent, with pine-forested draws alternating with rock outcroppings.

Camping

Camping along the Methow is difficult. Almost all of the land along the river is privately owned. Permission should be obtained prior to pitching a tent. There are, however, several state and Forest Service campgrounds within an easy commute of the river. Alta Lake State Park is only 2 miles off the main highway near Pateros. Campsites are about $6.00 per night and you should get there before the office closes at 8:00 P.M. Foggy Dew

Forest Service camp is about 7 miles up Gold Creek Road, which leaves the highway between Carlton and Methow.

Rapids

The lower section below Methow has many powerful class 3 rapids and one class 4 drop. Generally, experienced boaters can easily read the river and avoid large holes.

The **Black Canyon Rapids** are right where Black Canyon Creek joins the Methow. There is a substantial drop next to a sheer 100- to 150-foot river bluff. The drop starts after a sharp left bend and has a huge hole near the left side. The hole is known by an assortment of names, including Greyhound (so large it can swallow a bus) and Oarlock. However, the tag the Black Hole seems to have stuck. At most water levels there is a second, almost equally fearsome, hole somewhat downriver to the right. The best run is usually starting right center; when abreast of the Black Hole, move left and thread between the holes, running the large waves along the cliff on the left bank. Generally, it is better to err on the side of being too far right rather than too far left.

At log time 3 hours, you'll reach an island with most of the rivers flow going right. You should take the right channel but be prepared to pull left around a huge hole below the right side of the right channel.

A large rock formation is on the inside of a right bend at log time 3 hours, 19 minutes, forming the **Meteorite** (or the Lizard, or Crocodile). It forms a hole over 9,000 cfs and is an obstacle at lower water levels.

The holes make great playspots. (NW Outdoor Center photo)

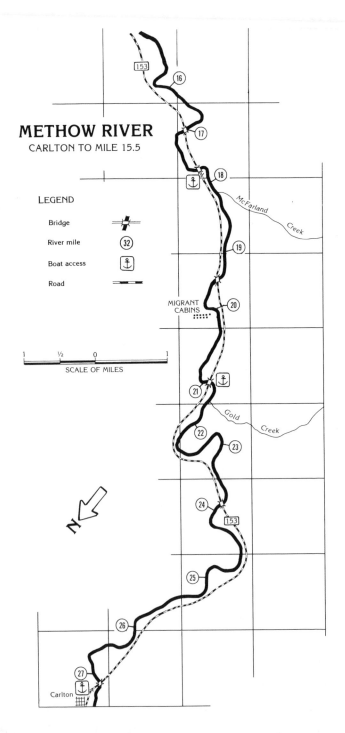

METHOW RIVER
CARLTON TO MILE 15.5

LEGEND

Bridge

River mile

Boat access

Road

SCALE OF MILES

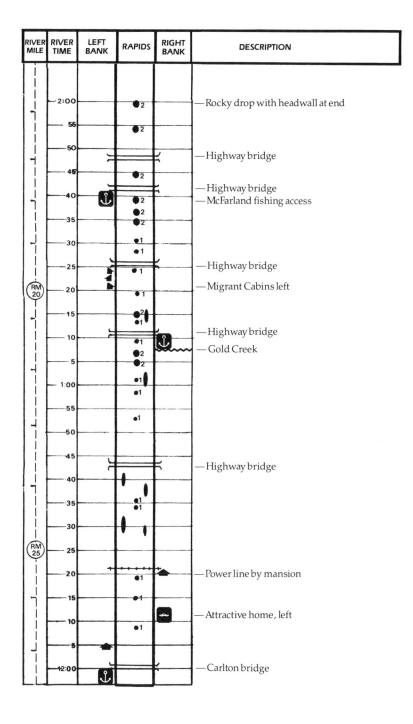

RIVER MILE	RIVER TIME	LEFT BANK	RAPIDS	RIGHT BANK	DESCRIPTION
	2:00		●2		—Rocky drop with headwall at end
	55		●2		
	50				—Highway bridge
	45		●2		
	40	⚓	●2		—Highway bridge —McFarland fishing access
	35		●2 ●2		
	30		●1 ●1		
	25		●1		—Highway bridge
RM 20	20				—Migrant Cabins left
	15		●2 ●1		
	10		●1	⚓	—Highway bridge —Gold Creek
	5		●2 ●2		
	1:00		●1 ●1		
	55				
	50		●1		
	45				—Highway bridge
	40				
	35		●1 ●1		
	30				
RM 25	25				
	20		●1		—Power line by mansion
	15		●1		
	10		●1		—Attractive home, left
	5				
	12:00	⚓			—Carlton bridge

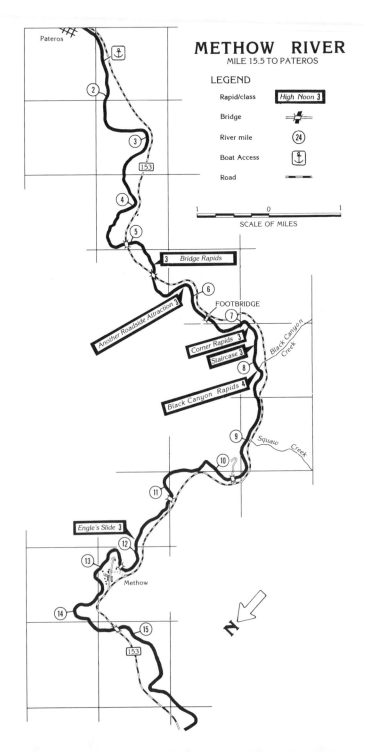

Pateros

METHOW RIVER
MILE 15.5 TO PATEROS

LEGEND

Rapid/class   High Noon 3

Bridge

River mile   24

Boat Access

Road

1   0   1
SCALE OF MILES

Bridge Rapids 3

Another Roadside Attraction 3

FOOTBRIDGE

Corner Rapids 3

Staircase 3

Black Canyon Creek

Black Canyon Rapids 4

Squaw Creek

Engle's Slide 3

Methow

N

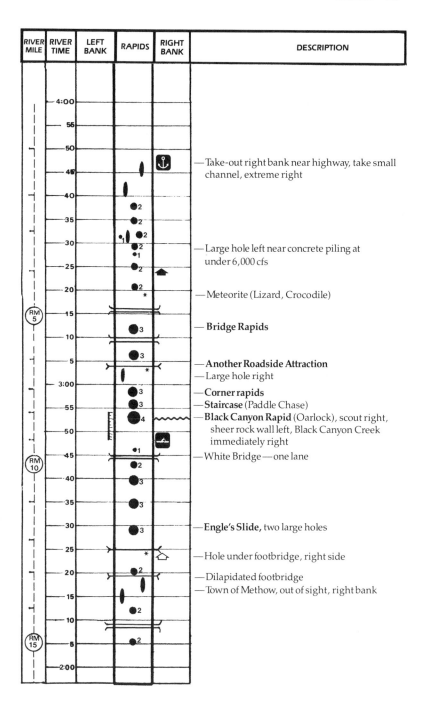

RIVER MILE	RIVER TIME	LEFT BANK	RAPIDS	RIGHT BANK	DESCRIPTION
	4:00				
	55				
	50				
	45			⚓	—Take-out right bank near highway, take small channel, extreme right
	40				
	35		●2		
	30		●2 ●2 ●2 ●1		—Large hole left near concrete piling at under 6,000 cfs
	25		●2		
	20		●2 *		—Meteorite (Lizard, Crocodile)
RM 5	15				
	10		●3		**— Bridge Rapids**
	5		●3		
			*		**—Another Roadside Attraction** —Large hole right
	3:00				
	55		●3 ●3 ●4		**—Corner rapids** **—Staircase** (Paddle Chase) **—Black Canyon Rapid** (Oarlock), scout right, sheer rock wall left, Black Canyon Creek immediately right
	50				
	45		●1		—White Bridge—one lane
RM 10	40		●2 ●3		
	35		●3		
	30		●3		—**Engle's Slide,** two large holes
	25		*		—Hole under footbridge, right side
	20		●2		—Dilapidated footbridge —Town of Methow, out of sight, right bank
	15				
	10		●2		
RM 15	5		●2		
	2:00				

EXPERT RIVERS

28

Chewuch

Logged at -	6,000 cfs Pateros gauge
Recommended water level -	5,000 to 10,000 cfs
Best time -	Late May and June
Rating -	Expert
Water level information -	NOAA Tape (206) 526-8530
River mile -	20.9 to 7.9; 13 miles
Time -	2 hours, 46 minutes; 4.7 mph
Elevation -	2,390' to 1,960'; 33' per mile

Camp Four to Five Mile Bridge

The Chewuch alternates between exciting rapid sections and quiet drifting. The rapids come in bunches near the mouths of the principal creeks feeding into the river. In between, you have ample opportunity to contemplate the clear water of the Chewuch framed by the red-brown bark of the ponderosa pines that line its banks. The forested Chewuch provides a wonderful contrast to the sagebrush-dry Methow into which it empties.

Getting There

The Chewuch flows into the Methow River at Winthrop, which is at the eastern end of the North Cascades Highway (State Route 20).

Winthrop was named after Theodore Winthrop, who published his account of his 1853 trip around Washington territory in *The Canoe and the Saddle*. Recently Timothy Egan retraced Winthrop's journey and published his account in *The Good Rain*.

On older maps the name of the river is spelled "Chewack." The spelling was recently changed to make the pronunciation more like that of the Indian word. The final "ch" is pronounced like a "k" so that the word sounds liked "Chewuck."

Put-ins and Take-outs

The take-out is at the bridge 5 miles above Winthrop. There is a small eddy on the right-hand side of the river just downstream from the bridge.

From the take-out, you should drive 0.2 mile up the Forest Service 37 road on the east side of the river. Look down over the edge of the slope next to the river to inspect the irrigation dam, which you will have to run if you boat the last mile of the trip.

The main road, and the shuttle route, is the West Chewuch road, Forest Service 51 road. Up this road 0.75 mile from the bridge, you'll find a dirt road that turns off toward the river. It has no sign other than a number—015. It leads to the site of the old Memorial Campground and provides a rough take-out point for those who wish to avoid the furious rapids between here and the bridge.

About 1.5 miles farther on the main road, you'll pass the entrance to the Eightmile Ranch (signed) on the right. About 3 miles upstream, the West Chewuch road crosses Falls Creek and you reach Falls Creek Campground. Above the campground 0.5 mile is a dirt road that turns off toward the river, signed "082." At the upstream end of this road is the put-in spot at log time 1 hour, 9 minutes.

The uppermost put-in is at the Camp Four Campground, just downstream from the only bridge over the upper part of the river.

Water Level

The Chewuch is an exciting run from 5,000 to 10,000 cfs on the Pateros gauge. The Chewuch itself provides about 20 percent of the flow recorded on the Pateros gauge. Take a careful look at the last mile above the

Pine trees line the bank along Falls Creek Rapids.

take-out before you run it at high levels; it has continuous, powerful rapids that develop huge holes at high water levels.

Chewuch
Pateros Gauge
Recommend 5,000 to 10,000 cfs

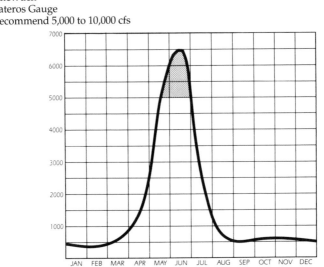

Special Hazards

Check the irrigation diversion **dam** at log time 2 hours, 43 minutes, before you run the last mile of the trip. At most of the recommended water-level range, it can safely be run, but it might form a dangerous keeper at other levels. Low water levels reveal a piece of **metal** sticking up from the dam to the left of the center channel; stay to the right of center.

The Chewuch has many **logs** in it and is a small enough river that they could easily block the channel. Check the rapid sections for blocking logs before you run the river, and stay alert!

Scenery

The Chewuch flows through a pretty valley covered with semi-open pine forest. The ponderosa pines along the banks of the river are beautiful. There is little evidence of human activity along the river above Eightmile Creek. The trip provides a contrast to the bigger, more developed Methow. The Okanogan National Forest has recommended the Chewuch for addition to our national Wild & Scenic Rivers system. If you would like to help get permanent protection for this outstanding river, contact the Rivers Council of Washington (see the Preface).

Camping

There are several campgrounds situated right along the Chewuch: Falls Creek, Chewuch and Camp Four. After mid-May, a fee is charged for the use of Falls Creek Campground.

Rapids

Twentymile Creek Rapids give you a taste of the Chewuch's excitement. There are several more sets of fast boulder and hole dodging, lasting from 200 yards to a mile. Check out **Boulder Creek Rapids**, the last mile of the trip, before you run it. It is continuous class 3 to 4 with no eddy large enough for a raft below the mouth of Boulder Creek. I like to think of it as "Mr. Toad's Wild Ride." There is an eddy on river left just below the mouth of Boulder Creek. You may want to stop here and secure your gear. Once a raft leaves this eddy, it is committed to going all the way to the take-out—there is no place to stop!

Falls Creek Campground allows you to camp right by the river.

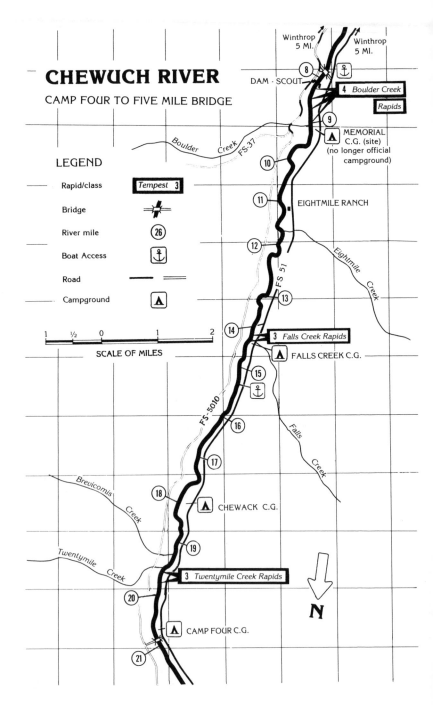

CHEWUCH RIVER

CAMP FOUR TO FIVE MILE BRIDGE

Winthrop 5 MI.

Winthrop 5 MI.

DAM · SCOUT

4 *Boulder Creek*

Rapids

MEMORIAL C.G. (site)
(no longer official campground)

Boulder Creek

FS-37

EIGHTMILE RANCH

Eightmile Creek

FS 51

LEGEND

—	Rapid/class	3 *Tempest*
	Bridge	
	River mile	26
	Boat Access	⚓
	Road	═══
	Campground	🅰

SCALE OF MILES

1 ½ 0 1 2

FS-5010

3 *Falls Creek Rapids*

🅰 FALLS CREEK C.G.

⚓

Falls Creek

Brevicornis Creek

🅰 CHEWACK C.G.

Twentymile Creek

3 *Twentymile Creek Rapids*

🅰 CAMP FOUR C.G.

N

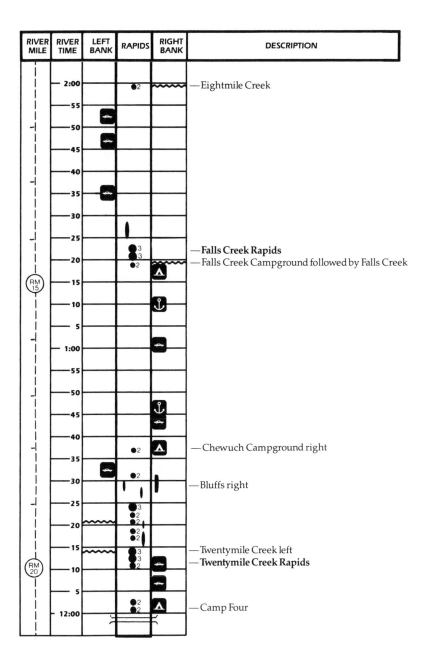

RIVER MILE	RIVER TIME	LEFT BANK	RAPIDS	RIGHT BANK	DESCRIPTION
	2:00		●2		—Eightmile Creek
	55				
	50				
	45				
	40				
	35				
	30				
	25				
	20		●3 ●3 ●2		—**Falls Creek Rapids** —Falls Creek Campground followed by Falls Creek
RM 15	15				
	10				
	5				
	1:00				
	55				
	50				
	45				
	40				
	35		●2		—Chewuch Campground right
	30		●2		—Bluffs right
	25		●3 ●2		
	20		●2 ●2		
	15		●3 ●3 ●2		—Twentymile Creek left —**Twentymile Creek Rapids**
RM 20	10				
	5				
	12:00		●2 ●2		—Camp Four

A rock wall on the right bank marks the entrance to Boulder Creek Rapids.

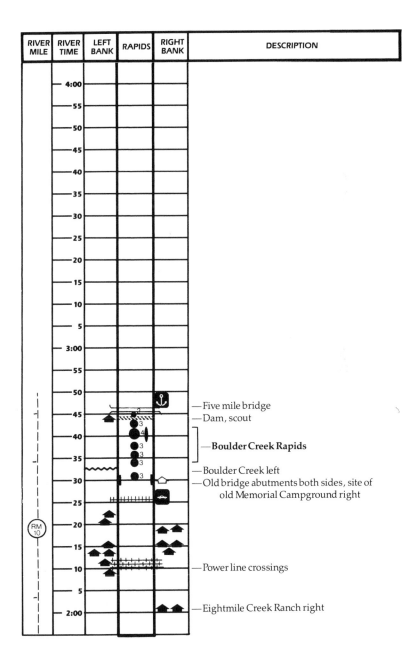

RIVER MILE	RIVER TIME	LEFT BANK	RAPIDS	RIGHT BANK	DESCRIPTION
	4:00				
	55				
	50				
	45				
	40				
	35				
	30				
	25				
	20				
	15				
	10				
	5				
	3:00				
	55				
	50			⚓	—Five mile bridge
	45		2		—Dam, scout
	40		3 4		
			3		⎫ —**Boulder Creek Rapids**
	35		3 3		⎭
	30		3		—Boulder Creek left
					—Old bridge abutments both sides, site of
	25				old Memorial Campground right
	20				
RM 10	15				
	10				—Power line crossings
	5				
	2:00				—Eightmile Creek Ranch right

29

Toutle

Logged at - 1,900 cfs
Recommended water level - 1,500 to 3,500 cfs
Best time - April through early June
Rating - Expert
Water level information - NOAA Tape (206) 526-8530
River mile - 16.3 to 6.8; 9.5 miles
Time - 1 hour, 58 minutes; 4.3 mph
Elevation - 420' to 115'; 32' per mile

Toutle to Tower Road Bridge

A trip on the Toutle provides a fascinating glimpse of the enormous destruction caused by the 1980 eruption of Mt. St. Helens. Enormous mudflows roared down the Toutle valley, destroying forest, homes and bridges. Left behind are high water mud lines on the trees, many downed trees, chunks of concrete and twisted metal.

Hollywood Gorge remains an awe-inspiring solid rock cleft through which the river swirls, however, and the Toutle is rapidly cleansing itself of the enormous amount of silt and mud that choked its channel just after the eruption.

Getting There

Take exit 49 (Castle Rock) from I-5 and go 2.1 miles east on State Route 504 to Chuck's Chevron and Grocery. Just before Chuck's, Tower Road turns off of the highway to the left. Follow Tower Road 2.7 miles to the new Tower Road bridge across the Toutle.

Put-ins and Take-outs

The take-out is on the left bank on the upstream side of the bridge. The bank on this Department of Wildlife site (conservation license required) is steep, but it's the only place available. To reach the put-in, either go back to Chuck's and continue 9.2 miles up State Route 504 to the new Toutle bridge (just beyond the town of Toutle), or continue across the Tower Road Bridge and follow Tower Road 10.1 miles to where it connects with State Route 504 again. If you have taken Tower Road, you should make a right and drive west on State Route 504 3.2 miles and turn left at an unmarked gravel road. Those taking State Route 504 from Chuck's will find this turn-off on their right, just 0.3 mile after crossing the Toutle Bridge. The road quickly deteriorates to dirt and winds back through the trees and ends up under the Toutle Bridge—the put-in.

Water Level

The Toutle has an active gauge on it at Tower Bridge. With the stabilizing of the channel in recent years, this gauge is now an accurate indicator of flows in the river. Good flows for a first trip are between 1,500 and 3,500 cfs. Boaters who know the river well may wish to run it at higher levels, but first-timers would do well to stick to these levels because it becomes very fast in both of the gorges at higher levels.

Toutle
Tower Bridge Gauge
Recommend 1,500 to 3,500 cfs

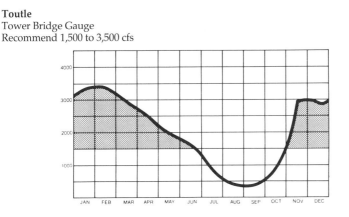

Debris from the flood caused by the eruption of Mount St. Helens

Charging through Hollywood Gorge Falls

Special Hazards

The Toutle demands your respect. The silt carried by the water makes it very difficult to read. The water is a uniform brown-gray, making it difficult to distinguish waves and holes. It's also important to recognize that, outside of the two gorge stretches, the river channel is still unstable and subject to change. Over ten years after the eruption, the ash and mud are solidifying rapidly and plants are re-establishing themselves everywhere, greening a landscape that was all gray in 1980.

The river is gradually recovering from the eruption; the silt decreases and the channel becomes more stable every year. The Army Corps of Engineers has built a dam on the river above the mouth of Green River to allow the silt to settle out. The dam does not have any effect on the water flow. While this dam clears the water, it prevents salmon and steelhead from reaching the upper Toutle by themselves; they must be trapped and trucked around the dam.

Scenery

Both gorge sections are spectacular, particularly the Hollywood Gorge from log time 1 hour, 11 minutes, to 1 hour, 41 minutes. The upper gorge (from log time 3 minutes to 27 minutes) is also constricted and studded with house- and automobile-size boulders, creating interesting rapids.

The area between the gorges, from log time 38 minutes to 1 hour, 10 minutes, exhibits the enormous scouring power of the eruption. The flood plain is littered with downed trees and the land is scarred by many abandoned river channels. A particularly interesting side trip is a visit to a destroyed home, marked by the chimney, at log time 43 minutes. It's easy to land on the right bank at about log time 45 minutes and walk back to the site. The house has been buried in silt nearly 8 feet deep, so that only the chimney above the mantel shows. Near the end of the devastated area, you will see mounds of material that the Army Corps of Engineers has cleared from the river channel. Bear right to stay in the main channel.

Camping

Seaquest State Park is just off State Route 504 about 4 miles east of Chuck's, near Silver Lake. Some additional camping is also available on a road off to the right, about 3 miles farther east, on the east end of Silver Lake.

Rapids

The first significant rapid of the trip is **Staircase** (or **The Steps**) at log time 11 minutes. There are huge boulders in the middle of the rapid and nasty ledges and holes to the left of them. The rapid is on a right bend in the river; stay to the right (the inside of the bend).

Tea Kettle (or **Tempest in a Teapot**) follows after a few hundred yards of fast water. It is around a left-hand bend and definitely deserves a scout. Land on the left bank, just below some huge boulders and above the left bend. The run threads a number of large boulders. The best route is usually just left of center in the main channel, avoiding the large hole next to the huge rocks on the right bank at the bottom.

The other rapid you should definitely scout is **Hollywood Gorge Falls** at log time 1 hour, 30 minutes. You should have no difficulty recognizing the horizon line with the huge boulder in the middle of it (covered by a mound of water at higher water levels). Land at a small beach between two rocky headlands on the right-hand side. Climb the lower headland and scramble down the rocks to get a look at the rapid. Most runs are to the left of the central rock in the falls, but at higher water levels it is also possible to spin off the rock to the right.

The major challenge of the rapid is not the falls, though you should beware the nasty lateral waves, which are a lot bigger than they look from shore, but rather the hole in the center of the river about 30 yards downstream. At most water levels, this hole is preceded by a large smooth wave that saps the momentum from your boat and drops you in the hole that can easily flip an 18-foot raft. The trick is to get around the hole either to the left (very technical at high water) or the right (a tough pull in a raft).

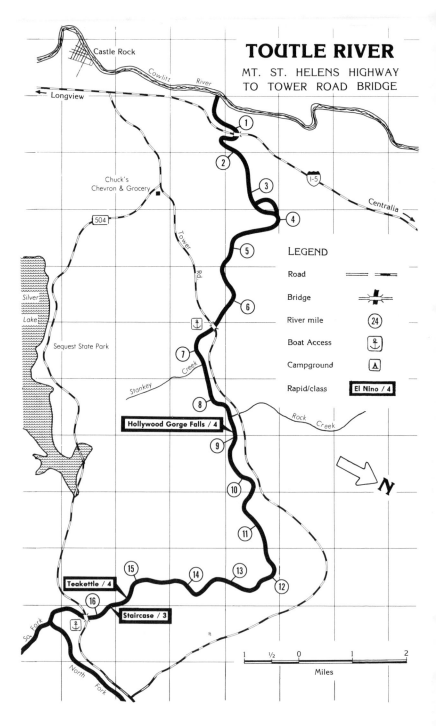

TOUTLE RIVER

MT. ST. HELENS HIGHWAY
TO TOWER ROAD BRIDGE

Castle Rock

Cowlitz River

Longview

Chuck's
Chevron & Grocery

504

Tower Rd

Silver Lake

Sequest State Park

Stankey Creek

I-5

Centralia

LEGEND

Road	
Bridge	
River mile	(24)
Boat Access	
Campground	(A)
Rapid/class	El Nino / 4

Hollywood Gorge Falls / 4

Rock Creek

Teakettle / 4

Staircase / 3

So. Fork

North Fork

N

| 1 ½ 0 1 2 |
| Miles |

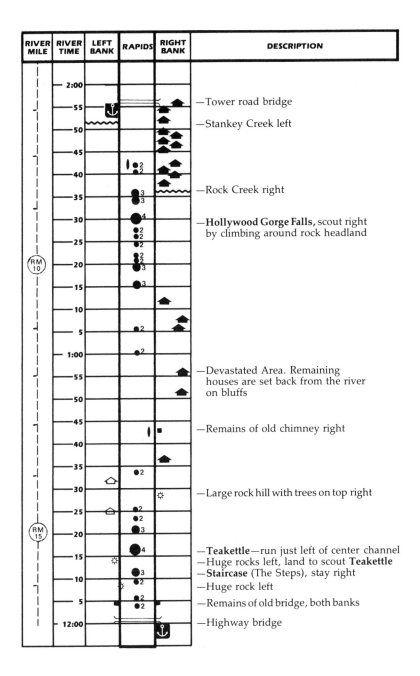

RIVER MILE	RIVER TIME	LEFT BANK	RAPIDS	RIGHT BANK	DESCRIPTION
	2:00				
	55				—Tower road bridge
	50				—Stankey Creek left
	45				
	40		2 2		
	35		3 3		—Rock Creek right
	30		4		—**Hollywood Gorge Falls,** scout right by climbing around rock headland
	25		2 2 2		
RM 10	20		2 2 3		
	15		3		
	10				
	5		2		
	1:00		2		
	55				—Devastated Area. Remaining houses are set back from the river on bluffs
	50				
	45				—Remains of old chimney right
	40				
	35				
	30		2		
	30				—Large rock hill with trees on top right
	25		2 2		
RM 15	20		3		
	15		4		—**Teakettle**—run just left of center channel
	15				—Huge rocks left, land to scout **Teakettle**
	10		3 2		—**Staircase** (The Steps), stay right
	10				—Huge rock left
	5		2 2		—Remains of old bridge, both banks
	12:00				—Highway bridge

30

Middle Sauk

Logged at - 6,900 cfs Sauk gauge
Recommended water level - 4,000 to 9,000 cfs
Best time - Late April to late July
Rating - Expert
Water level information - NOAA Tape (206) 526-8530
River mile - 31.7 to 21.4; 10.3 miles
Time - 2 hours, 4 minutes; 5.0 mph
Elevation - 900' to 502'; 39' per mile

White Chuck to Darrington

The Sauk derives its name from the Sah-kee-ma-hu band of the Skagit Indian tribe, which lived in the area. The Upper Sauk, above White Chuck, was covered in Chapter 6. The White Chuck adds significantly to the amount of water in the river, but because this section is much rockier than the upper section a good run requires the same readings on the Sauk gauge. The White Chuck also adds considerable glacial silt to the Sauk, turning it deep green.

Since most of the flow of the Sauk comes from melting snow and ice, it is very cold. Wetsuits are strongly advised even when the weather is warm. Helmets are also advisable because the Sauk is rocky. Anyone thrown from a raft may well hit his or her head on a rock. Commercial rafting companies require both wetsuits and helmets for all of their passengers.

At the recommended water levels, the Middle Sauk is one of the most exciting and scenic whitewater trips in Washington. It is protected as a scenic river under the national Wild & Scenic Rivers Act and is one of the most challenging half-dozen regularly rafted rivers in the state.

Getting There

The river is approached through Darrington, which is 65 miles northeast of Seattle on State Route 530.

The Mountain Loop Highway provides access to the Sauk. It leaves the south side of Darrington near the river and eventually crosses the Sauk just above the mouth of the White Chuck River. To get to it, go one block east of the 90-degree turn in the main road in Darrington, turn right, and

Helmets and wetsuits are advised on the Middle Sauk because it is rocky and cold.

then, after several blocks, left at a T intersection and follow the signs to "Mountain Loop Highway, Granite Falls."

An alternative road (sometimes impassable) is a narrow, winding dirt road on the northeast side of the river. To reach it, take a right immediately after crossing the bridge over the river near Darrington.

Put-ins and Take-outs

The take-out is at an unimproved boat ramp just downstream from the west (Darrington) side of the bridge over the river near Darrington.

An alternative take-out for those who want a shorter trip is at Snohomish County's Bachman Park at log time 1 hour, 34 minutes. This take-out is not easy to see from the river and you should memorize some landmarks in advance. It's just a little downstream from the end of the large tree-covered island around the right side of which the river has cut a new channel (the best boating route).

The put-in is at the boating access site just downstream from the mouth of the White Chuck River. To reach it, turn left off the Mountain Loop Highway about 200 yards after crossing the bridge over the Sauk.

Water Level

The recommended water level ranges from 4,000 cfs to 9,000 cfs on the Sauk gauge. To avoid scraping bottom, a large raft needs approximately 4,000 cfs. Kayaks and small inflatables may enjoy the river at lower levels, however.

Maximum recommendation is 9,000 cfs. Above 9,000 cfs the level of difficulty increases significantly. The river is likely to be carrying a number of logs that present a hazard in rapids. The river also carries more silt above 9,000 cfs, turning it gray and making river reading difficult, as

Into a hole in Jaws

whitewater does not stand out from the river. Holes are often seen only from some 20 to 25 feet away, requiring quick maneuvering. At higher levels, the water also flows more quickly, bringing you up on rocks and holes very rapidly.

At flows above 15,000 cfs, the rapids in the first 30 minutes of the trip should all be increased one level in difficulty. The stretch becomes class 4 to 5. There are NO eddies, NO opportunities to bail, NO time to rest, and LITTLE opportunity to rescue someone if necessary. This becomes a very dangerous stretch of water at higher flows.

The Sauk River gauge is located below the confluence of the Suiattle and the Sauk. The approximate percentage of the Sauk gauge reading that is actually present in the Middle Sauk varies by months as follows:

May	June	July	Aug	Sept
57%	52%	51%	41%	40%

Middle Sauk
Sauk Gauge
Recommend 4,000 to 9,000 cfs

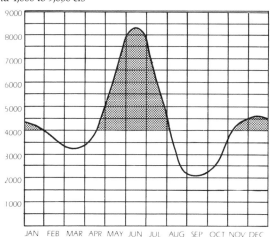

Special Hazards

You should be very careful to obtain the most recent gauge readings possible and to watch the weather. The Sauk is subject to **rapid fluctuations** in water level and can come up so fast after a rain or a period of hot weather that you can almost see it rise. Great caution must be exercised with regard to the water level. It could be at 8,000 cfs yesterday and 16,000 cfs today, making it a very dangerous run.

Scenery

The river flows through heavily forested banks between snow-covered mountains. The first two-thirds of the trip is quite remote. You're likely to see wildlife, particularly deer.

Camping

Camping is available at Bachman County Park—one of the possible take-outs—and at the Forest Service's Clear Creek Campground, just upriver from Bachman Park.

Rapids

The first few miles of the trip (up to log time 28 minutes) are very demanding. It is very difficult to scout any of the rapids on this section due to the twisting river channel, steep gradient and heavily forested banks. The rapids are choked with boulders and good river-reading skills are essential. This section of the river is very dangerous at flows above those recommended in this book.

The **Alligator Drop** takes its name from a large, flat rock in the middle of the river. This rock forms a hole capable of flipping a raft at flows over 8,000 cfs.

Jaws (or **Demon Seed**) is the most difficult rapid on the river. It is well worth scouting, which can be done on the right side. Land above the island on the right (watch for a small portion of the river heading right, through boulders—this is the water going to the right of the island). Wade across the channel to the island and walk downriver to scout. There is a good trail in the middle of the island once you get below the logs piled at its head. Below the island is a large rock, known as Demon Seed.

The rapid is usually run down the left side of the island and around the right side of Demon Seed. Then you should ferry to the left of the rocks in the center below. For many years, there was a logjam on the right below Demon Seed at the location shown in the diagram. The logjam was washed away in 1987 but may return in future years. If it does, it is important to ferry well left, away from the logs.

Oar rafts and kayakers can often make the ferry to the left of Demon Seed, avoiding the need to make the strong ferry below it. For a raft, this largely depends upon your ability to avoid filling your boat with water in the numerous holes on the approach down the left side of the island.

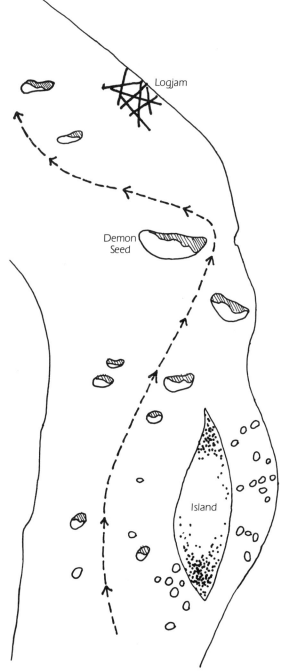

Jaws
Diagram courtesy of
Kimberly Piper

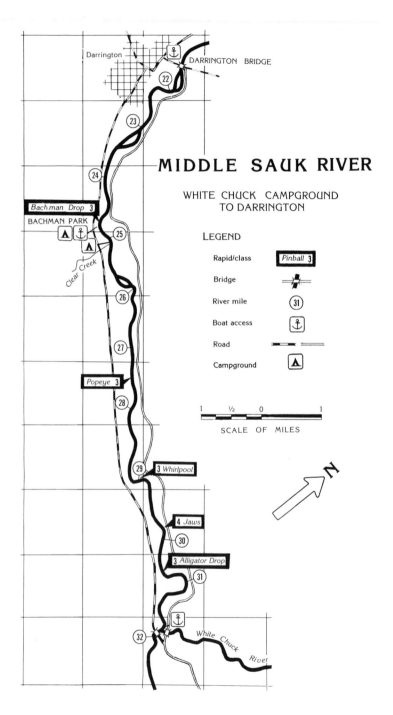

MIDDLE SAUK RIVER

WHITE CHUCK CAMPGROUND
TO DARRINGTON

LEGEND

Rapid/class	Pinball 3
Bridge	
River mile	31
Boat access	⚓
Road	
Campground	⛺

SCALE OF MILES

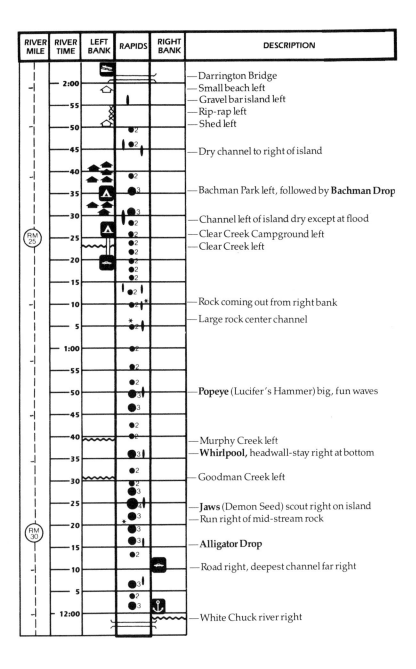

RIVER MILE	RIVER TIME	LEFT BANK	RAPIDS	RIGHT BANK	DESCRIPTION
					—Darrington Bridge
	2:00				—Small beach left
					—Gravel bar island left
	55				—Rip-rap left
	50		●2		—Shed left
	45		●2		—Dry channel to right of island
	40		●2		
	35		●3		—Bachman Park left, followed by **Bachman Drop**
	30		●3		—Channel left of island dry except at flood
	25		●2		—Clear Creek Campground left
			●2		—Clear Creek left
	20		●2		
			●2		
	15		●2		
			●2		
	10		●2 *		—Rock coming out from right bank
	5		* ●2		—Large rock center channel
	1:00		●2		
	55		●2		
	50		●2		
			●3		—**Popeye** (Lucifer's Hammer) big, fun waves
	45		●3		
	40		●2		
			●2		—Murphy Creek left
	35		●3		—**Whirlpool,** headwall-stay right at bottom
	30		●2		—Goodman Creek left
			●2		
	25		●3		
			●4		—**Jaws** (Demon Seed) scout right on island
	20		* ●3		—Run right of mid-stream rock
	15		●3		—**Alligator Drop**
	10		●2		—Road right, deepest channel far right
	5		●3		
			●2		
	12:00		●3		—White Chuck river right

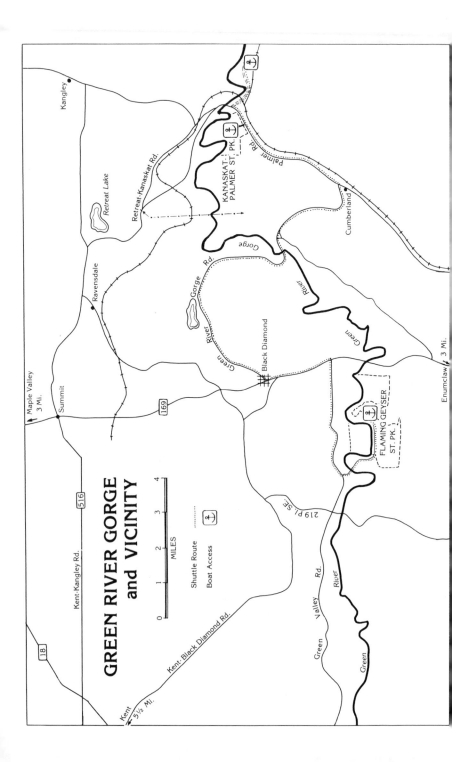

GREEN RIVER GORGE and VICINITY

Kent-Kangley Rd.

516

18

Maple Valley
3 Mi.

Summit

169

Kangley

Retreat Lake

Ravensdale

Retreat-Kanaskat Rd.

KANASKAT-
PALMER ST. PK.

Palmer Rd.

Gorge

Gorge Rd.

Green River

Green River

Gorge Rd.

Black Diamond

Cumberland

Green River

Kent-Black Diamond Rd.

Kent
5½ Mi.

Green Valley Rd.

Green River

Green River

219 Pl. SE

FLAMING GEYSER
ST. PK.

Enumclaw
3 Mi.

MILES

0   1   2   3   4

Shuttle Route · · · · · · ·

Boat Access

31

Green

Logged at - 1,800 cfs Howard Hansen gauge
Recommended water level - 1,100 to 2,300 cfs
Best time - April and May
Rating - Expert
Water level information - NOAA Tape (206) 526-8530
Corps of Engineers (206) 764-6702
River mile - 59.0 to 45.1; 13.9 miles
Time - 3 hours, 37 minutes; 3.8 mph
Elevation - 820' to 205'; 44' per mile

Palmer to Flaming Geyser Park

The Green River Gorge is one of the most beautiful river canyons in Washington State. The Green River has cut its way through a plateau approximately 30 miles southeast of Seattle. It descends from about 800 to 200 feet above sea level and then emerges into a broad valley. From this point it calmly flows north into Elliott Bay in Seattle.

This gorge has been proposed as a "Hanging Gardens" state park and the river is being considered for addition to our state scenic rivers system. There are numerous mines hereabouts, and the town of Black Diamond is named for the nearby coal deposits. In addition to coal, mercury has been found in this area. Flaming Geyser State Park (the take-out) acquired its name from a flame that still burns atop an abandoned gas well.

The river cannot be run much above Palmer, because it forms the Tacoma watershed and access is restricted. The Army Corps of Engineers' Howard Hansen Dam is a few miles above the put-in and controls the flow of water through the gorge.

Getting There

Black Diamond, where most boaters meet to run the Gorge, is on State Route 169. State Route 169 can be reached by taking exit 4 from I-405 to Renton toward Enumclaw and Maple Valley or, from the south, by exiting I-5 on State Route 18 and going 11 miles until it intersects State Route 516, the Kent–Kangley road, which in turn intersects State Route 169 in 5 miles.

The Green River can then be reached on a number of small county roads, which are shown on the vicinity map.

There's a great playspot at Paradise Ledge. *(NW Outdoor Center photo)*

Put-ins and Take-outs

The uppermost put-in is reached on an unmarked gravel road that turns off Palmer Road just south of the river in Palmer. Cross a pair of railroad tracks and drive about 1.1 miles until you see a 20-foot section of dirt road on your left (toward the river) connecting with a dirt road paralleling the gravel one you are on. Turn down onto the dirt road and drive about 20 yards back toward Palmer. The put-in is below a clearing on your right. It is a steep carry down to the eddy.

Two put-ins are available in Kanaskat–Palmer State Park. Enter the park and bear left at the first intersection, then follow the boating signs (which look just like the light boat put-in and take-out symbols in this book) to the put-ins. The signs to the right will lead you to a parking lot.

From here a wide 40-yard path leads through the bushes to the river and the "Dangerous River Conditions Ahead" sign just above Ledge Drop 1. The signs to the left lead to a parking area from which a somewhat longer and steeper path leads down to a large eddy just above Ledge Drop 2.

Light boats can also put in or take out at the Green River Gorge Resort, right by the Franklin Bridge. There is a $2.00 charge for using the steep (150 vertical feet) 300-yard trail down to the river.

The take-out is on the lawn of the picnic area at Flaming Geyser State Park. Follow the signs to the park from State Route 169. The picnic area is about 1.5 miles into the park.

Water Level

The most accurate gauge for judging river conditions in the gorge is the Howard Hansen gauge. Good levels for running are between 1,100 and 2,300 cfs. Good boaters, who are familiar with the gorge, will run it at higher levels, but many of the rapids increase a half class in ranking at those levels. If you are willing to make the tough carry to put in below Franklin Bridge at the resort, the lower gorge can be run at 900 cfs. Kayakers can scrape down the upper gorge on about 800 cfs and the lower gorge on about 600 cfs. A call to the Army Corps of Engineers office, at (206) 764-6702, puts you in touch with a regulator who can explain how much water will be released at various times for about the next 24 hours. The spillways on the dam are set Friday afternoon, and river flow remains constant all weekend unless there is sudden flooding.

Green
Howard Hansen Gauge
Recommend 1,100 to 2,300 cfs

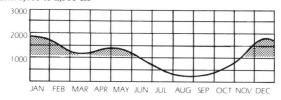

Special Hazards

Water is usually high enough to run the gorge only when the weather is **cold** or it is raining. Wetsuits are a must. Because the channel is very rocky, helmets are advisable for rafters. Kayakers should always wear helmets.

Scenery

The Green River Gorge is 150–300 feet deep and is protected under state law as a special conservation area. Almost 2 miles of Eocene sedimentary rocks and fossils are exposed, revealing layers of geological history.

Wolf Bauer in a *Seattle Times* article commented, "Down its cliffs and gentler draws remain untouched first-growth stands of evergreens, hiding moss and fern-covered grottos and myriads of tiny waterfalls seeping from the canyon walls. Freshness and moisture permeate the floor of the canyon in its shadowy twilight to nurture rain-forest type vegetation, water oriented birds, and man's awed senses within its massive cathedral-like halls. Placid pools like miniature chain lakes create an occasional corridor of silence into which only faint and muffled hints of rushing water may penetrate from around the bend—disturbed only by an occasional kingfisher, merganzer, water ouzel or trout rippling the water's impatient slack."

Camping

There are many good campsites at Kanaskat–Palmer State Park near the put-in. A fee is charged for camping at the park.

Rapids

The gorge can perhaps best be described as twisting and boulder-choked. There are so many rocks in the channel that even expert paddlers and oarsmen will find it difficult not to scrape some rocks in many areas. As can be seen from the log, the main gorge stretch from river time 40 minutes to river time 2 hours is very demanding. Class 3 water is nearly constant, and you must be prepared to run it at all times. It is pointless to discuss scouting these rapids or which way to run many of them, as they are often upon you before you know it. This is a small, technical stream requiring very precise maneuvering to avoid destroying your craft, or yourself, on the rocks.

The upper section, above the outlet of the fish hatchery at river time 40 minutes is quite straightforward and could even be canoed by experts, with the possible exception of **Railroad Bridge Drop**. As you approach this drop, there is a definite horizon line. The river drops about 4 feet in 7 or 8 feet. The drop can usually be run just to the right of center, but there are several rocks and holes that could be dangerous to the unwary.

Ledge Drop 1 is just around the bend below the outlet from the fish hatchery. There is also a sign visible from the river at this point warning of dangerous river conditions. Again, you will see a horizon line from above, followed by boiling whitewater. The drop can be scouted by landing on the right side, just below the fish hatchery outlet. To scout, you must scramble over the hillside and down around the bend. The run is usually right down the center. You must pay attention, however, to the powerful hydraulics and numerous holes. Ledge Drop 1 is marginally a class 4 rapid at 1,800 cfs, but with 20 percent more water (still within recommended discharge ranges for the run) the hydraulics become very powerful.

You will encounter **pipeline** (Ledge Drop 3) at a fairly sharp right bend in the river. A boulder bar extends out from the inside of the bend and considerable water works its way through it. There is enough water to boat only on the left or outside of the bend. After getting around the bend, work back toward the right, as a very large hole forms on the left. This large hole can have a breaking reversal that resembles the famous Pipeline Surf in Hawaii. The drop is a steep one, and much maneuvering is required to avoid the rocks and hit the reversal squarely at the bottom.

A high-tension powerline crossing the canyon high overhead is the warning for **Mercury** and **The Nozzle**. These two class 4 rapids are quite difficult because they occur about 50 yards apart. "Screw up on the Mercury and you'll get Nozzlized," say the old hands. Just below the powerline there is a brush-covered boulder bar in the middle of the river. Take the right channel and, after rounding the end of the bar and a short

Shooting through The Nozzle

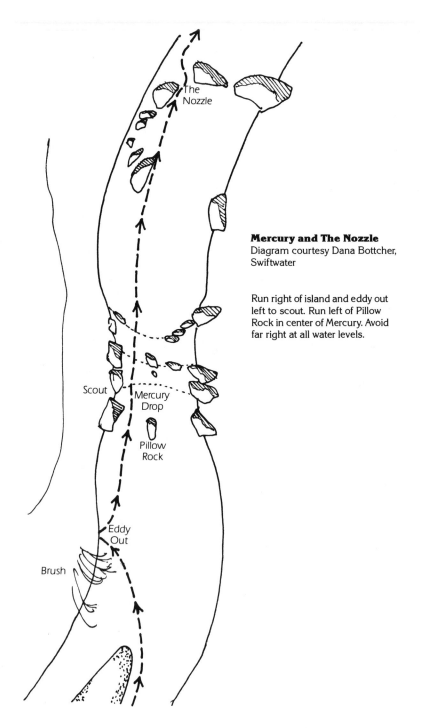

Mercury and The Nozzle
Diagram courtesy Dana Bottcher, Swiftwater

Run right of island and eddy out left to scout. Run left of Pillow Rock in center of Mercury. Avoid far right at all water levels.

(10 yards) class 3 rapid, pull into the left bank and scout Mercury and The Nozzle. Stay well left; if you're in the center of the channel, you'll never make it to the eddy. Scouting is not easy, because the bank is steep, rock strewn and brushy. However, even an expert river runner would have difficulty running these two rapids without first scouting them.

Usually the best run is to the left of the pillow rock at the center top of Mercury, then down just to the right of the large sloping rock forming the left side of The Nozzle.

The Nozzle is formed by three large rocks nearly choking off the flow of the river. Most of the water hits the upstream rock to the left and is deflected to the right, where it slams into the middle rock and then squirts to the left between the two rocks through a gap only 10–12 feet wide. Some of the water passes through a passage too small to be boated to the right side of the middle rock. This flow of water around both sides of the middle rock threatens to broach or wrap your boat on the rock. A good run skirts the upstream side of the left-hand rock while paddling or rowing to slow your approach to the middle rock, and then quickly turning left as soon as you come abreast of the opening, to shoot through The Nozzle.

The class 3 rapid just below The Nozzle has been christened "Let's Make a Deal" because there are three possible slots through the rocks. It is the hardest rapid on the water at flows over 3,000 cfs.

Below the Franklin Bridge near the Green River Resort, the difficulty eases, though kayakers should beware the "squirrely" water just below the bridge on the left. Shortly below the resort, you will reach **Paradise Ledge**, a great kayak playspot. A hotspring, caused by an underground fire in a coalmine, is on the left side at log time 2 hours, 18 minutes. It is marked by an old telephone pole set in a gully above it. The plastic that has been used to line a pool for the hot spring is also visible, and there is a good eddy to pull into. The hotspring is only about 70–75 degrees, but it can be very welcome on a cold day.

The difficulty of **Slide Drop** has eased greatly in the last few years because the river has cleared much of the channel. The rapid was created by rocks, trees and earth sliding into the river from the left side of the gorge. It can be scouted by landing on the left, just above the slide area. The best run of the drop is to the left of the pillow rock in the center. Although Slide Drop has become easier recently, remain alert. The instability of the cliffs in this area could easily result in new slides. The drop should be approached with caution. In a recent year, a fallen tree extended all the way across the river, requiring either a hair-raising run under the log or a carry around.

A new class 3 rapid, not shown on the log, was created on the river below Kummer Bridge by a landslide in 1994. There are good-sized waves in the main passage near the left bank.

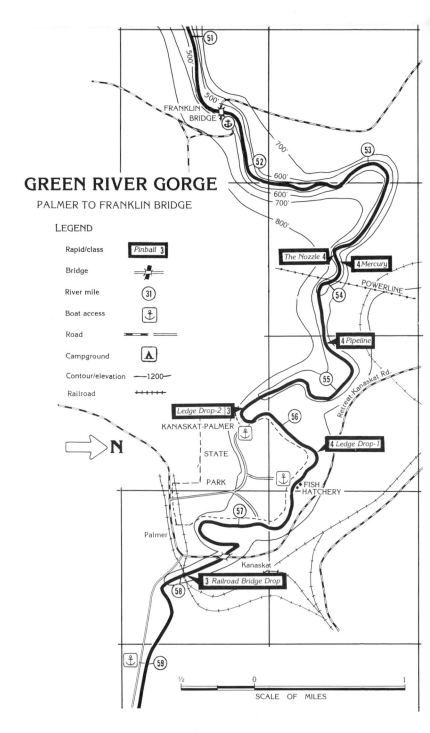

GREEN RIVER GORGE

PALMER TO FRANKLIN BRIDGE

LEGEND

Rapid/class	Pinball 3
Bridge	
River mile	31
Boat access	⚓
Road	
Campground	▲
Contour/elevation	—1200—
Railroad	+++++

N

500'
500'
FRANKLIN BRIDGE
51
52
53
700'
600'
600'
700'
800'
The Nozzle 4
4 Mercury
POWERLINE
54
4 Pipeline
55
Retreat-Kanaskat Rd.
Ledge Drop-2 3
KANASKAT-PALMER
56
4 Ledge Drop-1
STATE
PARK
FISH HATCHERY
57
Palmer
Kanaskat
3 Railroad Bridge Drop
58
59

½   0   1
SCALE OF MILES

RIVER MILE	RIVER TIME	LEFT BANK	RAPIDS	RIGHT BANK	DESCRIPTION

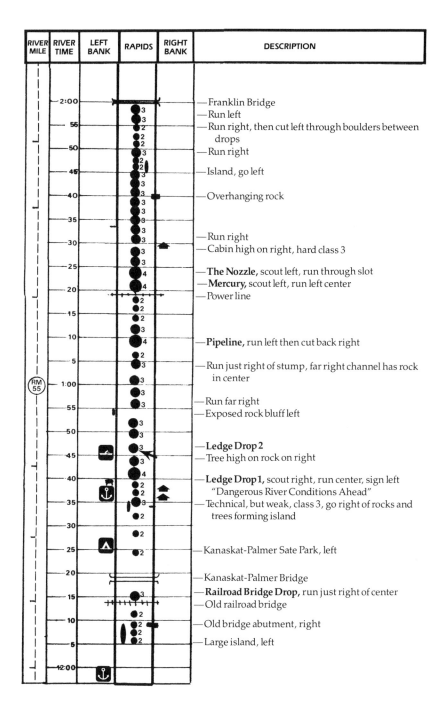

—Franklin Bridge
—Run left
—Run right, then cut left through boulders between drops
—Run right
—Island, go left
—Overhanging rock
—Run right
—Cabin high on right, hard class 3
—**The Nozzle,** scout left, run through slot
—**Mercury,** scout left, run left center
—Power line
—**Pipeline,** run left then cut back right
—Run just right of stump, far right channel has rock in center
—Run far right
—Exposed rock bluff left
—**Ledge Drop 2**
—Tree high on rock on right
—**Ledge Drop 1,** scout right, run center, sign left "Dangerous River Conditions Ahead"
—Technical, but weak, class 3, go right of rocks and trees forming island
—Kanaskat-Palmer Sate Park, left
—Kanaskat-Palmer Bridge
—**Railroad Bridge Drop,** run just right of center
—Old railroad bridge
—Old bridge abutment, right
—Large island, left

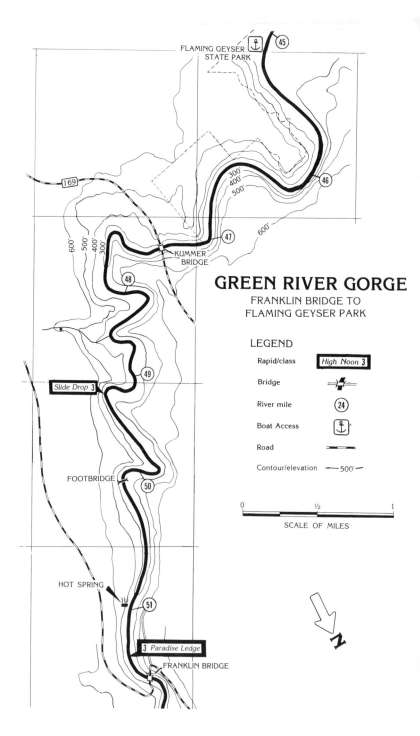

FLAMING GEYSER
STATE PARK

169

300
400
500

KUMMER
BRIDGE

600

GREEN RIVER GORGE

FRANKLIN BRIDGE TO
FLAMING GEYSER PARK

LEGEND

Rapid/class   High Noon 3

Bridge

River mile   24

Boat Access

Road

Contour/elevation   500'

Slide Drop 3

FOOTBRIDGE

0   ½   1

SCALE OF MILES

HOT SPRING

3 Paradise Ledge

FRANKLIN BRIDGE

N

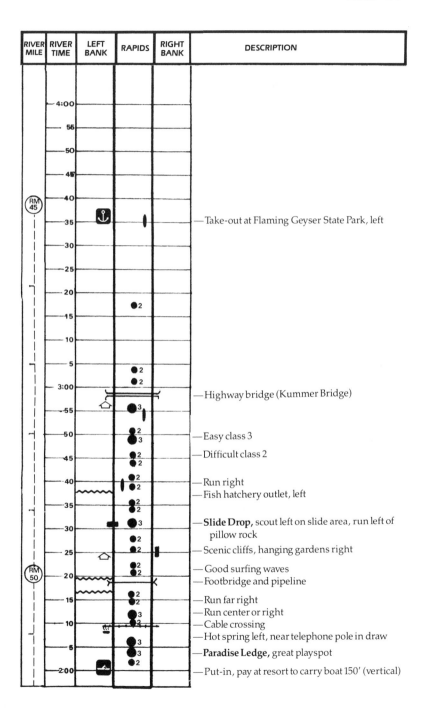

RIVER MILE	RIVER TIME	LEFT BANK	RAPIDS	RIGHT BANK	DESCRIPTION
	4:00				
	56				
	50				
	45				
RM 45	40				
	35	⚓	●		Take-out at Flaming Geyser State Park, left
	30				
	25				
	20				
	15		●2		
	10				
	5		●2		
			●2		
	3:00				
	55	⌂	●3		Highway bridge (Kummer Bridge)
	50		●2 ●3		Easy class 3
	45		●2 ●2		Difficult class 2
	40		● ●2 ●2		Run right
	35	∿∿∿	●2 ●2		Fish hatchery outlet, left
	30	▬	●3		**Slide Drop,** scout left on slide area, run left of pillow rock
	25	⌂	●2 ●2	▮	Scenic cliffs, hanging gardens right
RM 50	20	∿∿∿	●2 ●2	✕	Good surfing waves
					Footbridge and pipeline
	15		●2 ●2		Run far right
	10	≈	●3 ●3		Run center or right
					Cable crossing
	5		●3		Hot spring left, near telephone pole in draw
			●3		**Paradise Ledge,** great playspot
	2:00	⬛	●2		Put-in, pay at resort to carry boat 150' (vertical)

32

Skykomish

Logged at	-	2,400 cfs Gold Bar gauge
Recommended water level	-	2,000 to 5,000 cfs
Best time	-	July to early August
Rating	-	Expert
Water level information	-	NOAA Tape (206) 526-8530
River mile	-	50.0 to 43.5; 6.5 miles
Time	-	1 hour, 40 minutes; 3.9 mph
Elevation	-	455' to 255'; 31' per mile

Powerline to Gold Bar

The Skykomish River is the charter river in Washington State's scenic river program and provides a wide variety of river trips. Most of the rapids are above the town of Gold Bar (named by prospectors in 1869) because of a change in the underlying geology. Below Gold Bar the rocks of the Western Metamorphic Zone are relatively soft sandstones and mudstones, which erode easily to create a smooth, constantly sloping riverbed and a broad valley. Above Gold Bar, the rocks of the Eastern Metamorphic Zone are considerably harder and make for more rapids and a narrower river valley.

This section of the Sky is in the Eastern Metamorphic Zone and has the best rapids on the main stem of the river. The most outstanding rapid, Boulder Drop, is class 4 at most of the water levels recommended in this guide but is shown as a class 5 because it reaches that level of difficulty at the upper end of the recommended range. Due to the difficulty of the section, county law requires that all boaters wear both helmets and lifejackets. Wetsuits should also be worn because the water is cold and the chances of a long swim are good. For those who are prepared, the Sky provides one of the most exciting and beautiful whitewater experiences in Washington.

Getting There
US 2 parallels the Skykomish River about 50 miles northeast of Seattle.

Put-ins and Take-outs
From Gold Bar the put-in is reached by turning off US 2 onto Mt. Index Road south of the river, immediately before the US 2 bridge that crosses the river near Index. Drive approximately 0.5 mile on a dirt road and pull

Flying through the Airplane Turn in Boulder Drop *(Rocky Perko photo)*

off on the left (river side) just beyond some powerlines crossing overhead. From here, a steep trail leads down through the woods to a pool in the river, just above a series of powerlines. This is one of the few spots along the river that is National Forest land. You should not put in farther upriver because private property must be crossed to do so. The state of Washington has developed a management plan for the river. The plan calls for easements at many spots along the river. The State has acquired a site for a day use picnic area just below The Maze but has not yet acquired a site creating an easier put-in. Most property along the river is privately owned, and trespassing is not permitted. Parking is available near the put-in but is limited.

The take-out is reached on an unmarked dirt road about 100 yards east of the US 2 bridge just above Gold Bar. A Department of Wildlife conservation license is required to use this access—a dirt parking area next to an eddy just below the bridge.

An alternative put-in or take-out point is just below the railroad bridge at log time 50 minutes. It is a steep 100-yard carry and recommended for

There are a lot of good playspots on the Sky.

light boats only. It is found at a small dirt turnout on the outside of a bend on US 2 about a mile above Zeke's drive-in. There is only room for about four cars, so park all the rest of your vehicles elsewhere and leave only one shuttle car here.

Water Level

The Skykomish is a good run at 2,000–5,000 cfs on the Gold Bar gauge. Only those who know the river well should run it at above 5,000 cfs.

Skykomish
Gold Bar Gauge
Recommend 2,000 to 5,000 cfs

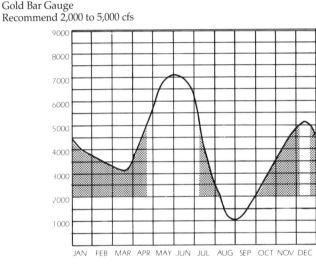

Special Hazards

None, other than **Boulder Drop**.

Scenery

This pool-and-drop river is a very pretty blue-green but uninvitingly cold. A boulder-choked part of the Washington State Scenic Rivers System, the Sky provides breathtaking views of Mt. Index and Mt. Persis. Both of these peaks tower some 5,000 feet above a riverbank that is covered by evergreen and deciduous trees. It is one of the cleanest rivers in western Washington, with very few logs to mar its granite boulder bed.

Camping

Forest Service campgrounds can be found at Money Creek, about 11 miles up US 2, or at Troublesome Creek and San Juan, 11 and 13 miles, respectively, up the North Fork of the Skykomish River.

Rapids

Powerline, the first rapid, can be seen from the put-in. Normally a class 3 drop, at high water levels (above 3,500 cfs to 4,500 cfs), the drop may be considered class 4. You should start your run on the left to avoid a large hole near the top of the rapid and then move to the center. The entire rapid can be scouted from the left side.

At log time 30 minutes, the Skykomish enters a rapid that kayakers have long referred to as **Garbage** (it is also known as the **Maze**). The favored route is to the left with the majority of water.

Anderson Hole is just over 30 minutes from the put-in. It is formed by a large rock and hole in the middle of the river where Anderson Creek enters the Skykomish. This hole can flip a kayak or raft. A safe run can be made through a small gap to the left and through an easier and larger passage to the right. The right route is recommended, as Boulder Drop is reached some 150 yards after Anderson Hole and should be scouted on the right bank.

Boulder Drop is recognized from upstream by a large number of house-sized boulders crossing the river as it constricts. Scouting from the right bank will reveal that the rapid consists of at least three distinct drops. Each drop must be carefully negotiated through a narrow passage. All scouting or portaging must be done on the right bank on National Forest land; the left bank is privately owned and no trespassing is allowed. The first drop is run on the right over a number of completely or partially submerged boulders that, at some water levels, can create troublesome holes. Approximately 20 yards below this drop, the boater reaches the second and principal drop. It is known as the Pickets because of four large boulders staggered at regular (more or less) intervals across the river. Two routes are commonly run through this section: the Needle or the Airplane Turn.

BOULDER NOTES (Drawing at 4,000 cfs)
- A. Entrance to rapid, small reversal; push through—don't hold back.
- B. Submerged rock and breaking wave. Use wave to push boat to left.
- C. Bad reversal; go left.
- D. The Needle. Reversal at bottom pushes boat hard left.
- E. The Dragon's Back. Easy to hang up on after Needle; run just to the right but avoid breaking wave downstream on the right.
- F. The Airplane Turn route. Run right of double reversals.
- G. Alternative route.
- H. House Rock.
- I. Combination reversal and breaking waves. Run left portion.
- J. Mercy Chute.

Boulder Drop
Diagram courtesy of Casey Garland,
Downstream River Runners

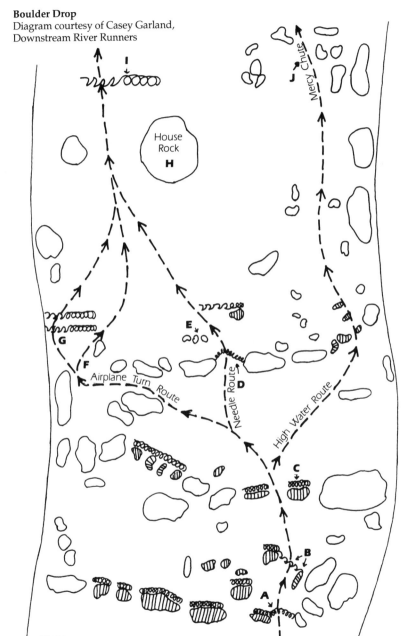

House
Rock
H

Mercy Chute

J

E

Needle Route

D

Airplane Turn Route

G

F

High Water Route

C

B

A

Entrance

Note
= Submerged Rock
= Reversals
= Breaking Waves

Riding out the tail-waves of Boulder Drop

The Needle is the steep route, directly between the two middle rocks. Most of the water pours through the Needle. However, due to the number of rocks at the bottom of the drop, the Needle cannot ordinarily be run with less than 2,000 cfs. Below the Needle, you are usually pushed to the left against an exposed rock by the force of the water. After pushing by this rock, it is necessary to move even farther left. There is a considerable drop alongside the house-sized rock below, but it is easily negotiated if you are still in control of your craft.

The Airplane Turn is probably the easier route to take if you can make the ferry to reach the turn. After negotiating the first drop, it is necessary to make a strong ferry to the left of the river, going around the left end of the Pickets. This route is not immediately obvious and requires careful study. Once you have managed to get far enough left to avoid the pull of the current toward the Needle, the water will carry you to the left into the turn. Turn 90 degrees and sweep right, back over a small ledge, toward the center of the river. After the Airplane Turn, the run to the left of the house-sized rock is usually not difficult.

If you decide to portage Boulder Drop, it should be done on the north bank of the river. The landowner on the south bank does not want boaters on his property. The portage can be made over the large boulders along the bank or up the slope to the railroad grade, along the grade, and then back down to the river.

After running Boulder Drop, you soon reach **The Ledge**, **Marbleshoot** and **Lunch Hole**. Lunch Hole should be run on the right, as a huge hole forms on the left on the outside of the bend.

At log time 50 minutes, you reach the Burlington Northern railroad bridge. Kayakers often take out here because most of the whitewater is over. From the bridge on, the river remains exciting, although not quite of the same class, and more private property dots the shore as the river broadens.

The take-out is easily recognized by the US 2 highway bridge. For the unwary, the last few yards before the take-out can be quite a surprise. The river unexpectedly drops under the bridge, and most of the river runs right, ending the trip with a jolt. Stay left of the gravel bar at flows below 3,000 cfs. The take-out itself is on the left bank next to a large eddy just downstream of the bridge.

Surfing the blue-green waters of the Sky

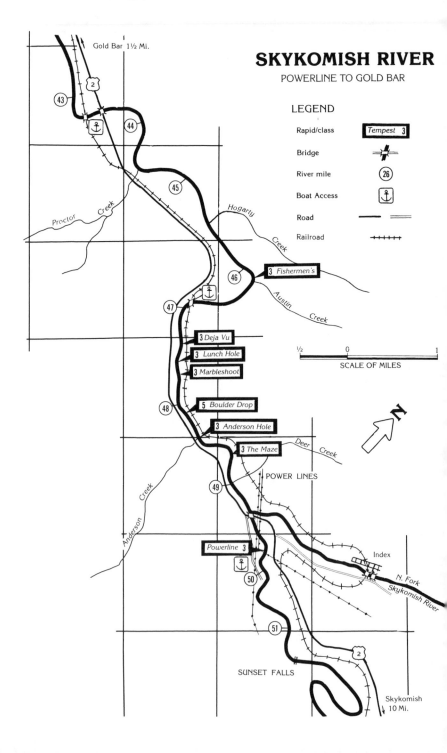

SKYKOMISH RIVER

POWERLINE TO GOLD BAR

LEGEND

Rapid/class	Tempest 3
Bridge	
River mile	26
Boat Access	
Road	
Railroad	+++++

SCALE OF MILES ½ 0 1

Gold Bar 1½ Mi.

Proctor Creek

Hogarty

Creek

Austin Creek

3 Fishermen's

3 Deja Vu

3 Lunch Hole

3 Marbleshoot

5 Boulder Drop

3 Anderson Hole

3 The Maze

Deer Creek

POWER LINES

Anderson Creek

Powerline 3

Index

N. Fork Skykomish River

SUNSET FALLS

Skykomish 10 Mi.

N

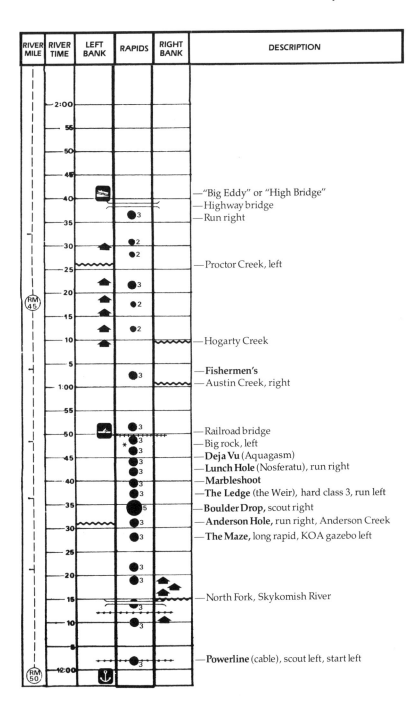

RIVER MILE	RIVER TIME	LEFT BANK	RAPIDS	RIGHT BANK	DESCRIPTION
	2:00				
	55				
	50				
	45				
	40	🚣			—"Big Eddy" or "High Bridge"
					—Highway bridge
	35		●3		—Run right
	30	▲	●2		
			●2		
	25	〜〜〜			—Proctor Creek, left
	20	▲	●3		
	15	▲	●2		
RM 45	10	▲	●2	〜〜〜	—Hogarty Creek
		▲			
	5				—**Fishermen's**
	1:00		●3	〜〜〜	—Austin Creek, right
	55				
	50	🚣	●3		—Railroad bridge
			●3		—Big rock, left
	45	*	●3		—**Deja Vu** (Aquagasm)
			●3		—**Lunch Hole** (Nosferatu), run right
	40		●3		—**Marbleshoot**
			●3		—**The Ledge** (the Weir), hard class 3, run left
	35		●5		—**Boulder Drop,** scout right
	30	〜〜〜	●3		—**Anderson Hole,** run right, Anderson Creek
			●3		—**The Maze,** long rapid, KOA gazebo left
	25				
	20		●3		
			●3	▲▲	
	15		●3	▲	—North Fork, Skykomish River
	10		●3	▲	
	5				
RM 50	12:00	⚓	●3		—**Powerline** (cable), scout left, start left

33

Upper Cispus

Logged at	-	2,100 cfs Randle gauge
Recommended water level	-	1,500 to 2,600 cfs
Best time	-	April to early July
Rating	-	Expert
Water level information	-	NOAA Tape (206) 526-8530
		U.S. Geological Survey
		(206) 593-6510
River mile	-	29.1 to 19.7; 9.4 miles
Time	-	1 hour, 44 minutes; 5.4 mph
Elevation	-	1,845' to 1,345'; 53' per mile

Road 23 Bridge to North Fork

The Cispus gathers its water on the west sides of Mt. Adams and the Goat Rocks and drops rapidly to the west toward its confluence with the Cowlitz. This river trip covers the portion of the Upper Cispus where its clear water tumbles through a narrow gorge in southwest Washington's Gifford Pinchot National Forest. This is one of the highest river trips possible in western Washington and snow could well block access to the river during the winter months.

The Army Corps of Engineers would like to study the feasibility of the Gravel Bar hydroelectric project, which would destroy the river above Blue Lake Creek. If you would like to help save the Upper Cispus, please contact the Rivers Council of Washington (see the Preface) and get involved in the campaign to protect the Cispus as a national Wild & Scenic river.

Getting There

The Cispus is usually approached through the town of Randle on US 12. Randle is about 54 miles east of I-5 and has a Forest Service Ranger Station. From the Puget Sound area north of Tacoma, the fastest way to Randle is on State Route 7, south through Spanaway, LaGrande and Morton to US 12.

Put-ins and Take-outs

From Randle, take the Forest Service 23 road south toward Trout Lake. You'll cross the Cowlitz just after leaving Randle and, in about 1 mile, bear left toward the Cispus Environmental Center and Trout Lake. After

Heading for Smoothrock Falls

driving about 10 miles through beautiful forest, the 28 road will turn off
to the right to cross the Cispus toward the Environmental Center.

To get to the put-in, you should continue straight ahead on the 23 road
toward Trout Lake. In about 10 more miles you will reach a fork in the
road. The pavement continues to the left toward Adams Fork Campground, but the main 23 road is the right fork. Take the right fork, which
becomes a gravel road. It winds down about 1 mile to the river; put-in at
the bridge.

There are several possible take-outs. The uppermost one, on the left
bank, at about log time 1 hour, 27 minutes, has become inaccessible because the river has shifted away from the bank here. The road on river left
is still useful for scouting. To get there, take the 28 road turn-off (toward
the Environmental Center) from the main 23 road and cross the bridge to
the south side of the Cispus. Just 100 yards south of the river, turn left on
the South Cispus road 2801. You can get a look at **Smoothrock Falls** by
driving 4.9 miles up the 2801 road. It continues another 5 miles upriver to
connect with the 23 road at the put-in.

You can take out a little below where the North Fork joins the river.
This take-out is on a broad gravel bar and requires a long carry of the
equipment unless you have a four-wheel-drive vehicle with high clear-
ance, which can negotiate the gravel bar. To reach this take-out, turn off
the main 23 road toward the river just on the Randle side of the North
Fork turn-off. A short drive will take you out on the gravel bar.

It is also possible to continue down the river to the 28 road bridge, the
starting point for the lower Cispus run. Taking out here will ordinarily require one or more portages, however. The river deposits logs in this slow
section of the river and all channels are usually blocked by logs in at least

one place. If you attempt this section of the river, you should stay to the right where the open gravel bars offer good portage routes; don't get into the narrow, forested channels on the left. We did on one trip and discovered the joys of pulling a raft upriver through the "Okeefenokee." Hopefully, as the beauty of this trip becomes more fully appreciated, either commercial outfitters running the river or the Forest Service will take responsibility for keeping a channel open through the logs.

Water Level

The water on this portion of the river makes up about 65 percent of the reading on the Randle gauge. Because this trip is so steep, a change of 300 cfs can make a big difference in the power of the hydraulics. At the minimum recommended level of 1,500 cfs, you will be bumping a lot of rocks and, at that level, I would not recommend the run to those with fiberglass kayaks. At the maximum recommended 2,600 cfs, you will find very powerful hydraulics and few eddies large enough for a raft. After you become familiar with the river, you may decide to run it at a higher level, but by all means, become familiar with it first because this is a very fast trip with some big drops.

Upper Cispus
Randle Gauge
Recommend 1,500 to 2,600 cfs

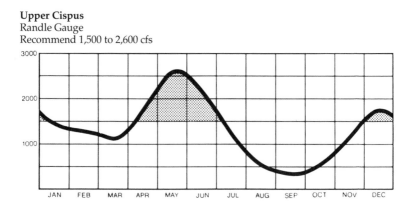

Special Hazards

Logs are a special hazard on the Upper Cispus. Besides the "Okeefenokee" waiting for you below the North Fork, there is potential for logjams forming at other places on the run. Keep alert. The main channel of the river is usually blocked by logs at log time 17 minutes. It is often easy to slide your boat down the small right-hand channel, which has too little water to boat. Recently, we have encountered a log jammed between two boulders at the entrance to **Picky-Picky**. Passage around it was possible on the left, but it wouldn't hurt to scout.

Scenery

You will see almost no signs of civilization on the Upper Cispus. The road is visible in a few places, but does not often intrude through the thick forest. There are beautiful rock-walled gorges at log time 42 minutes and again at 50–55 minutes. The rock is covered with a luxuriant moss and, in some places, towers 25 feet over the river. The upper part of the run has a fascinating channel; it has gravel bars, small islands and chutes studded with huge boulders. In the lower part of the run, views open toward 4,800-foot Tongue Mountain to the west. In the early season its crags are often still frosted with snow.

You can easily understand why the Cispus is on the inventory of potential Wild & Scenic rivers in Washington.

Camping

Numerous Forest Service campgrounds are available in the area. Adams Fork Campground is about 5 miles above the put-in, Blue Lake Creek Campground is just off the road about halfway through the run and North Fork Campground is near the take-out.

Rapids

Picky-Picky, just below Juniper Creek at log time 27 minutes, provides a good warm up for the technical whitewater ahead. It doesn't require any difficult moves, but it keeps you busy with nearly a quarter-mile of constant class 3 boulder dodging.

Big Bend follows a sharp left bend in the river. Pull in to the left bank to scout. It is usually run by threading through the boulders at the top to reach a pour-over ledge between a large boulder and the right bank. Then work back into the center and end the run by dropping over the bottom ledge in the center or next to the left bank. The water moves swiftly and you have to have your route well planned in advance.

White Lightning (it's white from bank to bank and you go through it like lightning) is easily recognized from upstream; you see a horizon line! A scout on the right bank will reveal a steep drop over a stair-like series of boulders. A large boulder protrudes from the water in the right-center of the channel. Stay to the right of this boulder, because the current on the left side will pin you against the rocks on the left bank. Watch the waves at the bottom; they're bigger than they look.

Smoothrock Falls is a small falls and definitely deserves a scout. A solid rock ledge extends all the way across the river and the river falls some 4–5 feet over it. At low water you can plunge over it nearly anywhere, but at higher water levels the nearly perfect hydraulic that it creates is very dangerous. Sometimes it should be run on the right where there is a notch in the ledge which allows the water to funnel through and break the perfect hydraulic; other times, the left is more promising. Check it out.

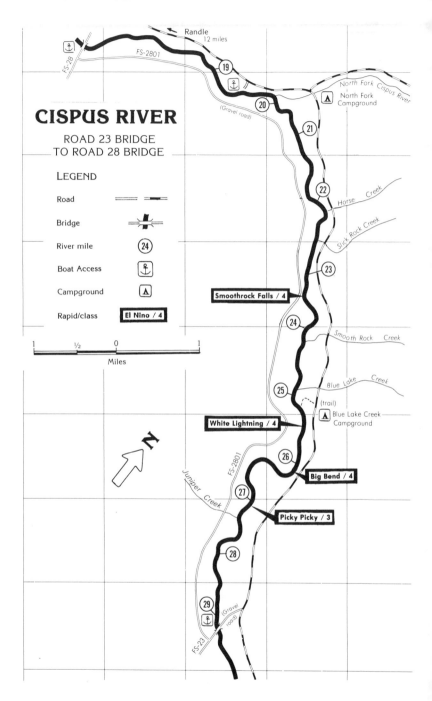

CISPUS RIVER

ROAD 23 BRIDGE
TO ROAD 28 BRIDGE

LEGEND

Road	
Bridge	
River mile	(24)
Boat Access	
Campground	
Rapid/class	El Nino / 4

Miles

Randle
12 miles

FS-2801

North Fork Cispus River

North Fork
Campground

Horse Creek

Slick Rock Creek

Smoothrock Falls / 4

Smooth Rock Creek

Blue Lake Creek

(trail)

Blue Lake Creek
Campground

White Lightning / 4

Big Bend / 4

Picky Picky / 3

Juniper Creek

FS-2801

FS-28

(Gravel road)

(Gravel road)

FS-23

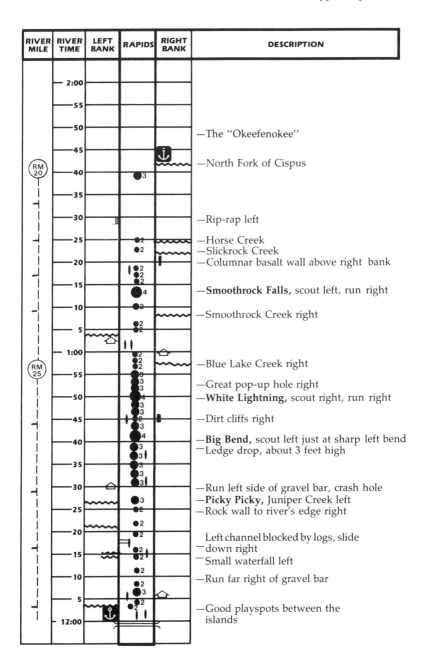

RIVER MILE	RIVER TIME	LEFT BANK	RAPIDS	RIGHT BANK	DESCRIPTION
	2:00				
	55				
	50				—The "Okeefenokee"
	45			⚓	
RM 20	40		●3	~~~	—North Fork of Cispus
	35				
	30	▨			—Rip-rap left
	25		●2	~~~~	—Horse Creek
	20		●2	⊦	—Slickrock Creek
			⏐●2 ●2 ●2		—Columnar basalt wall above right bank
	15		●4		—**Smoothrock Falls,** scout left, run right
	10		●2	~~~	—Smoothrock Creek right
	5	~~⌂	●2 ●2		
	1:00		⏐⏐	⌂	
RM 25	55		●2 ●2 ●8 ●3 ●3	~~~	—Blue Lake Creek right
	50		●4 ●3		—Great pop-up hole right
	45		●3 ⏐●2 ●3	⯀	—**White Lightning,** scout right, run right
	40		●4 ●3 ●3⏐		—Dirt cliffs right
	35		●3 ●3		—**Big Bend,** scout left just at sharp left bend
	30	⌂	●3⏐		—Ledge drop, about 3 feet high
	25	~~~	●3 ●2		—Run left side of gravel bar, crash hole
	20	~~~	●2		—**Picky Picky,** Juniper Creek left
			●2		—Rock wall to river's edge right
	15	~⯐	●2⏐ ●2⏐		Left channel blocked by logs, slide down right
	10		●2		—Small waterfall left
	5	~~~	●2 ●3	⌂	—Run far right of gravel bar
	12:00	⚓	●2 ⏐⏐		—Good playspots between the islands

34

Skykomish, North Fork

Logged at	-	7,500 cfs Gold Bar gauge
Recommended water level	-	6,000 to 12,000 cfs
Best time	-	Mid-May to June
Rating	-	Expert
Water level information	-	NOAA Tape (206) 526-8530
River mile	-	10.7 to 0; 10.7 miles
Time	-	1 hour, 59 minutes; 5.4 mph
Elevation	-	1,140' to 440'; 56' per mile

Galena to Confluence

Are you ready for a river that drops so fast that it disappears down through its granite boulders when you approach a major rapid? The North Fork of the Sky offers you beautiful views of the North Cascades while it puts your boating skills to the test. Hold onto your paddle—If you find the excitement is gone from the other trips in this guidebook, this one will knock your socks off!

Getting There

The name Skykomish comes from the Indian words meaning "inland people." You can reach the North Fork by turning off US 2 toward the town of Index about 7.5 miles east of Gold Bar. Index's 100 or so inhabitants are a mere remnant of the 1,000 greed-crazed gold miners who pitched their tents in this valley in the 1890s.

Put-ins and Take-outs

About 1 mile up the road from US 2 toward Index, you will pass under a railroad bridge. Just before getting to the bridge, there is a small dirt turn-out toward the river. This is the take-out for those running the North Fork or the put-in for those who wish to run the last mile and half of the North Fork before running the Sunset Falls stretch of the main Sky (covered in Chapter 32). Don't block this small access area by parking here. Load and unload, but park in the area off to the right (when you are coming from US 2) just *after* going under the railroad bridge. I've included the river below this point in the log for those who want to combine this trip with the main Sky.

Another put-in or take-out in this area is just across the road bridge into Index, upstream at Index City Park.

Threading through the boulders of El Nino

To reach the put-in continue up the North Fork road nearly 10 miles to where the road crosses the river on a new concrete bridge. About 150 yards beyond the bridge is a large turn-out next to the river: the put-in. The eddies amongst the rocks here are small and a raft has to be tied up because at least part of it is going to be out in the current.

Alternative put-ins for those who would like to reduce the amount of white-knuckle whitewater but still see most of the scenery are just above Trout Creek and just below the bridge near Howard Creek (on the left bank) at log time 18 minutes. This bridge is reached by turning off toward the river about 1 mile short of the bridge near the upper put-in, or about 9 miles above the take-out.

Water Level

The North Fork provides 39 percent of the water recorded on the Gold Bar gauge. Because of the enormous number of boulders studding its course, a lot of water is needed to boat the river. Kayakers can boat the river at 4,000 cfs and rafts can run the river from the bridge above Howard Creek on 5,000 cfs, but 6,000 cfs is necessary to raft the upper part of the river.

Boaters familiar with the North Fork will run it at higher levels than recommended here, but there is little margin for error at higher flows. At

291

the logged level of 7,500 cfs there were few eddies large enough for a raft and landing was difficult in the upper part of the run.

Special Hazards

Find out about logs on the river before you go; the logs change position every year. You must often avoid logs, particularly in the section a little below the bridge at log time 18 minutes, where the river has recently cut a new channel for itself through the forest. In 1986, a flood deposited a log in this area which completely blocked the river channel. The best way to find out about log conditions is to contact the Washington Kayak Club (WKC), whose members regularly run the North Fork of the Sky. Join the WKC and stay on top of boating conditions in Washington: Box 24264, Seattle, WA 98124. If you can't find anyone who has run the river recently, walk along the bank to check for logjams *before* you start down the river in your boat. Logs have been particularly bad in the area around log time 1 hour.

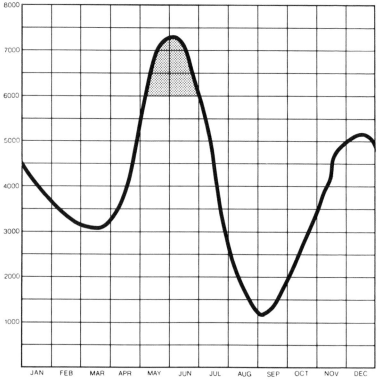

Skykomish, North Fork
Gold Bar Gauge
Recommend 6,000 to 12,000 cfs

Scenery

Although there are numerous cabins near Index and at two other points farther upriver, the riverbanks are largely natural. Huge granite boulders punctuating the narrow upper river channel make the first mile of the trip very interesting, if you can find a moment to think of anything besides the rapids. Gorgeous views of snow-capped Gunn Peak to the east and Mt. Index and Mt. Persis to the south open up as you descend to the middle of the run and the whitewater lets up enough to allow you to look around occasionally. As you approach the end of the trip, you will have good views of the Index Town Wall, behind the town of Index to the northwest, and may see a few of the many rock climbers who train there.

The North Fork of the Skykomish is a wintering area for bald eagles. They are particularly active in feeding during December and January, so it is best to avoid boating the river during those months when you might disturb them.

Unfortunately, the beauty of the North Fork is endangered. Boaters and conservationists are working on legislation to have the North Fork designated as a national Wild & Scenic river to stop the dam planned for the river upstream of the boating section. If you'd like to help save the North Fork, contact the Northwest Rivers Council (see the Preface).

Camping

Troublesome Creek is about 1 mile and San Juan Forest Service Campground is about 3 miles up the North Fork valley above the put-in. These campgrounds are usually open only between Memorial Day and Labor Day.

Rapids

Ah, the rapids. These are long, rocky haircurlers that challenge you with 200 yards of continuous class 3+ and then end up in a substantial class 4 drop. After running the first 2 miles of the North Fork for the first time, I was shell-shocked. Most of the class 3 rapids in the first 35 minutes are hard class 3s. Around river mile 10 the river slope is about 120 feet per mile, nearly the steepest that can be rafted. The clear waters of the North Fork offer some of the best whitewater in Washington. County ordinance requires everyone to wear helmets and lifejackets on both the North Fork and main Skykomish above Gold Bar.

The first big drop, **El Nino** (Guardrail), is right next to the road and should be obvious on the shuttle because the road is generally screened from the river by trees, but not here. Take a look at **El Nino** on the shuttle—You won't have much time to look at it when you're on the river. The other stand-out piece of whitewater is the **Minefield**, full of unexpected holes. You may want to scout it on the left; it's trickier than it looks from the river. The North Fork offers the most continually challenging run covered by this guidebook.

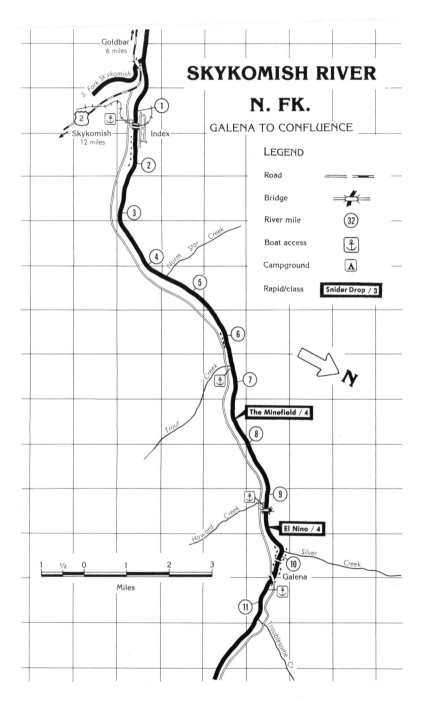

Goldbar
6 miles

S. Fork Skykomish

SKYKOMISH RIVER

N. FK.

GALENA TO CONFLUENCE

2

Skykomish
12 miles

Index

1

LEGEND

Road	
Bridge	
River mile	32
Boat access	⚓
Campground	Ⓐ
Rapid/class	**Snider Drop / 3**

2

3

North Star Creek

4

5

6

Creek

7

Trout

The Minefield / 4

8

9

Howard Creek

El Nino / 4

Silver Creek

10

Galena

11

Troublesome Cr.

1 ½ 0   1   2   3

Miles

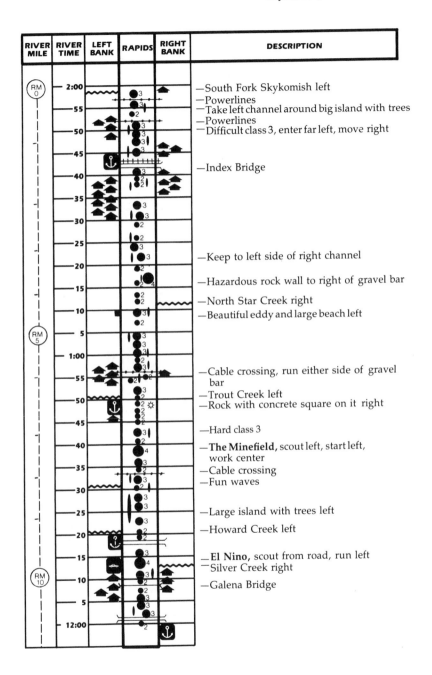

RIVER MILE	RIVER TIME	LEFT BANK	RAPIDS	RIGHT BANK	DESCRIPTION

—South Fork Skykomish left
—Powerlines
—Take left channel around big island with trees
—Powerlines
—Difficult class 3, enter far left, move right

—Index Bridge

—Keep to left side of right channel

—Hazardous rock wall to right of gravel bar

—North Star Creek right
—Beautiful eddy and large beach left

—Cable crossing, run either side of gravel bar
—Trout Creek left
—Rock with concrete square on it right

—Hard class 3

—**The Minefield,** scout left, start left, work center
—Cable crossing
—Fun waves

—Large island with trees left

—Howard Creek left

—**El Nino,** scout from road, run left
—Silver Creek right

—Galena Bridge

The Green River Gorge has challenging whitewater and beautiful scenery.

Appendix

In 1986, the Washington State Legislature passed a law governing commercial river running. While the provisions apply only to commercial trips, all river runners should comply with some of the sections. 91.14.020 requires that all watercraft be operated in a careful and prudent manner and that no watercraft interfere with other watercraft or proper navigation of the river. 91.14.080 spells out the reporting requirements in the event that a person dies or disappears.

Chapter 91.14—Passenger Watercraft for Hire—Operation

Sec.

91.14.005. Purpose

The purpose of this chapter is to further the public interest, welfare, and safety by providing for the protection and promotion of safety in the operation of watercraft carrying passengers for hire on the rivers of this state.

Enacted by Laws 1986, ch. 217, [§] 1.

91.14.010. Definitions

Unless the context clearly requires otherwise, the definitions in this section apply throughout this chapter.

(1) "Watercraft" means every type of watercraft carrying passengers for hire used as a means of transportation on a river, including but not limited to power boats, drift boats, open canoes, inflatable crafts, decked canoes, and kayaks.

(2) "Carrying passengers for hire" means carrying passengers by water-

craft for valuable consideration, whether given directly or indirectly or received by the owner, agent, operator, or other persons having an interest in the watercraft. This shall not affect trips where expenses for food, transportation, or incidentals are shared by participants on an even basis. Anyone receiving compensation for skills or money for amortization of equipment and carrying passengers shall be considered to be carrying passengers for hire. Individuals licensed under chapter 77.32 RCW and acting as a fishing guide are exempt from this chapter.

(3) "Operate" means to navigate or otherwise use a watercraft.

(4) "Operator" means any person operating the watercraft or performing the duties of a pilot or guide for one or more watercraft in a group.

(5) "Passenger" means every person on board a watercraft who is not an operator.

(6) "Rivers of the state" means those rivers and streams, or parts thereof, within the boundaries of this state.

Enacted by Laws 1986, ch. 217, [§] 2.

91.14.020. Operation of watercraft

(1) No person may operate any watercraft in a manner that interferes with other watercraft or with the free and proper navigation of the rivers of this state.

(2) Every operator of a watercraft shall at all times operate the watercraft in a careful and prudent manner and at such a speed as to not endanger the life, limb, or property of any person.

(3) No watercraft may be loaded with passengers or cargo beyond its safe carrying capacity taking into consideration the type and construction of the watercraft and other existing operating conditions. In the case of inflatable crafts, safe carrying capacity in whitewater shall be considered as less than the United States Coast Guard capacity rating for each watercraft. This subsection shall not apply in cases of an unexpected emergency on the river.

Enacted by Laws 1986, ch. 217, [§] 3.

91.14.030. Watercraft rights of way

(1) Except as provided in subsection (2) of this section, watercraft proceeding downstream have the right of way over watercraft proceeding upstream.

(2) In all cases, watercraft not under power have the right of way over motorized craft underway.

Enacted by Laws 1986, ch. 217, [§] 4.

91.14.040. Operators—First aid card required—Exception

(1) No person may operate on the rivers of this state a watercraft carrying passengers for hire unless the person has been issued a valid Red Cross standard first aid card or at least its equivalent.

(2) This section does not apply to a person operating a vessel on the navigable waters of the United States in this state and who is licensed by the United States Coast Guard for the type of vessel being operated.

Enacted by Laws 1986, ch. 217, [§] 5.

91.14.050. Safety equipment

While carrying passengers for hire on whitewater river sections in this state, the operator and owner shall:

(1) If using inflatable watercraft, use only watercraft with three or more separate air chambers;

(2) Ensure that all passenger and operators are wearing a securely fastened United States Coast Guard approved type III or type V life jacket in good condition;

(3) Ensure that each watercraft has accessible a spare type III or type V life jacket in good repair;

(4) Ensure that each watercraft has on it a bagged throwable line with a floating line and bag;

(5) Ensure that each watercraft has accessible an adequate first-aid kit;

(6) Ensure that each watercraft has a spare propelling device;

(7) Ensure that a repair kit and air pump are accessible to inflatable watercraft; and

(8) Ensure that equipment to prevent and treat hypothermia is accessible to all watercraft on a trip.

Enacted by Laws 1986, ch. 217, [§] 6.

91.14.060. Whitewater river sections—Use of alcohol prohibited—Watercraft to be accompanied by other watercraft

(1) Watercraft operators and passengers on any trip carrying passengers for hire shall not allow the use of alcohol during the course of a trip on a whitewater river section in this state.

(2) Any watercraft carrying passengers for hire on any whitewater river section in this state must be accompanied by at least one other watercraft under the supervision of the same operator or owner or being operated by a person registered under RCW 91.14.090 or an operator under the direction or control of a person registered under RCW 91.14.090.

Enacted by Laws 1986, ch. 217, [§] 7.

91.14.070. Whitewater river sections—Designation

Whitewater river sections include but are not limited to:

(1) Green river above Flaming Geyser state park;

(2) Klickitat river above the confluence with Summit creek;

(3) Methow river below the town of Carlton;

(4) Sauk river above the town of Darrington;

(5) Skagit river above Bacon creek;

(6) Suiattle river;

(7) Tieton river below Rimrock dam;

(8) Skykomish river below Sunset Falls and above the Highway 2 bridge one mile east of the town of Gold Bar;

(9) Wenatchee river above the Wenatchee county park at the town of Monitor;

(10) White Salmon river; and

(11) Any other section of river designated a "whitewater river section" by the interagency committee for outdoor recreation. Such river sections shall be

class two or greater difficulty under the international scale of whitewater difficulty.

Enacted by Laws 1986, ch. 217, [§] 8.

91.14.080. Death or disappearance from watercraft—Notification of authorities

(1) When, as a result of an occurrence that involves a watercraft or its equipment, a person dies or disappears from a watercraft, the operator shall notify the nearest sheriff's department, state patrol office, coast guard station, or other law enforcement agency of:

(a) The date, time, and exact location of the occurrence;

(b) The name of each person who died or disappeared;

(c) A description of the watercraft; and

(d) The names and addresses of the owner and operator.

(2) When the operator of a boat cannot give the notice required by subsection (1) of this section, each person on board that boat shall either give the notice or determine that the notice has been given.

Enacted by Laws 1986, ch. 217, [§] 9.

91.14.090. Registration of persons carrying passengers for hire on whitewater river sections—List of registered persons—Notice of registrants' insurance termination—State immune from civil actions arising from registration

(1) Any person carrying passengers for hire on whitewater river sections in this state may register with the department of licensing. Each registration application shall be submitted annually on a form provided by the department of licensing and shall include the following information:

(a) The name, residence address, and residence telephone number, and the business name, address, and telephone number of the registrant;

(b) Proof that the registrant has liability insurance for a minimum of three hundred thousand dollars per claim for occurrences by the registrant and the registrant's employees that result in bodily injury or property damage; and

(c) Certification that the registrant will maintain the insurance for a period of not less than one year from the date of registration.

(2) The department of licensing shall charge a fee for each application, to be set in accordance with RCW 43.24.086.

(3) Any person advertising or representing themselves as having registered under this section who is not currently registered is guilty of a gross misdemeanor.

(4) The department of licensing shall submit annually a list of registered persons and companies to the department of trade and economic development, tourism and promotion division.

(5) If an insurance company cancels or refuses to renew insurance for a registrant during the period of registration, the insurance company shall notify the department of licensing in writing of the termination of coverage and its effective date not less than thirty days before the effective date of termination.

(a) Upon receipt of an insurance company termination notice, the department of licensing shall send written notice to the registrant that on the effective date of termination the department of licensing will suspend the registration unless proof of insurance as required by this section is filed with the department of licensing before the effective date of termination.

(b) If an insurance company fails to give notice of coverage termination, this failure shall not have the effect of continuing the coverage.

(c) The department of licensing may suspend or revoke registration under this section if the registrant fails to maintain in full force and effect the insurance required by this section.

(6) The state of Washington shall be immune from any civil action arising from a registration under this section.

Enacted by Laws 1986, ch. 217, [§] 11.

91.14.100. Enforcement—Chapter to supplement federal law

(1) Every peace officer of this state and its political subdivisions has the authority to enforce this chapter. Wildlife agents of the department of game and fisheries patrol officers of the department of fisheries, through their directors, the state patrol, through its chief, county sheriffs, and other local law enforcement bodies, shall assist in the enforcement. In the exercise of this responsibility, all such officers may stop any watercraft and direct it to a suitable pier or anchorage for boarding.

(2) A person, while operating a watercraft on any waters of this state, shall not knowingly flee or attempt to elude a law enforcement officer after having received a signal from the law enforcement officer to bring the boat to a stop.

(3) This chapter shall be construed to supplement federal laws and regulations. To the extent this chapter is inconsistent with federal laws and regulations, the federal laws and regulations shall control.

Enacted by Laws 1986, ch. 217, [§] 10.

91.14.110. Civil penalty

A person violating this chapter shall be subject to a civil penalty of up to one hundred fifty dollars per violation.

Enacted by Laws 1986, ch. 217, [§] 12.

INDEX

The author taping notes
on a whitewater trip.

About the author:

Doug North began running Washington rivers eleven years ago as a whitewater canoeist. He was surprised to find out that little information on Washington's whitewater rivers was available in print; particularly lacking was information on good water levels for each trip. So he began compiling information that resulted in his guidebooks—first, *Washington Whitewater 1*, then *Washington Whitewater 2*, and now this revised second edition combining the two books.

North is a Washington native and practices law in Seattle. A long-time outdoor enthusiast, he also hikes, climbs and skis cross-country. In addition to boating Washington rivers, he has run more than a dozen rivers in Colorado, Oregon, Idaho, and British Columbia. A founder of Northwest Rivers Council, he has been very active in protecting the rivers of the Northwest from development that would interfere with their free-flowing qualities and the recreation, fish, and wildlife dependent on them.